collection, processing, and analysis for research projects.

- Part VI **The Implement** — Howard Freeman and be considered in desig ing a research project, kon discusses cooperati in the research setting.

- Part VII **Integrating Research and Practice** — Robert Leonard and James Skipper examine the cultural and structural components that account for the separation between research and practice. William Usdane discusses a research utilization program, and A. D. Puth presents the practitioner's viewpoint on the problem.

It is Dr. O'Toole's conviction that the commanding articles in this book will provoke the improvements and refinements that he believes are necessary to the vital processes of social research.

Since 1968 Richard O'Toole has been Research Director of the Vocational Guidance and Rehabilitation Services in Cleveland. In September, 1971 he begins his new appointment as Chairman of the Department of Sociology at Kent State University. After receiving his B.A. and M.A. from the University of Oklahoma, he was awarded his Ph.D. by the University of Oregon. Dr. O'Toole has taught at both these schools and at Case Western Reserve. He has also worked in a research capacity for various private and governmental agencies, mainly in the fields of vocational guidance and rehabilitation. Professional journals have published a number of his articles.

$8.95 cloth

THE ORGANIZATION, MANAGEMENT AND
TACTICS OF SOCIAL RESEARCH

The Organization, Management and Tactics of Social Research

Edited by

RICHARD O'TOOLE

Vocational Guidance and
Rehabilitation Services and
Case Western Reserve University

SCHENKMAN PUBLISHING COMPANY, INC. 1971
Cambridge, Massachusetts, U.S.A., and London, England

This investigation was supported, in part, by Research Grant No. RD-2875-G
from the Division of Research and Demonstration Grants, Social and Rehabilitation Service, Department of Health, Education, and Welfare, Washington, D.C.,
20201.
The Social and Rehabilitation Service reserves a royalty-free, nonexclusive, and
irrevocable license to reproduce, publish, or otherwise use, and to authorize others
to use, all copyrightable or copyrighted material resulting from the grant-
supported activity.

To my teachers
ROBERT DUBIN
NORMAN R. JACKMAN
MUZAFER SHERIF
GILBERT GEIS
JAMES L. PRICE
JOEL BERREMAN

CONTENTS

ACKNOWLEDGEMENTS

I want to thank the contributors for the thought and work they put into the chapters and for the candid manner in which their own research experience is reported.

Ed Suchman not only contributed a major chapter, but freely gave advice during the planning of the symposium, and was a stimulant to the fruitful discussions during the meetings. We will all miss him.

My colleagues in the Department of Sociology of Case Western Reserve University provided many suggestions and comments during the course of the work. My Chairman, Marvin B. Sussman taught me a great deal about the organization, management and tactics of holding a symposium and editing the papers for the book.

The staff of Vocational Guidance and Rehabilitation Services were instrumental in the success of the symposium and in preparing the manuscript: Margaret Mitchell, Anita Werner, Sue Morgan Herne, Miriam Erb and Joyce Susa. My special thanks to Mrs. Olive K. Banister for her active support of the symposium.

I also want to express appreciation to William M. Usdane, Joan H. Criswell and Nathan E. Acree and the staff of the Division of Research and Demonstration Grants for their support and advice, and the Social and Rehabilitation Service for providing funding for the project.

My wife's daily encouragement and my daughter's delight in seeing her father's name in print served as both support and impetus to produce this book.

RICHARD O'TOOLE
August, 1970

CONTRIBUTORS

MELVIN E. ALLERHAND, Ph.D., *Director, Consumer Participation in Health Planning Project, Lecturer, School of Management, Case Western Reserve University.*

EDGAR F. BORGATTA, Ph.D., *Professor of Sociology, The University of Wisconsin.*

ROBERT DUBIN, Ph.D., *Professor of Sociology and Administration, The University of California at Irvine.*

HOWARD J. EHRLICH, Ph.D., *Associate Professor of Sociology, The University of Iowa, and Director, Program in Social Psychology, University of Iowa.*

WILLIAM H. FORM, Ph.D., *Research Professor of Sociology, Michigan State University.*

HOWARD E. FREEMAN, Ph.D., *Professor of Social Research, The Florence Heller Graduate School for Advanced Studies in Social Welfare, Brandeis University.*

MARIE R. HAUG, Ph.D., *Assistant Professor of Sociology and Research Director, Institute on the Family and the Bureaucratic Society, Case Western Reserve University.*

ROBERT C. LEONARD, Ph.D., *Associate Professor of Sociology, The University of Arizona.*

A. D. PUTH, *Assistant Director, The National Rehabilitation Association.*

PETER H. ROSSI, Ph.D., *Chairman, Department of Social Relations, The Johns Hopkins University.*

JAMES K. SKIPPER, JR., Ph.D., *Associate Professor of Sociology, Case Western Reserve University.*

EDWARD A. SUCHMAN, Ph.D. (deceased), *Professor of Sociology and Public Health, The University of Pittsburgh.*

MARVIN B. SUSSMAN, Ph.D., *Chairman, Department of Sociology, Case Western Reserve University. Visiting Professor at the Carolina Population Center and Department of Mental Health, University of North Carolina at Chapel Hill.*

GEORGE H. WOLKON, Ph.D., *Research Director, Center for Training in Community Psychiatry, Los Angeles, California, Department of Mental Hygiene.*

Powhatan J. Wooldridge, Ph.D., *Associate Professor of Sociology, The University of Iowa.*

William M. Usdane, Ph.D., *formerly Chief, Division of Research and Demonstration, Social and Rehabilitation Service, Department of Health, Education, and Welfare. Presently, Research Director, U.S. Department of Labor, Office of the Assistant Secretary.*

Richard O'Toole, Ph.D., *Editor, Research Director, Vocational Guidance and Rehabilitation Services and Adjunct Associate Professor of Sociology Case Western Reserve University.*

INTRODUCTION

Scientists and philosophers have long been concerned with the inter-relationships between scientific activities and their societal settings. The sociology of science, and sociology of knowledge, for example, are traditional areas of interest. Yet only within recent years has there been interest in systematic study of research as a social and behavioral process.

This book analyzes and presents guidelines on the relationships between the organization, management, and tactics of research, the research process and its outcomes, and the impact of research on programs for individual and societal change. It is based on the assumption that as many research efforts fail to meet their full potential because of such managerial problems as fail because of more traditional methodological problems, such as faulty designs, or measurement techniques. It assumes that given such methodological knowledge the researcher is still not fully prepared to conduct research. In fact, organizational, managerial, and tactical problems may lead to the outright failure of a research project. Thus, it is not a methodological work in the traditional sense but a necessary supplement to texts on methods and treatments of particular data collection and analytic techniques.

In our research we must be more aware of how various features of the organizations in which we work, the way in which we manage relations with respondents, and the manner in which data are processed, for example, affect research results. Scientific operations are influenced by the social systems which relate researchers, research organizations, organizations for directing, administering and funding research, and particularly in the social and behavior sciences by the new social systems which relate researcher and subject. The reliability and validity of the data collected, the amount of error in data processing, and the analysis and dissemination of results are affected. Interpersonal relations with subjects must be initiated and conducted in a manner which does not affect the data gathered through the relationship. Inter-organizational relations between the research organization and the organization being researched must be managed to allow the research to be initiated, conducted and completed. Within the research organization, administrative procedures must be developed and carried out so that the various research tasks are accomplished accurately and efficiently.

In these days of funded research the various research tasks must be accomplished according to a pre-determined time schedule and according to budget agreements. The model which orients the book calls attention to the effects of these relations on the many phases of the research process and its results, including the impact of research on practice. Only a short time ago there were only a relatively few individuals involved in social and behavioral research. However, today we live in a society oriented toward change and large governmental and private organizations have been formed to fund and conduct programs to intervene and correct individual and societal ills. We have also become oriented to the view that scientific research is the best means of discovering the basic principles to be used in designing programs and the most efficient means to evaluate their effectiveness. Thus, more and more research is being conducted which utilizes social and behavioral science research techniques as evaluative tools. It is therefore imperative that we analyze the processes which are involved in the management of social research and present guidelines for the solution of such problems.

Ideally, empirically tested social and behavioral science theories would explain the research process and the contingencies that are involved so that an administrative science and procedural guidelines could be derived from them. However, although our methodology has reached a level of sophistication where some techniques such as the social survey and some experimental procedures have become routine, we have not yet systematically investigated the effects of many contingencies that arise as these and other techniques are organized and managed in the course of research. Much of the knowledge in this area is still in the form of uncodified and largely unresearched folk wisdom. For the most part it is communicated and learned only on an informal basis in the researcher-apprentice and colleague relationships during the course of research. Much has to be gained in a costly trial and error process throughout a researcher's career. In one sense this book is an attempt to get on paper what has been learned by experienced researchers in the "school of hard knocks."

The aims of the book are both theoretical and practical. The papers should be a contribution to the sociology of research, an area well worthy of study in its own right for its significance to sociological theory. It is practical for researchers in that it deals with the everyday problems of organizing, managing and conducting research. It is also practical in another sense, because it continues on where most past work has left off and deals with the problems of the integration of research and practice.

In regard to the aims, the book was designed for several major audiences: researchers in the social and behavioral sciences, practitioners in the helping professions, and, of course, students in both groups. It is also hoped that it will be of value to funding organizations which have a major responsibility in administering research programs and securing a closer relationship between research and the utilization of research findings in practice.

In view of these aims it seemed that a logical step would be to gather a group of successful researchers and representatives of the helping professions and divide the labor according to the design of the book and by interests and past experience. Contributors were also selected on the basis of their experience in research that has been directly relevant to programs for individual rehabilitation and social policy.

Although the contributors address their discussions for the most part to sociological research, the issues have relevance to all the social and behavioral sciences. In these disciplines research is a social process which takes place through and is affected by interpersonal, organizational and inter-organizational relationships. (I'm also sure that many of the statements are relevant for the biological and physical sciences.)

Also, while in discussing practice the specific referent is to rehabilitation, yet I feel that the issues discussed are relevant to all the helping professions. Thus, the use of the word practitioner refers to all the helping professions.

Specifically to Practitioners

Research is no longer an avocation for a few practitioners but has become a basic part of service program planning and development. Today's practitioner in the helping professions has many opportunities to be involved in research and one of the aims of this book is to help practitioners understand research.

The practitioner is often asked to conduct evaluative research to justify the expenditure of scarce resources on service programs and innovations in established programs.

State and private support of demonstration programs most often requires a research component before funds are made available to test new concepts of service. In short, evaluative research has become one of the required means of providing the proof of the pudding. The practitioner is also asked to cooperate in research endeavors. If he is to do more than sanction a research project, to fully cooperate in research, he should have a basic understanding of the research, for his practical knowledge can be very beneficial to the success of the project. And, he may be able to get greater program benefits from a project in which he plays an active part. The practitioner-administrator must successfully play both of these research roles and he may also have the administrative task of coordinating and integrating a research division with the other departments under his supervision.

And, the practitioner is a major consumer of research findings. In this role he must be able to sort through and evaluate research results and interpret findings in order to apply them to particular individuals and settings in which he works. In this process he does not receive much help from researchers or from the system by which research results are disseminated. As discussed throughout the book, but particularly in the last section, we are faced with tremendous problems in attempting to bring about a closer relationship between research and practice. Thus, the practitioner participates in the research process as a practitioner-researcher, participant in the conduct of research by others, administration, and consumer of research findings.

I believe that practitioners will find the chapters included in this book very helpful in understanding and carrying out their various research related roles. Formal training for practice does not often include a great deal of research methodology or procedures and many practitioners have not had the opportunity to gain much research experience. Theory and research have an aura of awe about them, for many practitioners, and there has been a tendency to withdraw from research — to leave research and theory up to the researchers. At the same time there is a tendency to disregard research as something unrelated to practice and recently some practitioners have called for de-emphasis on research.

It is hoped that by providing practitioners with a greater understanding of research the book will aid in making a step toward correcting this situation. Therefore, I would like to offer some suggestions to practitioners in reading the book. You may want to read the chapters by Suchman and Allerhand and then the section on the integration of research and practice before proceeding to the remaining chapters.

The Organization of the Book

The book is divided into seven sections each comprised of a major chapter and discussion chapter, the last topic includes two discussion chapters. The authors of the discussion chapters were given the freedom to develop any issue or issues which they felt should be included under the guidelines of their assigned topic.

PART I   *A Sociological Analysis of Research* — The papers by Form and Ehrlich set the stage for the analysis by conducting a sociological analysis of the social structures and social processes that are involved in research.

PART II   *Theory and Theory Building* — Dubin and Wooldridge provide further orientation through a discussion of theory, theory building, the functions of theory, and the relationship of theory to research. These chapters are a necessary background for an analysis of managing research.

PART III   *Demonstration and Applied Research* — As a result of the importance of evaluative designs a special section is devoted to models for demonstration and applied research. Suchman presents guidelines for this research, discusses common problems encountered, and suggests solutions. Allerhand presents his own experiences in evaluative research as case studies illustrating the general principles he has derived for managing such projects.

PART IV   *Organizational Structures for Research* — Rossi and Sussman take up an analysis of the structures by which research is organized. They describe and analyze alternative research organizational structures, their relative advantages and disadvantages, their relations with other organizations such as funding organizations and universities, and their advantages and disadvantages to the individual researcher.

PART V   *The Management and Tactics of Research* — Professors Borgatta and Haug were assigned the task of discussing the managerial and tactical problems involved in data collection, processing, and analysis that so often cause serious problems in research projects. Guidelines and practical techniques to solve these problems are suggested.

PART VI   *The Implementation of Research* — In the major paper in this section Freeman analyzes elements to be considered in designing and managing a research project under the headings of cooperation of subjects and relevant organizations, reliability, validity, precision and accuracy, and efficiency. Wolkon discusses cooperation with persons in the research setting as a major determinant of the quality of research and its outcomes.

PART VII   *Integrating Research and Practice* — The problem which orients the last section is the "interface" between research and practice. Leonard and Skipper analyze the cultural and structural components which account for the separation between research and practice. The authors then present their solution to the problem and discuss how it can function to bring about a closer relationship between research and practice. Usdane discusses the problem of the utilization of research findings and describes the research utilization program developed under his administration of the Division of Research and Demonstration Grants of the Social and Rehabilitation Service as a solution to the problem. Puth presents the practitioner's viewpoint on the problem — the viewpoint of a man vitally concerned with developing means of dealing with human problems.

Finally, it is hoped that the ideas presented and the questions raised in the following chapters will lead to more of the research process being viewed as problematic. If the book stimulates further research and refinement in the theories and procedures with the organization, management and tactics of social research, then our efforts will have been worthwhile.

RICHARD O'TOOLE

A SOCIOLOGICAL ANALYSIS
OF RESEARCH

CHAPTER ONE

The Sociology of Social Research

WILLIAM H. FORM

An Overview of the Problem

Research is a social activity whose problems and methods are affected by the milieu in which it takes place. In order to increase awareness of this milieu, we propose to consider research as a social system comprised of sponsors, researchers, and hosts. All three may affect the selection of problems to be studied, the methods used in research, and the dissemination of the results. The sociology of social research examines the decision-making process in the research system.

Just as surely as the technological and organizational revolutions transform society, they also transform the organization of research. A shift of emphasis is taking place away from the craft researcher studying interpersonal relations to research institutes studying interorganizational relations. Thus, in the future, more research will be done in an organizational context. In the craft situation, the researcher's primary management problem is to exert effective personal influence in the research system in order to obtain maximum cooperation. When research is conducted by an agency, however, the primary problem becomes one of effective collective bargaining with the sponsors and hosts. Different ethical dilemmas flow from different political dilemmas in each type of research situation. However, in both types of research social systems, the more the research itself studies problems of power between collectivities, the more resistance will researchers encounter in their work. The task of sociologists is to try

3

to anticipate the power situation they will confront in different types of research situations and to devise the most appropriate methodology to achieve their goals.

Research as a Social System

Among the social scientist's ubiquitous anxieties is doubt about the validity of his data. He is worried that his presence, instruments, and modes of operation somehow filter and distort the data he collects. Ideally, he would like to collect information without influencing the behavior of the people he is studying. Unfortunately, he cannot always do so, for social research itself is a social process, in which the investigator *participates* in a social milieu that existed long before he entered the field, influences him while he is in the field, and continues to affect his future research. Yet, while his occupational *raison d'être* is to analyze social phenomena, he has hesitated to study research itself in this context.

He must overcome this hesitancy for several reasons. First, since he is often a variable in the situations he is studying, any approach that fails to take his own behavior into account results in distortion. Second, today social research is itself a significant area worthy of study. Thousands of people derive a living from research and they spend millions of dollars annually doing it. This vast enterprise now constitutes a distinct social and cultural pattern to which people respond in predictable ways. Third, sociology is sufficiently mature and secure to risk the testing of specific hypotheses concerning how social situations in research may affect the quality of its data. Such knowledge needs to be fed back systematically into the discipline to guide future research strategies.

Different relationships are probably formed at different stages of the research: e.g., formulating ideas, raising money, training a field staff, securing permission to do the research, contacting respondents, analyzing data, securing a publisher, communicating research results to the sponsors, and so on.[1] It may be that different types of social systems are associated with different research techniques (survey, participant observation, non-participant observation, panel analyses, experimentation, etc.). This essay will concentrate primarily on social relationships encountered in the entry and fieldwork stages of research because these stages require personal interaction.

The concept "research social system" has advantages for our analysis because it emphasizes the relationship between the researcher and persons and agencies with whom he interacts and avoids an exclusive emphasis on the researcher. Of course, sociologists are aware that their research occurs in a social context, but they acknowledge this fact only obliquely. Generally sociologists assume that people in the organizations they study have positive feelings toward them. Yet, at times, they recognize that respondents won't cooperate and they must be induced to, preferably without their knowledge. For example, the technique of pretending that an interview is completed, when in fact it isn't, is a standard artifice. There is a general tendency to avoid ethical confrontations by assuming that both researchers and respondents will be honest.[2] In short, although the "Heisenberg principle" and the "Hawthorne effect" are well known, researchers generally ignore the phenomena in their own research.[3] Traditionally, researchers have neglected to report how their data may have been affected by adverse situations in the field.[4] When reported, they are typically evaluated as shortcomings in field techniques; i.e., they are swept under the methodological carpet. Recent exceptions to this general trend are found in the collected works of Adams and Preiss (1960), Hammond (1964), Vidich, Bensman, and Stein (1964), and Sjoberg (1967). The problems and insights raised in these works are somewhat different from mine, but they do contribute to our fund of knowledge about research as a social phenomenon.

Sponsors, Researchers, and Hosts

Research situations may vary in social complexity: e.g., one researcher working with accumulated records and requiring no social interaction, a dyadic relationship between researcher and respondent (e.g., a questionnaire or interview situation), or a team of researchers studying a large number of community organizations. At a later point I shall specify some characteristics of these different types of research social ·systems. Here let us explore the characteristics of a moderately complex research situation in which there are at least three interacting parties: sponsors, researchers, and the researched (hosts). Any of the three may be a person, a small group, or a complex set of organizations. Whatever the situation, each may be thought of as a sub-system having a distinct set of values, a characteristic organization (or personality), and a set of expectations toward the others. The "success" of the research would seem to depend on how well the sponsors, researchers, and hosts relate to the others throughout the study.

There are two main types of sponsors, financial and social, and both may be involved in the research. Whyte (1959) and Orlans (1967), among others, have examined in detail how financial sponsors may participate in the research social system. The politics of research patronage (who gets money for research) are too well known to require elaboration here, but the sponsor's influence on research design and methodology remains shrouded from public scrutiny. Yet the trend is clear: financial sponsors are becoming increasingly powerful because they can afford to hire the most talented researchers to look after their interests. Indeed, this talent may even be represented by a person who is hired to monitor the work of a colleague. Gerard Piel (1967) observed that in this situation the sponsor is judge, jury, plaintiff, and defendant. Sometimes the financial sponsor is a private or governmental bureau that has close ties to the group being studied. The sponsor can influence the research by advising its clientele (the research host) how to "cooperate" with the researcher. The financial sponsor can influence the research social system not only by exerting financial pressure, but also by influencing the research design, general methodology, field operations, and publication and dissemination of the data.[5] In short, there is an increasing amount of formal and informal bargaining between sponsor and researcher on what research will be done, how it shall be done, and how its results shall be presented.[6]

The researcher must, in some way, gain acceptance of himself and his project by the people or organizations he is studying. He cannot avoid justifying himself and his research because he needs cooperation to obtain valid and reliable data. It may be helpful to label the people and groups whose cooperation he needs as his "hosts" since, in a real sense, his presence among them is at their sufferance, and they can refuse to cooperate.

The researcher–host relationship is often facilitated by an intermediary or a social sponsor. Sometimes the investigator feels that he needs no sponsor to gain acceptance of the groups he is studying.[7] He sponsors himself in the name of science, the ultimate social utility of his research, or other values that he feels appeal to his "hosts." At other times, he may feel that he needs a sponsor who either is a member of the group he wants to study or has access to it. In both instances, the sponsorship decision may affect the design of research, so the selection of the sponsor should not be made haphazardly. To my knowledge, social scientists have not systematically studied research sponsors and how their behavior affects research decisions.

The folklore of sponsorship encourages blundering behavior. Researchers typically solicit the most powerful or prestigious person they know in an organization for permission to conduct a study, or they identify an intermediary who will introduce them to someone in the organization.[8] This person is then asked to introduce the researcher to someone higher in the organization until the most powerful person who can "grant permission" for the study is located. Three errors may occur in this strategy: the belief that (1) the social credit of the original relationship can be effectively transferred up the hierarchy; that (2) the position of the original sponsor in his social system permits him to render the services expected of him;[9] and that (3) a powerful and prestigious person can, in fact, sponsor effectively at all organizational levels. Sponsorship, like prestige, is not necessarily transferable; it can be contested at any time by any faction in an organization.

The effective sponsor typically participates in two systems (the researcher's and host's), is accepted in both, and can be helpful to both. Other positions are known to have these characteristics: the fixer, the middleman, the marginal man, the broker, and the mediator. The researcher may learn much about sponsorship by studying these positions. In large and complex organizations, no one person can assume the sponsorship role because even the best sponsor has unequal status, access, and power in different parts of an organization. Sponsorship then involves different types of persons who can perform different services depending on the demands of the research and the social climate of the research situation.

Reciprocal Role-Sets and Functions

Social scientists have recognized some of the relationships that develop between them and their hosts (respondents, interviewees, organizations, or complex of organizations). The relationship that has been studied most is that between the interviewer and his respondent. (Riesman and Benny, 1956; Hyman, 1954; Kohn and Cannell, 1957; American Journal of Sociology, September, 1956.) Unfortunately, how respondents to a questionnaire evaluate the researcher has received less attention. Yet a degree of cleavage between the researcher and his host may be inevitable because the researcher occupies a unique position in the relationship: he is a temporary "intruder" or an inquisitive stranger who has ideas of the appropriate supplementary behavior he expects of his hosts.[10] The host may have different ideas about how he should behave.[11] In other terms, the role-sets or the intergroup relationships may not be symmetrical, and this situation may result in conflicts or misunderstandings that can invalidate the data. Although Sjoberg and Nett (1968: 80–95) briefly examined the problem of how the scientist legitimizes his behavior to the public, they did not examine systematically the reciprocal responses of the public.[12] It may be useful to list here some of the possible reciprocal role sets between the researcher and host in interpersonal social situations. At a later point, we shall review social exchanges between researcher and host in complex organizational situations.

1. *Social photographer or ethnographer.* Often parading as social historians, researchers try to present themselves as neutral observers of the way of life, problems and situations that confront the people they are studying. The host is expected to "act naturally" (pretend the researcher is not there) while his picture is being taken, a most difficult thing to do.

2. *Public relations expert.* Researchers sometimes present themselves as community relations publicists who will so dramatize the problems and difficulties their hosts face that a compassionate public will somehow help them. In exchange for good publicity, the host is expected to reveal all to the empathic observers.

3. *Social engineer.* Sometimes researchers suggest that their findings may be directly useful to the host, but the particular use can be specified only after prolonged consultation. During this period the host may be expected to cooperate in some "experiments" to reveal "latent patterns." Sometimes there is no "payoff," and conflict ensues.

4. *Teaching.* In self-surveys, researchers define their role as teaching the host how to gather systematic social knowledge about himself. Such studies are sometimes inexpensive because the data are collected by the client himself or the host. However, the data are made available to the researcher who uses them for his own purposes. Thus, sometimes the host is expected to play the role of a cooperative and exploited student. Some consequences of this type of relationship are folk knowledge in the profession.

5. *Scientist.* Occasionally the researcher defines himself as a pure scientist who wants information and offers his host nothing in return. Both are the handmaidens of science, but the host is expected to yield to the superior intellect and knowledge of the researchers.

6. Other role sets are possible, and sometimes all of them are found in the same situation (Vidich and Bensman, 1964).

Several observations may be made about the reciprocal role-sets or researcher–organization relations. First, while the researcher may change his behavior during the study, he may expect the host to behave uniformly. This asymmetry is apparent in the description of the five role-sets: the variation is greater in the behavior of the researcher than in the responses he expects from his hosts.[13] Second, the researcher may define his functions differently than do his sponsors and hosts. While such disagreements may be inevitable in all functionally differentiated systems, some of them may result from the researcher's decision to mask his role.[14] Since most academicians are not professional actors, their deceptions are often clumsy and they expose themselves. Third, misunderstandings may arise among researchers, sponsors, and hosts as they redefine their relationships during a study. Research needs to be done on how such misunderstandings arise and how confrontations are resolved.

Two illustrations of the interview situation reveal the variability of the relationships that can develop in it and the possibly injurious consequences for gathering reliable data. A common ritual at the end of an interview is for the interviewer to ask the respondents what they thought about the interview. Since their comments are rarely used to interpret data, this solicitation is a form of deceit or an attempt to reduce the tension of the situation (Goffman, 1952). Unless social scientists take into account how the attitudes and behavior of their sponsors and hosts affect their research, they may accumulate data of uncertain validity. In this connection the recent work of Irwin Deutscher (1966, 1969) should be studied. He clearly demonstrated, in a review of studies on ethnic prejudice, that, while the reliability of findings has increased over time, their validity may have diminished. The primary reason for this situation has been that the researchers are increasingly less inclined to take into account the social context of the research situation.[15]

In one of my studies, follow-up interviews with respondents evoked the following reactions to a single interviewer:

"It was a great experience! I learned a lot."
"He was kind of a nut, wasn't he?"
"What a waste of time that was."
"I gave him only enough to satisfy him."
"He was kind of naive, wasn't he? No sense telling him everything."

If this interviewer performed consistently, he obviously did not evoke a consistent role definition from his respondents, and the data he recorded may be biased.

Cannell and Axelrod (1956) reported the reactions of interviewees in four surveys. Despite near unanimity that they were not pressured, that interviewers were friendly, that the survey aims were made clear, 22 to 28 per cent of the respondents did not want to be interviewed again and 15 to 36 per cent found some of the questions too personal. The substantive replies of these people should be compared with those of the more enthusiastic respondents. In short, to assess the value of data they collect, sociologists need to know more about how people respond to them. It is indeed strange that sociologists do not apply their knowledge of group structure and processes to their own research.

The social organization of the host affects the type of reception the researcher will receive and his behavior toward the host. In survey research situations, in which the individuals interviewed are scattered ecologically and have no social contacts with one another, the relationship between the researcher and host is a dyadic one — whether the researcher represents himself or a research organization. Although, as we have demonstrated, problems can arise in the relationship, they are not primarily problems of power because respondents cannot easily organize against the researcher. Since the researcher is not studying social organization directly, no organizational response can be made toward him. He can collect data and publish his results with relative impunity.

If the host is a social organization, its response to the researcher, whether he is an individual or an organization, depends in large part upon its degree of internal integration, the amount of communication among its members or units (organization), and the power relationships among them. If the host is a community, its social structure tends to be diffuse, so the constituent organizations are not likely to respond to the researcher consensually and this lack of consensus enables the researcher to work out a specific strategy toward each organization.

The researcher faces the most difficult problems when his host is a single organization, such as a bureaucracy. Here a great deal of daily communication occurs among the members of the constituent units, and the units stand in a clear power relationship to one another. The research, irrespective of its content, will be perceived as having some effect on the internal relations of the organization. Therefore the researcher will experience more difficulty in gaining access to do the study and he will be blocked from studying important problems of power.

Structural Changes in Research Organization: Craft and Organizational Models

The technological and bureaucratic revolutions that are changing the economy and other institutions also affect science and its methodology (Scott, 1966). Traditionally, social science has been a craft. The master and his apprentice performed all of the research tasks. Singly or together they designed the research, did all the field work, analyzed the data, and published the results. Slowly and informally a methodology and a technology of field operations evolved that seemed to parallel those used by the physical and natural sciences.

J. A. Barnes (1963) points out that the methodology of social anthropologists and sociologists prior to 1925 was analogous to that used by natural scientists. Researchers did not disturb the social life of the people they studied, researchers did not want to become involved in policy questions, the people they studied did not know what social research was, and they did not read research reports. In short, researchers were relatively free to do what they wanted to do, and what they did had little effect on the people they studied.

Craft researchers typically work in two-person social systems which include the researcher and his respondent or the observed.[16] In the questionnaire, the observer is the instrument itself, and the respondent is the other in the dyadic relationship. Social research texts tend to be manuals on how the craftsman and his apprentice should gather data in these interpersonal contexts. Methods of studying organizational and community phenomena are meagerly developed. Where mentioned, the unit of analysis is not an organization but rather individuals behaving in organizational, institutional, or community settings.

Obviously, these observations on the craft model of research do not apply to the entire range of current social research. They are a caricature of the dominant type of research being conducted. While the craft pattern will continue to flourish, research increasingly will be done by large bureaus or institutes. Yet the field techniques used by these institutes still tend to be those developed in the craft tradition. They are predicated on a "human relations" or "psychiatric" model of interpersonal behavior. That is, the social relationship between the researcher and the host is built on the desire to have a warm, interpersonal, cooperative relationship. Moreover, the scientific questions typically pursued deal with interpersonal relations. Evidence that field techniques are dominated by a human relations model may be seen by analyzing the social relationships between researchers and hosts in the cases presented in *Human Organization Research* (Adams and Preiss, 1960) and similar collections.

To study issues where research is done in an interorganizational context, let us focus, by way of contrast, on a contemporary, complex, social research system. At the center is the research institute, which is a holding company that contains semi-autonomous units specializing in certain types of research but sharing some common services and specialists (e.g., sampling, data processing, field operations, and so on). This institute is often supervised by an advisory board that is attached to a larger organization such as a university, government bureau, or business. In addition, advisory research boards, professional associations, departmental faculties, and other organizations have quasi-official ties to the institute. Financial sponsors, who support the institute or a specific piece of research, may also be considered part of the research social system.

The *ad hoc* organizational arrangements in certain types of research situations may be complex. "Action research" in a community setting involves a large number of competing organizations, some of which have research bureaus of their own. Advisory boards, composed of representatives of the groups participating in the research or affected by the research, have their own experts who may be asked to monitor the research. In some instances, the organizations participating in the research social system may represent almost the total spectrum of the community (Brymer and Farris, 1967; Vidich, Bensman, and Stein, 1964). What is probably more important, no clear principles define the relationships among the organizations. Thus, although there may be no hierarchical or authoritative pattern within the emergent research social system, consensus sufficient to get the research job done is needed. The consequences of this type of structure for research operations are considered later.

The Research Institute

In an informed article, Rossi (1964) contrasts the research institute and the independent faculty researcher. He stresses that there are strong strains in the institute to build an organization in which the lines of authority are clearer than in a teaching department. The institute gradually develops autonomy from university departments and operates independently. Yet it can attract departmental members because it has the resources to increase their productivity. Often the institute engages in large surveys that are, by their nature, expensive ventures. Consequently the institute grows in size, division of labor, and specialization. The more it grows, the steeper is its hierarchy, the more elaborate its division of labor, and the more is its staff controlled by impersonal authority.

Campbell (1953) points out that the administrator of a large research institute is often a scholar raised in the craft tradition. Despite his desire to follow this tradition, subordinates, sponsors, and others expect and want him to behave bureaucratically. He must schedule each research stage, meet certain deadlines, mollify sponsors, adjudicate employee grievances, and so on. The administrator wants his study directors to assume some of these responsibilities, but they tend to resist him because they interpret administrative activities as antithetical to scholarship.

Thus, a persistent problem which research institutes face is the development, by its hierarchy, of a sense of common fate.

Record (1967: 33–34) explains how the research institute develops types of external relationships different from those of the individual researcher:

> Unlike the individual researcher, who is apt to define his relationship to an interest group in the context of a single study, the research institute needs to develop continuing associations to maintain open pipelines over long periods of time. The individual scholar may move on but the institute remains. Its purposes, needs, reputation, image, and rationale are closely bound up with, yet distinct from, the purposes, needs, reputation, image, and rationale of its individual staff members at any one moment and certainly of the personnel as it changes over time. . . . Perhaps the single most important determinant of the degree of cooperation an institute can gain for new studies is its reputation for "responsibility" and "trustworthiness" in previous projects. To maintain access to organizations in its area, the institute must develop a working relationship which embodies mutual confidence. Often the institute's community advisory committee helps it to gain entrée to specific groups and to achieve "respectability" among the organizations which operate in its field of study.

It is difficult to find a neutral description and evaluation of the research institute from social scientists reared in the craft tradition. The advantages of bureaucracies are quickly forgotten and their demonic characteristics emphasized. Research institutes are seen as constricting the creativity of the scholar, forcing him to lose contact with scientific problems, bending him to the coercive and conservative wills of the sponsors and administrators, insisting that he engage in scholastic inbreeding, permitting him to escape intellectual responsibility, and many other ills that befall the organization man (Record, 1960; Barnes, 1963; Vidich and Bensman, 1964). This ideological emphasis is not surprising given its honorable ancestry in the discipline (Weber, 1946; Merton, 1940), yet it does becloud an impartial analysis of the political context of the research social system.

In summary, the research institute is an internally differentiated agency containing many of the organizational attributes of a factory. It employs research directors, research specialists, and technical specialists who deal with problems of sampling, computer analysis, field supervision, and so on. It also employs workers of relatively low status who may not share the values of the research directors. The institute also supports a complex technology. Staff and technology are so expensive to maintain that the institute is *dependent upon a constant inflow of money* to keep operations going. Almost of necessity it must devote increasing energy to applied research. The sponsors who provide the money must be satisfied, and they will not subsidize research that will harm them. Thus constricted by institutional forces, the institute faces difficulties in studying the behavior of the high and mighty.

The shift of social research from an individualistic to an organizational effort should remind us of the kinds of changes that accompany the passing of a traditional society and the creation of a modern industrial one. In the latter, technology and the complex organization exert independent effects on research, and it is to these effects that we shall now turn.

Social Research in a Complex Organizational Milieu

Since research bureaus, the organizations they study, and the social milieu in which both function have characteristics of formal, large-scale, and complex organizations, the strategies they use in dealing with one another take the form of collective bargaining. Before specifying the strategies, let us examine some features of formal and complex organizations.

Complex organizations are comprised of units or sub-systems that are assigned specific tasks that fit into a pattern. The pattern may be clearly specified, as in some bureaucracies, or vaguely apparent as in some community associations. In both instances, tasks are assigned to sub-organizations and not to persons or roles. Although interdependent, sub-organizations have more internal than external interaction, and thus they develop unique goals and values. Since the attainment of these goals is often achieved at the expense of others, each sub-organization must know how the activities of others may affect its own welfare. An informal communication system arises to provide the information necessary for collective bargaining (Miller and Form, 1964: 275–80). One main problem of complex organizations is maintaining sufficient control over its units so that the integrational goals of the organization will take precedence over those of its units. This integration-segmentation struggle is a basic feature of complex organizations.

In what ways does this milieu affect the behavior of the research organization? Since research is a form of intervention into a system that has maintained some degree of equilibrium, it will be resisted as any other form of intervention. A copious literature documents how large-scale organizations resist innovations, reorganization, technological changes, and evaluations even when they are initiated from within (Gouldner, 1954; Whyte, 1955). Since research is usually defined by the members of the organization being studied as a prelude to change, it will be especially resisted. Sjoberg and Nett (1968: 119) summarize this situation very well:

> Most bureaucratic structures object to being studied in depth — except perhaps when the diffusion of results can be carefully controlled — because social research tends to expose their practices to outsiders, including competitors and opponents. . . . And whenever there are competitive relations among business organizations, between government and business, and so on, the accepted practice calls for controls of the information to be released to outsiders. Inasmuch as formal organizations are reluctant to expose their operations to public scrutiny for fear that politicians will object to or misinterpret various practices and consequently withdraw their support, social scientists tend to study relatively weak organizations. When they do study the very powerful ones, they usually skirt the sensitive issues. Thus most studies of bureaucracies in the United States have been of the middle-level management and not of the elite decision makers. Also relevant is the difficulty in gaining access to the power elements, unless one relies upon marginal informants.

Research intervention into a complex organization, whether by a single researcher or by an agency, necessarily increases the self-consciousness of the researcher and his visibility in the host organization. The formal and informal communication networks assure the researcher a type of "instant notoriety" he might not experience in the study of a more loosely-knit system. The more sub-systems he contacts, the greater will be his visibility and the more pressure he will feel to present a coherent account of what he intends to do. He must usually make a formal announcement of his entry and also specify his objectives according to the expectations he has of others. Since formal organizations allocate and make public the functions of each department or unit, employees are understandably uneasy with the researcher who does not do the same. Under these circumstances the researcher will have difficulty improvising statements and behavior to fit all situations.[17]

Understandably, research institutes tend to specify how researchers should behave in organizational studies. These specifications tend to be based on vague intuitions of what "will work" or get them by, and not on knowledge of how new positions or functions will fit into existing complex organizations. Clearly, sociologists should design alternative strategies on the basis of their knowledge about how organizations function. They should be able to conduct experiments, for example, on whether an increased awareness of the researchers affects their reception and the amount and validity of the data they receive.[18]

Whenever two or more sub-systems are coordinated to achieve common goals, their independence is curtailed; and this generalization applies to research institutes studying large organizations or a cluster of organizations. How sub-systems resolve problems of their mutual dependency reflects the distribution of power in an organization. Since the research agency is not a permanent part of the organization it is studying, it occupies a special status and probably has less power than the other sub-systems. The main source of this weakness, at least in the beginning of research, stems from the agency's inability to use knowledge about the organization to its advantage. However, as a specialist in accumulating knowledge, the research agency gradually acquires a comprehensive view of the organization, and in so doing, acquires more independence and power. Toward the end of the study the researchers often possess more knowledge of the organization than any of its members, including management. However, as soon as the research is completed, the institute departs and loses the power that it acquired. Thus, the institute may have a "career" in the research social system, extending from extreme dependency to considerable independence.

The dependency of the researchers is of two sorts, financial and informational; and the dependency is doubled if both are derived from the same source. This double dependency explains why house-sponsored research generally is inferior to research efforts where the two dependencies are separated. Rossi points out that the sources of research money are relatively few, so that the financial sponsors can put some pressure on researchers and monitor their operations. Yet financial dependency does not paralyze the research team because it has a monopoly on one important weapon: research expertise. The sponsor's dependency on it enables the researchers to engage in passive "robin-hooding," i.e., including in the research items of no interest to the sponsor, but which the sponsor must nonetheless support (Rossi, 1964: 1156).

Although financial dependency does affect research questions and methodology, informational dependency is more critical for obtaining valid and reliable data. This problem is more important for a research institute than for a lone researcher because ordinarily the institute has a relatively greater impact on the host organization than the researcher (Scott, 1965: 763). The individual researcher can pace his work more leisurely and so he has time to establish rapport with many people and become less conspicuous. The research institute, on the other hand, often moves into the host organization with a team of interviewers or observers to study several parts of the organization simultaneously. Merely the announcement that a heavily financed study has begun and an advisory board has been selected to help the researchers signals employees that changes are in the wind and they should prepare to defend themselves.

It can be argued that employees of bureaucracies and community associations accommodate easily to organizational innovations and that the introduction of research into an organization is not different than any other type of change. After all, the task of modern management is to initiate change. Since no study has attempted to measure the relative impact of research on employees as opposed to other types of managerially inspired changes, no *a priori* answer to the problem is possible. However, research intervention is a different order of change. Employees become unusually suspicious when changes are inspired by an outside research firm because "ordinary" innovations don't require this kind of legitimation. Internally inspired reorganizations come and go, but their impact is usually less than management anticipates. Employees are sophisticated in the ways of handling reorganizations and minimizing their impact on work. They will want especially to anticipate much of what the researchers want in order to minimize injurious findings. This desire is especially strong in cases where researchers are conducting experiments to forge new management policies.[19] Whether or not management establishes an advisory board to monitor the research team, the employees will certainly set up their own informal monitoring devices.[20] Undoubtedly monitoring affects the kind and quality of data researchers will collect. Moreover, each sub-system in the organization will respond differently to the researchers, depending on how each anticipates what the impact of the research will be. The researchers naturally will try to minimize their influence on the organization, but their efforts can only be partially effective because they have no direct control over the organization. The Heisenberg effect is inevitable.

The Exchange-Bargaining Process in Research

As we have seen, researchers who study complex organizations become conscious of their behavior, conscious of their dependency on others, and conscious of how others define them. They must therefore consider what tactics to adopt, especially when they need the cooperation of two or more interacting units of the organization. If this cooperation is not forthcoming, the researchers may try to stimulate it by engaging in a form of action research or collective bargaining. They do so when they are denied the cooperation earlier promised them.

Joan W. Moore (1967: 237) clearly recognized this situation in her study of Mexican–American relations in the Southwest. She reported on the problems that arose from the breaking of an implicit agreement with the Community Advisory Committee, which was part of the research social system:

> Many Anglo groups . . . who have attempted to establish relations with a group of Mexican–American leaders have become targets of an attack whose weapons are the old charges of discrimination and exploitation of Mexican–Americans by Anglos. Our project has been no exception: the Committee had been used as such a forum by a leader apparently motivated in part by a desire to reaffirm the legitimacy of his leadership to the audience of other Committee members. Though we would reject the relevance of the manifest content of his attacks on our projects, its latent content may have considerable validity, and it calls into question the underlying nature of the bargain between researcher and subject.

Later Moore (1967: 240) reported:

> The history of the exploratory phase of our project is one of modification of structure, technique, and locations for research in the course of nearly a year's communication with our subjects and their neighbors, and our fellow academics. The focus of the chronicle above has been to show how the research process itself is involved in the political process and has moral consequences.

Moore does not go far enough in her analysis because she does not recognize that the researchers themselves may initiate the political process. They are not always helpless victims caught up in politics for they sometimes intervene to structure relations to serve their own purposes.

In a bargaining situation, by definition, the participants must have resources that they can apply to achieve their goals despite the resistance of others. That no party has all the resources makes exchanges possible, for when one party has no resources it must submit to the will of those who do. The literature is replete with illustrations of unsuccessful research ventures in which researchers lacked sufficient power to gain acceptance, or, as happens more often, once having begun a study, were unable to obtain the desired information for "lack of cooperation," i.e., insufficient power to bargain for the desired information.

In most studies, the researchers seem the most powerless and the sponsors, advisory committees, host, and others seem to have all the weapons. Except for situations where the researchers operate as spies or uninvited guests, they need the cooperation of the parties being studied to get information.[21] The financial sponsor, host, and others control access to information, the quality of information given, access to persons who control information sources, space to work, time schedules, and so on. Any or all of these needs may be denied.

What weapons does the researcher have? What can he exchange in the bargaining? First, if he has permission to do a study, he has the status of an invited guest who can expect the cooperation and good will of his host. To be sure, the demands a guest can make on his host are limited, but they are often undefined and their specification may have a social cost: embarrassment to the host. The researcher can depend upon the "fund of good will" that all people have in normal personal encounters, but he also has the additional good will extended to the guest. Most researchers who work with "unsophisticated hosts" (people who have not had previous experience with researchers) can use this good will to obtain a great deal of cooperation and information. Good will is the primary resource of the craft researcher who works with individual respondents. His success depends upon how well he projects himself, how positive an identity he builds, and how influential a sponsor he can find. Brymer and Farris (1960: 305) reported that among Mexican–Americans, cooperation depended on being defined as a "good guy," while Whyte (1966: 111–114) emphasized in *Street Corner Society* that sponsorship was his primary resource.

Two factors in organizational research decrease the relative importance of the researcher's interpersonal competence and fund of good will: the research sophistication of the host and the impersonalization of the research process. In the United States, research is no longer rare, so people increasingly evaluate it according to their own objectives. Thus the researcher's fund of good will is shrinking. When research is defined in non-personal terms, i.e., as a business, people feel that they don't need to cooperate with it. Therefore, the research institute that studies an organization must increasingly rely on the other types of resources to obtain information.

One obvious resource is the prestige of the researcher as a university professor or as a man of great knowledge. Low status respondents especially gain prestige from interacting with the researcher. In large organizations, the researcher (or his organization) may require a long time to establish and communicate his prestige. Blau (1964: 30–31) indicated that when he first began his study of bureaucracy, he was marginal to the system and he was able to talk only to marginal people. As his prestige grew, he was able to "trade" on this resource and interview higher status people who gained respect in their systems by being interviewed. Others have reported that toward the end of their field work their prestige had grown so much that respondents vied to be interviewed. The prestige of the researcher is not as important a resource when an organization conducts the research, when the prestige of the field staff is low, and when the prestige of the respondent is high. Marcus (1965: 5) reported:

> It is no accident, then, that most studies are made of lower echelons in organizations. The researcher's own anxiety tends to increase as he interviews and observes those who more closely approximate his status. Higher management personnel tend to be more familiar with research techniques and can usually employ sophisticated verbal skills to parry questions. All this makes upper echelons more difficult to interview even though they appear more friendly, affable and accepting. The entire problem is compounded by the fact that upper management personnel possesses a vocabulary which is glib but incapable of describing work which often has no definite pattern or structure.

The prestige of the researcher is derived not only from his occupational level but also from his knowledge, which is only vaguely apparent to employees at the early stage of research but becomes increasingly obvious as the research progresses. At some point researchers cannot help but reveal that they know more about the organization than any of its members. Rossi (1964), Blau (1964), Scott (1965), and others have shown that this knowledge can be used to increase a respondent's cooperation. Although certain ethical problems arise from using knowledge as pressure, information exchanges can be made. Gouldner (1967) obtained access into a division because he had earlier provided the division head with information that he used in a successful presentation before top management. Dalton (1964) also built up obligations with intimates in order to obtain confidential information.

A more complex situation involving exchange of information is confronted when the cooperation of two or more units of an organization is needed. Form and Gale, in a study of automobile workers in Argentina, needed access to the personnel files in order to obtain the roster of employees from which to select a sample. They needed the consent of the industrial relations manager, the personnel manager, and the president of the local labor union to conduct the study. The personnel and the industrial relations manager were competing for the support of top management for certain pet projects, and the union president was trying to demonstrate his independence from the industrial relations manager who informally controlled industrial relations. None was inclined to approve the study, but none would formally deny it. The consent of one might provide the researchers the leverage necessary to get the consent of the others. The researchers convinced the personnel manager that they could prepare a report on recruitment and turnover of company personnel from company files. They prepared a report that impressed top management, raised the status of the personnel manager, "sold" the utility of sociology, and provided evidence to the company that the researchers were not against management. Thus, the report was exchanged for access to the files (Form and Gale: 1967). However, the tactic had its costs, for the industrial relations director became less cooperative. To placate him, the researchers always visited him first whenever they entered the plant for any reason, including visits to the personnel director. The industrial relations director finally gave his consent; an added inducement in his decision was the threat that the researchers would approach the union without using the director as an intermediator, a tactic that would have undercut his status and reduced his influence on the research. The consent of the union was also obtained, despite the resistance of its president, by systematically developing rapport with lower level officers who aspired to and later succeeded in seizing control of the union. This tactic was successful because the president was losing control of the union and because the researchers recognized the growing power of the faction.

This case illustrates something more than an exchange; i.e., while attempting to gain access the researchers discovered allegedly confidential information about industrial relations. Discreet use of this information demonstrated to company and union officials that withholding certain kinds of information or giving misinformation was useless. Clearly, a formidable resource which the researcher has in bargaining is confidential knowledge of the local situation. He is in a race to gather enough information about the organization for bargaining before access may be denied him or before the situation becomes unfavorably balanced against him.

Bargaining is not necessarily a simple dyadic relationship. The researcher may forge a temporary alliance with one unit of the organization or he may serve as a channel of communication between previously isolated units and thus build general obligations. Although he may not be able to marshall sufficient resources to bargain for all the data he wants, he should exploit all of his resources. Research bargaining is so widespread and so important that social scientists should study it systematically and recommend policies for its use. Clumsy improvising of field tactics should be replaced by tested knowledge about how complex organizations bargain.[22]

Social Structure, Politics and Ideology

Whenever research takes place in complex social structures, it necessarily occurs within a political context, and, within this context, the ideology of the members of the sub-systems not only circumscribes the activities of the researchers (who themselves have a unique ideology) but also raises ethical dilemmas that differ from those that arise in simpler interpersonal research situations.

Two types of social organizations have been considered in the above discussion: a large bureaucracy and a complex of interacting community associations. In both examples the functions of the sub-systems that compose the larger organization are defined by reciprocal interactions. Since perfect reciprocities rarely exist, sub-systems tend to be reciprocally unbalanced, and this conditions leads to differences in how they view each other and the larger organization. Also, since resources of the larger organization are limited, competition or conflict between sub-systems is inevitable. Thus, in the context of conflict, differences in functions and goals, and differences in perspectives (views of the organization) provide the structural requisites for the development of ideologies peculiar to the sub-systems (Miller and Form, 1964: 368–429; Dalton, 1959). Ideological differences are commonly associated with different political strategies.

In short, complex organizations should be viewed as political collectivities, and sociologists studying them should be aware of this basic fact and take it into account in their research plans. The research institute operating within a larger organization may be considered a sub-system that has unusual structural properties and a distinctive ideology. Since researchers live in a political community, they must behave politically and consider politics in their methodology. Our task is to illustrate this reality.[23]

One unique feature of the research institute in the field is that it "participates" in more sub-systems than any other sub-system of the organization being studied.[24] This fact not only puts it astride the communication network of the organization (a source of power in itself), but permits it to learn and, if necessary, to expose the knowledge, secrets, and advantages that the sub-systems have accumulated over time. The power that sub-systems wield often depends upon keeping secret the amount and *sources* of their power. Once their sources of power are exposed, advantages quickly disappear and new strategies must be created to meet their opposition (Abramson *et al.*, 1958). So, while the greater access of the researcher gives him an advantage, it also makes others more suspicious of him.

Suspicion is an endemic feature of complex organizations, and secrecy is part of their way of life. Organizations with no secrets are vulnerable to the aggressive plans of others. As Mouzelis (1968: 163) points out, the fieldwork of organizational studies is expensive, and researchers are often dependent for funds upon those who control organizations. Consequently, researchers avoid findings which harm those who hold power, but people in lower echelons who may be harmed by the findings avoid giving researchers information that might increase the leverage of the powerful. Thus researchers who try to implement a scientific ideology are caught in a political situation in which science is suspect at all echelons.

Joan Moore (1967: 242) points out that, especially in the study of conflict, researchers are forced to validate their activities in a political context at all stages of the research.

> The academician's preoccupations are emphatically not those of the ethnic activist. Nor is the activist particularly interested in or sympathetic with the means by which conclusions are reached. Thus not only must the activist trust the researcher with "inside" interpretations of life . . . but he must accept and promulgate research conclusions on no basis stronger than faith. Pure research does not ordinarily inspire this kind of loyalty. This, unfortunately, is a problem for which the ideological background of academic sociologists fit them badly. Possibly the modern ideology of research is obsolete for research in a contemporary urban ethnic setting.

Brymer and Farris (1967: 307), who engaged in an action-research program to reduce juvenile delinquency among Spanish-speaking youth in a southwestern city, arrived at a similar conclusion.

> . . . The researcher seems to gather much of his data via methods over which he lacks firm control. . . . He is unable to control the definition that others make of him. And the data which the respondents provide the researcher tend to be in terms of their own definition of him.

Most American sociologists are caught in a dilemma. Although they acknowledge that they cannot adopt a perfectly value-free position in selecting problems, they cling to the idea that they can follow a value-free methodology. Yet in some research areas, particularly those dealing with economic and political issues, their experiences have demonstrated how difficult it is to pursue certain questions, get access to some research sites, use the methods best suited to the problem, and freely publish their findings. For example, the ideological identification of sociologists was made conspicuously apparent in industrial sociology. The "human relations in industry movement" was quickly labeled "managerial sociology," and academic sociologists generally abandoned the area to social psychologists and social scientists in business schools. The reluctance of sociologists to study the morale of workers effectively blocked their access to industry and the study of many other important problems. One consequence of this situation was that sociologists shifted their attention to the study of labor unions. Lipset, Wilensky, Dubin, Blau, Shephard, and many others have admitted that they had to identify themselves as pro-labor before they were permitted to study unions. Yet their work has not been labeled "labor sociology," which it clearly is. Neither have sociologists done much research in industrial relations or collective bargaining from a managerial, labor union, or a disinterested point of view. Here ideological opponents have closed ranks against the "neutral scientist" to keep their collective bargaining sessions secret.[25]

This striving for secrecy should not surprise social scientists. Political, class, racial, and other societal cleavages necessarily affect social scientists, who are a part of the society. That the political–ideological cleavages of American society have, until recently, been kept under control may account, in part at least, for the relatively rapid growth of a "disinterested social science." Some European countries have traditionally recognized the ideological cleavages of the society in the academic community. Catholic, Marxist, and conservative university chairs of political economy have been traditionally established by German, French, and Italian universities. In fact, a strange reversal in the ideological status of the social sciences may be occurring in Europe and the United States. While a disinterested sociology is gaining headway in Europe (perhaps accompanying a decline in ideology), an ideological splitting within the social sciences seems to be increasing in the United States (perhaps in response to rising racial and class consciousness). Ideological issues of the broader society are influencing the work of American sociologists, and many are experiencing increasing difficulty in working as disinterested investigators. Effective access into many Black communities is virtually impossible for most White sociologists irrespective of their ideological inclinations. Even Black sociologists find their entrée limited unless they espouse a position approved by the leadership. When granted access, their research is heavily monitored and they cannot publish results without "proper clearance." Advisory committees seem to be increasing their power over researchers and other participants in the research social system.

Undoubtedly sociologists will be found (as they always have been) who are not only willing to accept severe restrictions on their work, but who insist that their work is as scientifically valid as anyone's. That is, they not only accept the ideology of some groups but insist that no one can escape the impact of ideology on research. The cleavage between those who wish to maintain a value-free science and those who accept the impact of ideology on science runs deep and manifests itself in many issues.[26] We cannot pursue here the problems associated with the ideological splitting of the social science community (Gouldner, 1968). It should be apparent, however, that the political problems of conducting research will be exacerbated by the public acknowledgement of these ideological splits. While it may become easier for sponsors to select the kind of researchers they want, the researchers themselves may be faced with the more stubborn problems of managing intergroup relations in the field.

Joan Rytina (1968) has suggested that the political problems of research management vary with the research question and the social organization of the host. When the research takes place in a situation where power is concentrated, as in a bureaucracy, those in power (top management) will refuse entry to a researcher whose objective is to examine their behavior. They will tend to grant entry to researchers whose objective is to study the activities of underlings, if they are convinced that such research will enable them to maintain or increase their control in the organization. Thus, research in human relations is permitted but research on decision making within the elite structure is not.

Power in the community tends to be more diffused than it is in a bureaucracy. Therefore the study of community issues takes place in a more amorphous and sometimes more dynamic situation. Cooperation with the researcher depends upon *how* power is structured. Big businessmen, for example, need not cooperate with the researcher unless he can get other groups whose cooperation businessmen need (such as labor unions and ethnic groups) to bring pressure on business. Government officials may cooperate with researchers more readily than businessmen do not only because officials exert less imperative control over the political community but because officials are more exposed to external pressures.

Finally, in the type of research which explores individual attitudes, it is clear that the results will probably have no immediate impact on the interpersonal, organizational, or community relationships of the respondents. Here the researcher will gain cooperation to the extent that he is competent in his interpersonal relationships with the respondents.

Whether the researcher represents himself or an organization may also affect the degree of cooperation he receives in the different research settings just described. I have noted that the personnel from a research bureau tend to be more resisted than private researchers; yet the latter have fewer resources to do an extensive, empirically grounded piece of research of a large complex organization.

Ethics and Research Politics

The ethical problems facing the researcher also vary according to the type of problem he is studying and its organizational setting. Sjoberg and his colleagues (1967, 1968) have explored extensively the ethical dilemmas confronting sociologists doing research that requires the cooperation of several collectivities. They have documented many instances of ethical problems which arise from certain political dilemmas that confront all the parties in the research social system.

One basic ethical problem facing the researcher is whether or not he should disclose his full intentions to those whose cooperation he needs and those who will be affected by his findings. If he does so fully and explicitly, he will (many disagree) be less successful in gaining entrée than if he makes limited, vague, and inaccurate statements about his intentions. The prevailing practice seems to be to give the host as little information as is necessary to obtain entrée and cooperation. Dalton, Blau, Goldner, van den Berghe, and many others point out, by way of justification, that they would not have been able to conduct their research had they been completely honest with all concerned from the very beginning. They had hoped to allay suspicion as it arose. Generally this tactic is successful when informants are not apprehensive about research results. Sometimes, however, suspicion increases as the research progresses. For example, Dalton (1964: 65) confessed that, as his hypotheses became increasingly specified (as he focused on the conflicts between Catholics and Masons) in the organization, the dangers to his research increased. Yet he found no satisfactory solution to the problem of revealing his research intentions to everyone because every department he studied had its own ethics, and, as he moved across departments, he had to violate ethical understandings. Goldner (1967: 265) faced a similar problem because he realized that his data were more available to managers than to workers in the business, and thus gave the managers more power.

The crucial issue seems to be whether the interpersonal ethics which seemed adequate for the craft model of social research, can solve the *moral* problems confronting researchers working on problems of intergroup relations. I prefer using the concept moral (following Durkheim) rather than ethical, because moral traditionally applies to collective relations while ethics has an interpersonal connotation. Perhaps sociologists are attempting to follow an ethical code that is inapplicable to the collective bargaining situations they confront in social research. For example, Brymer and Farris (1967: 307) take the position that, since the researcher is unable to anticipate ethical questions beforehand, he "should perhaps shift his ethical concerns to those aspects of the research process where he does wield relatively full control — namely the storage, interpretation, and publication of the data." This suggestion avoids confronting the problems of what to do where there is disagreement on the aims of the research, the design of the research, and the type of data that will be collected. Once these questions are resolved, the storage, interpretation, and publication of the findings are relatively minor issues.

There are no easy solutions to the moral problems inherent in inter-organizational research situations, and codes of ethics promulgated by academic societies will not resolve them because the codes are not useful in collective bargaining. They are inherently vague, and conflict invariably ensues from efforts to clarify them and apply them to specific situations. If the experience in the area of industrial relations is considered, conflict increases when the parties focus on principles, morals, and ethics, and it decreases when discussion focuses on practices, procedures, and immediate objectives. Pluralistic bargaining moves from practice to principle and takes place in a developmental model of social power (Form, 1964). It works best when all parties accept research as a permanent feature of their lives, acknowledge the political character of the system in which they live, formally study (usually with the help of a social scientist) how their political system works, and participate in the implementation of research results. This solution can rarely be used to meet the political and moral dilemmas faced in most research situations. Dilemmas will remain, as all sides continue to bargain within a broad range of norms. Power, not ethics, will determine the tactics that parties will use to attain their ends.

Status Relations and Strategies of Access

Sjoberg and Nett (1968: 174) present an interesting hypothesis concerning the status problems of members of research social systems:

> Other dilemmas regarding status and role definitions emerge in modern complex industrial orders. One stems from the shifting status of researchers over time. As social scientists have climbed the social ladder, they have gained easier access to such groups as business and corporate organizations that

formerly were closed to direct observation. Simultaneously, these upper status groups have redefined the researcher's status and his redefinition affects what is being observed. Furthermore, as sociologists have experienced upward social mobility, their perception of the lower socio-economic groups has shifted, with the result that the former may be less able to empathize with the latter's way of life.

I doubt the validity of this hypothesis. Sociologists have probably been recruited from an increasingly wide span of the class–ethnic structure, so they should be able, given their backgrounds, to study and empathize with an increasingly wide range of socio-economic groups. Whatever the actual situation, the upward status mobility of sociologists has not automatically given them access to study higher status groups. Perhaps the prestige of the research organization is more important than the personal prestige of the scholar. We have already noted that scholars from highly prestigious universities have gained research access more easily to large corporations and government than scholars from less prestigious universities. The important question remains, What do sociologists study once they have gained access? Does their increased status permit them, for example, to study decision-making within top management circles? Probably not. Nonetheless Sjoberg and Nett's hypothesis that status equality among participants of a research social system promotes research cooperation deserves to be tested.

Unfortunately sociologists are not sufficiently aware of the impact that that their status and background have on their research. Two examples can be cited in which sociologists confused their influence on respondents with the respondents' own behavior. Strauss and Schatzman (1955) reported the responses of various social classes to the after-effects of a tornado in the Southwest. They found that middle-class respondents gave more accurate, more detailed, and more lengthy accounts of their behavior than lower-class respondents. They attributed this finding to the superior language and conceptual ability of the middle classes. While the explanation may have some validity, a study of victims of a tornado in Flint, Michigan, showed no class differences in the length of responses, accuracy of recall, and other responses that were coded (Form and Nosow, 1958). Such conflicting findings perhaps reveal more about the researchers than the people they are studying.

In the first study, the interviewers were midwestern middle-class college students interviewing people in Arkansas. They probably established easier rapport with the middle-class residents of the area and therefore obtained better protocols. Riesman and Benny (1956: 6), who reviewed the protocols of the study, suggest that the lower class, rural respondents wanted to talk about the theodicy of the disaster (why God had caused it), but that the NORC interviewers wanted to follow their questionnaire. In this situation the respondents answered the questions only perfunctorily. In the Flint study, interviewers were local college students who were sons of working-class fathers, and they had no difficulty getting equally good and lengthy protocols from both working- and middle-class respondents.

Perhaps a more dramatic illustration of the effect of status differentials in a research situation is the famous Hawthorne study in which, in 20,000 interviews, not one worker mentioned labor unrest to counselors during the time when the company was spending thousands of dollars fighting the unions (Gilson, 1940). If workers felt that the counselors were pro-management and anti-union, they would be careful not to express their union sentiments. Although the status barriers between researchers and respondents can be reduced by skillful interviewers, they cannot be completely eradicated. The inability to assess status dynamics when questionnaires, scales, and structured items are used in survey research is a serious shortcoming of those devices.[27]

Variables other than the prestige levels of the participants in the research system need to be considered. How the researcher structures his role is especially important for his access to the groups he is studying. Obviously his access is affected by the range of groups he studies, how much he needs to probe, and the methods he selects to gather data. His "acceptance" may be partial, uneven, or conditional (Hanna, 1965). The more conflictive and heterogeneous the inter-group relations, the more conditional the researcher's acceptance, the more problems he will encounter in establishing acceptable identities in various groups, and the greater risk he runs in obtaining equally valid data from all groups.

Although most researchers assume that high acceptance by the host is ideal, some feel that a marginal status is necessary at the early stage of research, and others feel that marginality is the best status to maintain throughout the research (Olmsted, 1965). It is remarkable that a profession that has collected so much information about social marginality has never bothered to apply this knowledge to guide its own research strategy.

Marginality is but one role the scholar can assume in a research situation. Some questions worth studying are: What other roles can researchers design for themselves in the systems they are studying? Can they play different roles (e.g., as "one of the boys," as marginal, as an outsider) in different parts of a complex organization? What happens to the quality of data when researchers are defined differently by different groups? Can researchers design different roles for themselves during different stages of research? If so, do they need training in "role taking" to learn how to play appropriate roles (Foote and Cottrell, 1955)?

Most researchers feel that they know whether they have made "errors" in gaining access to an organization and in establishing rapport after entrée. Their test is whether they were "resisted" or felt that they were. The test should be whether they received the best data possible, and the only way of knowing this information is to examine data received under different acceptance conditions. Sociologists should know what tactics are most appropriate under what conditions and for what purposes. Since such data are not available, experiments should be designed to get them.

Some research situations recur too often to allow the profession to depend upon folklore to guide its work. For example, in studying a bureaucracy, should the initial permission to conduct research be made at the highest echelon, the next highest echelon, or at several echelons simultaneously? Probably the final decision is made by second level managers, but do we really know this? What are the consequences for gaining the acceptance of people at lower levels when permission for the study was granted by the highest authorities? Is the best tactic to "fumble upstairs"?

Different types of organizations probably require different tactics to gain access. In six studies of American local labor unions, I found that to approach the top echelon of the International first was a mistake, but it was also a mistake not to inform the international after I originated contact with the locals. I also discovered that the best research sponsors for studies were teachers engaged in labor education in the extension division of the University. If this kind of knowledge is valid, it should become available to all researchers. Moreover, we should have some sociological basis for confirming hypotheses about access and not depend solely on successful experiences.

In my research of an Italian automobile factory, I needed the cooperation of four labor unions and management. I reasoned that I would be labeled a bourgeois sociologist from a bourgeois country, and that I would encounter the most resistance from the unions on the political left and the least resistance from the conservative unions and the company. I decided to approach the leftist unions first, then the other unions, and finally the company (Form, 1964). Actually, my reception was the opposite of my expectations, for I encountered most resistance from the conservative unions and the company. I should have chosen just the opposite tactic. At first, I attributed my error to being a neophyte in a foreign land, but later decided that ignorance of Italian social structure had nothing to do with my mistakes. I made equally serious ones in the United States where presumably I knew something about the society and labor–management relations. I can only suggest a hypothesis that should be tested: In an organizational complex marked by ideological conflict, the weakest unit will cooperate most with the researchers in the hope of exposing and weakening the position of the powerful.[28] The hypothesis may be incorrect, but it has the virtue of being testable in a wide range of situations.

Researchers should define their social relationships differently in different research situations. Most social scientists are aware, especially in field work, that an upper middle-class, white, male sociologist will be received differently when he studies adolescent gangs, divorce, student riots, community decision-making, race relations, union–management bargaining, drug addiction, and so on. In fact, an unpublished lore deals with "what kind of person" can get the most valid data most easily. To my knowledge this lore has not been accumulated systematically, and, what is more important, it has not been examined in a sociological framework. Considerable published information exists in certain areas (e.g., whether women make better interviewers than men in the study of family problems, whether Black interviewers get better information from Blacks than White interviewers), but this information is based largely on one type of research social system, an interpersonal one.

Abelson (1968) was interested in the problem whether people in an interview would provide valid information on their future voting behavior. He suggested that a person who distrusts Catholics would behave, "given the stimulus of a sweet lady interviewer asking whether he . . . would be willing to vote for a Catholic nominated by his own party," the same way as he would in a voting booth because there may be little discrepancy between the polling and the voting situation. Both situations, he contends, are not private, but socially parallel. His observation is an inference; it points to but does not test similarities in situations.

Social scientists should be most conscious of the effects of social structure on the results of studies when they perform laboratory experiments. Yet a review of such studies revealed that the behavior of the experimenters was not considered. Weik (1965) says that the methods of involving subjects in experiments are through instruction, hiring, making the performance visible (invidious), exchange (payment of some sort), feedback of data on the experiment to the subject, and increasing the subject's interest in the task. Clearly, these methods of involvement create different types of social systems in which the experimenter plays such different roles as the teacher, employer, peer, staff-expediter, and so on. Yet researchers have not analyzed how these different role-sets might differentially affect experimental outcomes: the researcher miraculously remains outside the social system. Finally, Weik (1965: 253) concluded, "An underlying theme in this discussion has been that subjects may ascribe the reasons for experimental happenings to themselves or to the experimenter. It was suggested that the more responsibility for the conduct of events the group assumes, the more involvement they will manifest in the experimental situation." This finding is hardly an analysis of the social system of the scientific experiment.

Social and Cultural Setting of Research

In their own research, sociologists often ignore their own maxim that no person, position, or group can be understood outside a larger social and cultural framework. Yet the profession has proposed many transcultural rules for getting information. For example, standard, survey research procedure insists that the respondent should answer questions only for himself, that the interviewer should pose questions directly and uniformly, and that he should not argue with the respondent. These rules may be interpreted as an effort by the researchers to erect a standard research social system. Yet Miller (1965) has shown in comparative studies of influentials in England and the United States that the researcher's field techniques must be accommodated to varying cultural definitions of the researcher, the research, and the subject of the research.

A colleague described his quandary in Italy when he knew that respondents were lying to him. He decided not to deviate from interviewing rules but to refocus his study and learn something about the structure of political rationalization. He later found that he learned more about his original research goals by arguing with people. In a society that prizes polemical skill, knowledge, and verbal fencing, the American rules of interviewing simply did not apply. I found in a study of Italian automobile workers that many phases of the investigation were cast in a bargaining context, and that I was expected to bargain for cooperation and information. In a situation marked by conflict, cleavage, antagonisms, and alliances, I played a special role in getting the unions and management to cooperate with the local university in the research (Form, 1964).

The inadequacy of the "rule of anonymity" in the interview was revealed in a study of community influentials in two border communities of Mexico and the United States (D'Antonio and Form, 1964). While "the line" assuring anonymity seemed to work while interviewing Americans, it did not apply in Mexico. At the end of one interview, when anonymity was being ritualistically assured, a Mexican respondent shouted, "I don't want anonymity. I want everyone to know how I feel about these things. If everything I've told you is to be disguised, then this interview has been a complete waste of my time."

In the same study, other differences that affected the research social system were noticed. The Mexican business and political influentials were ideologically more sophisticated than their American counterparts, and they were more willing to examine the relationships between business and politics. They relished the interviews, asked questions, and freely gave advice on how we should proceed in our work. Their greater spontaneity reflected the greater prestige accorded professors in Mexico and the greater cultural breadth of educated people in the country. Parallel findings are reported by Hunt, Crane, and Wahlke (1964), Lerner (1956), and Chaplin (1968).

Cross-national comparative studies force the researcher to confront differences in the social system of research because he tends to use the same methodology and techniques, yet he encounters different experiences in the field. He is forced to recognize different sponsorship patterns, different conceptions of research on the part of his respondents, differences in the status of the researcher, and so on. These differences force him to use different tactics to attain his goals, so much so that he cannot but wonder whether he is studying the "same thing" and whether his data are uniformly valid.

I attempted to study the social and occupational integration of automobile workers in the United States, Italy, Argentina, and India. The cooperation of unions and management was necessary in all four countries. The process of gaining access to company files and obtaining sponsorship from all the parties was different in all four countries. In India, the hierarchical principle worked; top management approved and everyone else went along. In Argentina, important second-level officials in labor and management had to be visited repeatedly over long periods in order to gain their confidence and approval. In Italy, bargaining and the use of external pressure was needed to get cooperation. In the United States, management gave only informal approval, and labor gave it only after ascertaining the ideological trustworthiness of the researchers. We are not certain whether these different experiences reflected national or cultural differences. But one conclusion is clear: the researcher had to be concerned constantly with the problem of how his status in the research system affected the quality of data he was trying to gather.

Conclusions

From a review of the above materials one may conclude that I have neglected problems of methodology altogether. To be sure, I have not made specific recommendations on research design. Suggestions for improvements of methodology do not flow automatically from observations on the research process. Perhaps the sociology of social research is at such a primitive stage of development that the only recommendation that can be made now is that researchers be more conscious of the social context of their research and consider it as they plan research and interpret data. But ultimately sociologists must design experiments, as some psychologists have already done, that will help them assess more precisely how the social context of research affects the problems they study and the data they collect.

In the meantime, a few suggestions can be tentatively offered. We now have sufficient evidence to demonstrate that the problems sociologists select for study, how they design their research, and the tactics they follow in the field do not follow the "logic" of science. Research represents a series of accommodations from what is desirable to achieve to what is possible within a given social context and within a given folklore of research practices. Some of the folklore is found in textbooks on methodology, but most of it is part of an informal tradition, which is passed on from generation to generation.

A first step in restructuring methodology should be the systematic collection of this folklore, noting discrepancies in it, searching out deviant cases, and evaluating the evidence, so that policies can be recommended. Undoubtedly such a compendium will have the effect of undermining some current practices now regarded as sacrosanct, especially in the area of field methods. Flexibility will be encouraged once certain practices are exposed for what they are: untested guesses.

Second, the research literature should be analyzed for situations in which social scientists were forced by circumstances to reformulate their original problems, how they did this, and how their results were affected. To have most value this analysis should be done for specific fields (e.g., complex organizations, community, social stratification, family, political sociology) and for different social contexts (e.g., unrelated individuals, primary groups, amorphous social systems, cohesive hierarchies). Researches should be examined for a number of conditions: those that forced changes in problems, those that forced changes in methods, those that blocked access to sources of data, and so on. Such a review of literature not only will have general programmatic relevance for research design, but will enable those interested in the sociology of research to identify variables that should be included in experiments dealing with alternative strategies for research access.

Third, since the amount and quality of published data on the sociology of research are limited, a movement should be launched to encourage sociologists to make protocols of their research experiences. These protocols should be as detailed, honest, and as self-critical as possible. Although most of them will not be published, they should be collected and made available to scholars who are preparing new studies. The repository may also serve as a pool of data for those wanting to study the sociology of social research.

Notes to the Chapter

1. Already a sizable literature exists on the sociology of hunting research funds from foundations, businesses, and governmental agencies, and how the hunt affects research questions, design, and findings (Orlans, 1967; Record, 1960).

2. Chris Argyris (1960). A rare document that details the experiences of a researcher who consciously deceived his respondents is that of Pierre L. van den Berghe (1967).

3. Howard Ehrlich, in a private communication, believes I exaggerate this problem, and that there has been a great deal of research on the issue. He feels that there was much in the 1930's, that research was quiescent until 1950, and that since, social psychologists have done a great deal of research on the problem. Yet he admits that in his own research on prejudice, people were always interpreting his work as commentaries on research technique although it actually dealt with the state of knowledge on prejudice. My position is that the study of research as a social system and process links problems of methodology to problems of validity of research findings. Illustrative of relevant research on the question: Cook (undated), Rosenthal (1966), Friedman (1967).

4. One important reason for this situation is the shortage of space in journals, and the insistence by editors that data be featured and that less space be devoted to research design and difficulties encountered in the field.

5. Arthur J. Vidich and Joseph Bensman (1964: 323–326) point out that multiple sponsorship creates a multiple reference group situation. Usually the sponsor's interest in the research varies with phases of the research.

6. Orlans (1967) points out that these discussions are clouded in administrative regulations in the research contract.

7. It may appear that social sponsorship is not necessary in certain types of research, e.g., survey research or public opinion polling. Here the researchers may

be their own sponsors (self-legitimizers). Letters of introduction, the interviewer's introductory "spiel," the prestigious names on the mastheads of stationery constitute self-sponsorship devices.

8. In large-scale survey research, in which there is only one brief contact with a respondent, the researcher's concern with the validation of his presence is minimal. He expects and usually gets (in the United States at least) a friendly reception and frank responses. In studies of communities, organizations, or institutions, or in studies that need the long-term cooperation of respondents (e.g., panels), the researcher is forced to consider the problem of sponsorship more deeply because these persons and organizations are more difficult to manipulate.

9. In a study of two cities along the United States–Mexico border, we discovered that a signed calling card from a prestigious sponsor introducing us to other respondents was a great asset in gaining access to influentials in Mexico, but such sponsorship was hard to get in the United States and, when obtained, was less effective (D'Antonio and Form, 1964: 249–267).

10. A complicating factor is introduced when research tasks are assigned to the sponsors or the hosts, as in self-surveys (Sower, Holland, Tiedtke, and Freeman, 1957).

11. Something may be learned by studying the host of a party (Riesman, Potter, and Watson, 1960). They suggest a typology: Institutional host, the inconspicuous host, and the social engineer.

12. They do enumerate three applied roles from the scientist's point of view: moralizer, mediator, and technician. Various roles of sociologists are also explored by Shostak (1966) and Gouldner and Miller (1965).

13. Orne (1962) says, "The totality of cues which convey an experimental hypothesis to the subject . . . is called the demand characteristics of the experimental situation: the study and control of the demand characteristics [constitute] an empirical issue to determine under what circumstances demand characteristics significantly affect subjects' experimental behavior."

14. Blau (1964) experienced difficulty in maintaining a consistent role definition in his research on bureaucracies.

15. In another systematic review of public opinion literature, Deutscher concluded, "The only instance in which an attitude or an opinion may be accurately described as 'unreal' is when it is elicited in a rigorously controlled interview situation by highly trained interviewers, employing a technically high-quality instrument." See *Public vs. Private Opinions: The Real and the Unreal* (unpublished manuscript, February 1, 1966), p. 1.

16. I am omitting a discussion of research based on the accumulation of records and unobtrusive methods and emphasizing research involving personal contact, even though it may be indirect, as in the questionnaire.

17. Blau (1964: 26–27) recorded the mistakes he made in defining his status and research objectives to different groups in the government bureaucracy he was studying. Hindsight suggests that he might have applied knowledge about bureaucracy more effectively in defining his position and intended tasks. Since

there has been little experimentation on the strategies of access, we cannot know whether his recommendation was a good one; namely, to present a concrete lecture on how bureaucracies behave.

18. One of the best discussions of this area is that by Scott (1965: 262–284).

19. As in the cases reviewed by Seashore (1964: 168).

20. An advisory board, as we shall see, is often created to equalize the power between the research organization and the host. When the host hires professional social scientists, the sophistication of the two parties is matched, and a more balanced power situation results.

21. Other exceptions are situations where documents or unobtrusive observation provide the primary source materials.

22. I have stressed bargaining from the researcher's point of view, but a complete understanding of the process involves analyzing it also from the perspective of other participants. For an extensive case study of research bargaining in a complex industrial setting, see Form, 1964.

23. Eugene Schneider (1950) believes that the conflictive character of industrial structures limits access to them and observations that can be made of them.

24. The number and range of a sub-system's participation in other parts of an organization has not been adequately studied. The accounting organization perhaps has the widest range, certain staff organizations also have a wide range, while others (usually at the bottom) have a very narrow range. In community systems, the range of interpenetration of the constituent organizations is relatively limited.

25. When Paul F. Lazarsfeld appointed me chairman of the sessions on industrial relations for the meetings of the American Sociological Association in 1962, I had to disband the meetings for lack of research in the area.

26. My colleague, Harry Perlstadt (1968), advises that the American Sociological Association should formally acknowledge this cleavage and make it the basis of a party system, similar to the party system of the International Typographical Union.

27. Lazarsfeld (1962) suggests that the instrumentation (technology) of research is related to its history, ideology, intellectual style, and its social organization.

28. The weakest and most cooperative unions in the company were the communist and the fascist.

REFERENCES

ABELSON, ROBERT P.
    1968   "Computers, polls and public opinion — some puzzles and paradoxes." *Trans-action*, **5** (September): 22–23.

ABRAMSON, E. H., *et al.*
    1958   "Social power and commitment: a theoretical statement." *American Sociological Review*, **23** (February): 15–22.

ADAMS, RICHARD N., and JACK J. PREISS (eds.)
1960   *Human Organization Research: Field Relations and Techniques.* Homewood, Illinois: Dorsey.
American Journal of Sociology, **61** (September).
1956
ARGYRIS, CHRIS
1960   *Understanding Organizational Behavior.* Homewood, Illinois: Dorsey.
BARNES, J. A.
1963   "Some ethical problems in modern fieldwork." *British Journal of Sociology*, **14** (June): 118–134.
BLAU, PETER M.
1964   "The research process in the study of The Dynamics of Bureaucracy." Pp. 24–32 in Philip E. Hammond (ed.), *Sociologists at Work.* New York: Basic Books.
BRYMER, RICHARD A., and BUFORD FARRIS
1967   "Ethical and political dilemmas in the investigation of deviance: a study of juvenile delinquency." Pp. 297–318 in Gideon Sjoberg (ed.), *Ethics, Politics and Social Research.* Cambridge: Schenkman.
CAMPBELL, ANGUS
1953   "Administering research organizations." *American Psychologist*, **8** (June): 225–230.
CANNELL, CHARLES F., and MORRIS AXELROD
1956   "The respondent reports on the interview." *American Journal of Sociology*, **62** (September): 177–181.
CHAPLIN, DAVID
1968   "Interviewing foreign elites." Unpublished manuscript.
COOK, DESMOND L.
undated "The relation of possible hawthorne effect components to stages of experimental investigation." Bureau of Educational Research and Service, Ohio State University (mimeographed): 63–133.
DALTON, MELVILLE
1964   "Preconceptions and methods in Men Who Manage." Pp. 50–95 in Philip E. Hammond (ed.), *Sociologists at Work.* New York: Basic Books.
D'ANTONIO, WILLIAM V., and WILLIAM H. FORM
1964   *Influentials in Two Border Cities.* South Bend: University of Notre Dame Press.
DEUTSCHER, IRWIN
1966a   "Words and deeds: social science and social science policy." *Social Problems*, **13** (Winter): 235–254.
1966b   "Public vs. private opinions: the real and the unreal." Unpublished manuscript (February).
1969   "Looking backward: case studies on the 'progress' of methodology in sociological research." *American Sociologist*, **4** (February): 35–41.

FOOTE, NELSON N., and LEONARD S. COTTRELL, JR.
  1955   *Identity and Interpersonal Competence.* Chicago: Chicago University Press.
FORM, WILLIAM H.
  1964a   "A bargaining model for social research." Unpublished manuscript.
  1964b   "Social power and social welfare." Pp. 83–85 in Robert Morris (ed.),
           Centrally Planned Change: Prospects and Concepts. New York: National
           Association of Social Workers.
FORM, WILLIAM H., and SIGMUND NOSOW
  1958   *Community in Disaster.* New York: Harper and Bros.
FORM, WILLIAM H., and RICHARD P. GALE
  1967   "The politics of research access." Unpublished manuscript.
FRIEDMAN, NEIL
  1967   *The Social Nature of Psychological Research: The Psychological Experiment
           as a Social Interaction.* New York: Basic Books.
GILSON, MARY B.
  1940   "Review of Roethlisberger and Dickson, management and the
           worker." *American Journal of Sociology,* **46** (July): 98–101.
GOFFMAN, ERVIN
  1952   "Cooling the mark out: some aspects of adaptation to failure."
           Psychiatry, **15** (November): 451–463.
GOLDNER, FRED H.
  1967   "Role emergence and the ethics of ambiguity." P. 248 in Gideon
           Sjoberg (ed.), *Ethics, Politics and Social Research.* Cambridge: Schenkman.
GOULDNER, ALVIN W.
  1954   *Wildcat Strike.* Yellow Springs, Ohio: Antioch Press.
  1968   "The sociologist as partisan: sociology and the welfare state." *American
           Sociologist,* **3** (May): 103–116.
GOULDNER, ALVIN W., and S. M. MILLER (eds.)
  1965   *Applied Sociology.* New York: Free Press.
HAMMOND, PHILIP E. (ed.)
  1964   *Sociologists at Work.* New York: Basic Books.
HANNA, WILLIAM J.
  1965   "Image making in field research." *American Behavioral Scientist,* **8**
           (January): 15–20.
HUNT, WILLIAM H., et al.
  1964   "Interviewing political elites in cross-cultural comparative research."
           American Journal of Sociology, **70** (July): 59–68.
HYMAN, HERBERT H., et al.
  1954   *Interviewing in Social Research.* Chicago: University of Chicago Press.
KOHN, ROBERT L., and CHARLES F. CANNELL
  1957   *The Dynamics of Interviewing.* New York: Wiley.
LAZARSFELD, PAUL F.
  1962   "The sociology of empirical social research." *American Sociological
           Review,* **27** (December): 757–767.

LERNER, DANIEL
    1956   "Interviewing Frenchmen." *American Journal of Sociology*, **62**
            (September): 187–194.
MARCUS, PHILIP M.
    1965   "Strategy and tactics in field research: the process of acceptance."
            Unpublished manuscript.
MERTON, ROBERT K.
    1940   "Bureaucratic structure and personality." *Social Forces*, **18** (May):
            460–568.
MILLER, DELBERT C.
    1965   "The impact of organization and research value structures on research
            behavior." Pp. 39–54 in Alvin W. Gouldner and S. M. Miller (eds.),
            Applied Sociology. New York: Free Press.
MILLER, DELBERT C., and WILLIAM H. FORM
    1964   *Industrial Sociology*. New York: Harper and Row.
MOORE, JOAN
    1967   "Political and ethical problems . . . of a minority population."
            Pp. 225–244 in Gideon Sjoberg (ed.), *Ethics, Politics and Social Research*.
            Cambridge: Schenkman.
MOUZELIS, NICOS P.
    1968   *Organization and Bureaucracy: An Analysis of Modern Theories*. Chicago:
            Aldine.
OLMSTED, DONALD W.
    1962   *Social Rules, Groups, and Leadership*. East Lansing, Michigan: Institute
            of Community Development, Michigan State University.
ORLANS, HAROLD
    1967   "Ethical problems in the relations of research sponsors and investi-
            gators." Pp. 3–24 in Gideon Sjoberg (ed.), *Ethics, Politics and Social
            Research*. Cambridge: Schenkman.
ORNE, MARTIN T.
    1962   "On the social psychology of the psychological experiment." *American
            Psychologist*, **17** (November): 776–783.
PERLSTADT, HARRY
    1968   "A challenge to sociologists." Unpublished manuscript.
PIEL, GERARD
    1965   "The treason of the clerks." *Philadelphia: Address at the Annual Meeting
            of the American Philosophical Society*, **39** (April).
POWDERMAKER, HORTENSE
    1966   *Stranger and Friend*. New York: W. W. Norton.
RECORD, JANE CASSELS
    1967   "The research institute and the pressure group." Pp. 33–34 in Gideon
            Sjoberg (ed.), *Ethics, Politics and Social Research*. Cambridge: Schenk-
            man.

RECORD, WILSON
1960   "Some reflections on bureaucratic trends in sociological research."
        American Sociological Review, 25 (June): 411–414.

RIESMAN, DAVID, and MARK BENNEY
1956   "The sociology of an interview." *Midwest Sociologist,* 18 (Winter):
        3–15.

RIESMAN, DAVID, et al.
1960   "The vanishing host." *Human Organization,* 19 (Spring): 17–27.

ROSENTHAL, ROBERT
1966   *Experimenter Effects in Behavioral Research.* New York: Appleton-
        Century-Crofts.

ROSSI, PETER H.
1964   "Researchers, scholars, and policy makers: the politics of large-scale
        research." *Daedalus,* 93 (Fall): 1142–1161.

RYTINA, JOAN
1968   "Politics in social research." Unpublished manuscript.

SCHNEIDER, EUGENE
1950   "Limitations on observations in industrial sociology." *Social Forces,*
        28 (March): 279–284.

SCOTT, NORMAN W.
1966   *The Social System of Science.* New York: Holt, Rinehart and Winston.

SCOTT, W. RICHARD
1965   "Field methods in the study of organizations." Pp. 261–304 in
        James G. March (ed.), *Handbook of Organizations.* Chicago: Rand
        McNally

SEASHORE, STANLEY
1964   "Field experiments with formal organizations." *Human Organization,*
        24 (Summer): 164–170.

SHOSTAK, ARTHUR B. (ed.)
1966   *Sociology in Action.* Homewood, Illinois: Dorsey.

SJOBERG, GIDEON (ed.)
1967   *Ethics, Politics and Social Research.* Cambridge: Schenkman.

SJOBERG, GIDEON, and ROGER NETT
1968   *A Methodology for Social Research.* New York: Harper and Row.

SOWER, C. E., et al.
1957   *Community Involvement.* Glencoe, Illinois: Free Press.

STRAUSS, ANSELM, and LEONARD SCHATZMAN
1955   "Social class and modes of communication." *American Journal of
        Sociology,* 60 (January): 329–338.

VAN DEN BERGHE, PIERRE L.
1967   "Research in South Africa: the story of my experience with tyranny."
        Pp. 198–244 in Gideon Sjoberg (ed.), *Ethics, Politics and Social Research.*
        Cambridge: Schenkman.

VIDICH, ARTHUR J., *et al.* (eds.)
  1964   *Reflections on Community Studies.* New York: Wiley.
VIDICH, ARTHUR J., and JOSEPH BENSMAN
  1967   "The Springdale case: academic bureaucrats and sensitive towns-people." Pp. 323–326 in Arthur J. Vidich, Joseph Bensman, and Maurice R. Stein (eds.), *Reflections on Community Studies.* New York: Wiley.
WEBER, MAX
  1946   "Bureaucracy." Pp. 196–244 in H. H. Gerth and C. W. Mills (trans. and eds.), *From Max Weber: Essays in Sociology.* New York: Oxford University Press.
WEIK, KARL E.
  1965   "Laboratory experimentation with organizations." Pp. 194–260 in James G. March (ed.), *Handbook of Organizations.* Chicago: Rand McNally.
WHYTE, WILLIAM FOOTE
  1943   *Street Corner Society: The Social Structure of an Italian Slum.* Chicago: University of Chicago Press.
  1955   *Money and Motivation.* New York: Harper and Row.
  1959   *Man and Organization: Three Problems in Human Relations in Industry.* Homewood, Illinois: Richard D. Irwin.

CHAPTER TWO

The Sociology of Social Research: A Discussion

HOWARD J. EHRLICH

William Form's provocative essay on the sociology of social research is an exciting overture to this symposium. Its thematic variations border on a new paradigm of social inquiry. I share these preparadigmatic impulses and I shall try to use his themes as background for my own composition.

Form and I are concerned with the fundamental problems of meta-sociological analysis. Metasociological ventures have four objectives: (1) to furnish criteria for determining the *domain* of sociology in general, and sociological theories in particular; (2) to specify criteria of *relevance* by which we can determine what statements can be admitted to this domain; (3) to supply criteria to determine the *quality* of relevant statements; and (4) to appraise the *ethics and morality* of the solutions offered to these three problems. While Form's specific concerns are not directed to the problem of domain, it should be clear that there may be no degrees of freedom. Let me illustrate this by exhibiting two statements which will be presented subsequently by Dubin and Freeman.

Dubin: "The theorist–researcher is not interested in the normative decisions as to whether the present state of affairs is to be continued or changed, the direction in which the change is to be oriented, or the evaluation of whether the change has been attained successfully."

Freeman: "If social research is going to prosper, however, it is necessary to make certain that a significant proportion of our studies be directed at

43

matters that are of concern to informants and that the potential of investigations be assessed in terms of their likelihood to result in progressive social change."

I find it difficult to reconcile the aseptic formulations of Dubin with Freeman's prescription for prosperity. While neither addresses the problem of domain directly, I think that they are bound to strategies which will yield different sociological paradigms. When Form addresses himself to the increasing politicization of American social science he anticipates not merely the differences between these two, but a developing ideological rift within the profession and within the academy.

The Sociologist in the Academy

When Professor Form delineates the social system of research as comprised of research sponsors, researchers, and research hosts, he surprisingly omits the setting in which most sociologists work. I do not believe that you can fully understand social research without studying the university which represents the major employer of most sociologists, and probably most social scientists. Similarly, I do not think you can complete this analysis without considering the social organization of sociology itself. I will consider the sociology of sociology in the final section of this paper.

My primary concern here in calling attention to the university is to indicate its contribution to the idea of a "neutral" social science. On almost all American campuses the dominant, if not exclusive, model of the academic man is built upon the premise that the role of academician and the role of citizen impose seriously conflicting demands. Discussions of the routine of acceptable activities for university scholars and scientists invariably and blandly terminate with the acceptance of all legitimate activities as appropriate — providing that these activities are segregated by role. There is presumably an individual's role as a scientist (or scholar) and an individual's role as a citizen. Advocacy of social policy is proscribed for the scientist: the scientist may scrutinize, systematize, and theorize. He may not advocate. Only the scientist-transmogrified-to-citizen may advocate. Even then, the citizen who is also a scientist may claim no special knowledge. To do so would be to violate the segregation of roles.

I could discharge this entire argument by simply declaring that it is based on a serious misconstruction of role theory. It is that; but such a refutation would be trivial since the argument can be reformulated without using the concept of role in any formal sociological framework.

I suspect that I could also dismiss this argument by exposing its history as deriving from the attempts of American social science to achieve academic respectability by deliberately eschewing involvement in social philosophy and social planning. Or I think that I could dismiss the argument on the basis of its essentially anti-intellectual and conservative political implications. However, independent of the origin of this issue and regardless of its potential social consequences, many scientists and scholars do insist on its current validity.

In whatever way the argument is formulated, it necessarily centers on what it means to advocate the acceptance of a scientific (or a scholarly) statement and what it means to advocate the acceptance of a policy statement. Measurement, experiment, and the construction of theory are normative procedures of science and the standards for a decision on the test of an hypothesis are in most circumstances predetermined. Facts never speak for themselves in science, only scientists speak. It is not a simple matter to make a serious scientific statement. And a major part of the training in all sciences is in methodology, the procedures by which one can make such statements.

The institution of science and its mechanism of recruitment and socialization have been so successful in the history of science that despite the privacy and isolation of the laboratory, the instances of scientific fraud are incredibly rare. Claims that go beyond the data are institutionally proscribed and socially controlled. Science operates with a committed coldness, and the scientist may well be the prototype of the oversocialized man. The drive for the control of error is so excessive, and the extravagant claim so obscene in the panoply of science, that few scientific statements ever escape specification in the most qualified of qualified prose. This zealous pursuit of truth has its psychological cost.

Consider the scientist in the arena of policy where error has no control and where the demand is for the extravagant claim. Clinically we may observe in most subjects two behaviors: first, a rigid adherence to the norms of procedure; and second, a reiterated and plaintive cry — "we need more research on that." The psychological cost for the oversocialized scholar is that he may be transmuted into a professional witness to life.

The basis for the acceptance of scientific statements is primarily procedural rather than evaluative. In contrast, the rules for the acceptance of policy statements are primarily evaluative.

The scientist, nevertheless, is inextricably involved in evaluation. He is always called upon to assess the value of his procedures, the outcomes of his test, and the value of his theory. The scientist as a scientist must make value judgments. To be sure, these judgments are generally construed as nonmoral, but they do have real consequences for the behavior of other scientists, for students, and for a limited but unknown posterity.

Problems of Ethics and Morality

Social research is still of such novelty in society that we have few ethical or legal precedents and certainly no well-developed language for the analysis of the ethical and moral dilemmas of research. The shift from a craft to an organizational model of social research, which Form highlights, and the technological innovations in observing and recording behaviors have aroused the professional conscience. It is my feeling that social research, as presently developed, is more likely to result in social injury than it is to contribute to the social benefit.

I want to discuss two issues which were not explicitly developed in Form's essay. The first is the issue of confidentiality. The nature of the confidentiality of data is often described as being defined by the researcher-subject agreement. Through this unwritten and necessarily vague contract, researcher and host enter into their peculiar relationship. Although most social scientists probably take seriously their pledges to confidence (when made), the fact remains that the social researcher is granted no legal protection, no privileged status for his research materials. Personal or organizational guarantees of confidence, then, are without institutional support: neither the state nor the professional association provide much protection.

Even where legal entanglements are not a problem (and as yet they have not been very frequent), it still remains that neither the meaning of confidence nor the procedures for its maintenance are well-established. The sociological literature is replete with pseudonymously identified communities and organizations, but it is also replete with those which have been openly identified. Furthermore, there is no tradition of respect for this confidence, and it is not uncommon to observe researchers publically name the units studied by someone else.

The confused circumstances regarding confidentiality was dramatized for me in a recent issue of the *American Sociological Review*. Two sociologists treated anonymously a sub-area of a major metropolitan city, using the same data which I used in three earlier publications — including one in the *Review*. In my articles I explicitly identified the area studied. I made this identification because I thought that a knowledge of the research site was essential to understanding the limits of my data. It should be clear that the researcher who studies organizations or communities which have unusual properties must seriously confront the problems of disclosure by publication for the subject and for the discipline.

The nature of the relation between the researcher and his host can seldom be fully anticipated, particularly given the bargaining aspects of this relation that Form displays. Under these circumstances, the researcher can not initially obtain the informed consent of his host regarding confidentiality because he may not know until after the research has been completed what the scope and significance of his data are. I do not want to confront the issue of informed consent directly, although it is clearly a major problem. I want, rather, to consider the issue of informed consent in the context of the maintenance of confidentiality. The problems generated here center about the effects of the communication of our research results.

Now I want it clear that I am not talking about the unintended or deliberately evil applications of research. (On this point, we may confront the tragic flaw of all science). The results of most research can not easily be controlled, and any scientific breakthroughs can be applied for quite opposite political objectives. For those who fear the misuse of their research, I do not believe that there is any alternative but to opt out. I know, in fact, of two scientists who have done so.

The publication and communication of research may present the host with a view of himself that he did not invite, that he finds offensive or mortifying. Unless the researcher himself publishes under a pseudonym and/or does so some specified number of years later, there is probably no way the products of social research can be insulated from the visibility of its subjects. There is in fact no reason why such insulation should occur, nor is it the case that the researcher should be prepared to take the consequences of his action. The consequences, after all, are not his alone.

Although communication through professional journals serves to decrease the public visibility of research, I believe this restriction violates the subjects' trust under some conditions. Publication of research in solely professional media may do injury to the subjects of study who have neither the access nor resources to obtain and interpret our scientific language. This may be particularly true for some ethnic and political minorities.

Finally, the communication of research through public media may serve to change or rigidify existing levels of consensus or even to accelerate the diffusion of ideas and social practices. It may be a source of great amusement to learn from the Iowa Poll that 1 out of 10 Iowans believe flying saucers are here from other planets. But when I learn from Harris and Gallup that 4 out of 5 Americans think "Negroes are pushing too fast," I find nothing amusing in the responses of established political leaders and white and black militants.

If the social scientist continues to license only social scientists (or journalists) to adjudicate what may be published, then I believe the scope of his mandate will become more and more restricted to the laboratory. While I think the laboratory and formal model building have been seriously neglected in sociology, I do not believe you can have a sociology without a continued exchange between field and laboratory sites. The social science of tomorrow will flourish not on the basis of the tolerance or even cooperation of the host, but on the basis of collaboration. The "ideological fracturing of the social sciences" that Form reports is a signal of the increasing exchange between academic sociology and the communities it ostensibly serves.

Problems of Quality

The closing theme of Form's presentation is a call for the systematizing of reports on the process of social research. If we were to undertake this task seriously, it might be helpful to distinguish between research which seeks primarily to test hypotheses which are part of a larger network of explicit statements, and research which is oriented primarily to the description of phenomena and the formulation of hypotheses. I suspect that problems of error-control may be more variable by research objective than by the formal content of research. Nevertheless, it might be worthwhile to start by trying to develop a scheme for the classification of measurement errors. It seems to me that there are three major classes of measurement errors: response errors, i.e., those generated mainly by the personal characteristics of individual respondents; instrument errors, i.e., those generated by the research instrument (and the testing situation) itself; and researcher errors, i.e., those generated by the behavior of the researcher through his manipulation of subjects and/or instruments. (Researcher errors do not include errors of research design.) We might begin, then, with a scheme something like this:

A. *Response errors*
   1. deliberate error (e.g., lying, evasiveness).
   2. reporting error (e.g., errors of knowledge, recall).
   3. stylistic error (e.g., acquiescence, indecisiveness).

B. *Instrument errors*
1. commitment error (e.g., inadequate alternatives, meaningless options).
2. errors of order (e.g., primacy effects, effects of repetition).
3. errors of structure (e.g., ambiguity, difficulty level).
4. errors of measurement (instrument-generated changes).

C. *Researcher errors*
1. errors derived from the communication of expected results.
2. errors of nonstandard research operations.
3. errors of deceptive/manipulative designs.
4. errors of sponsorship.
5. errors of bargaining.

Such a taxonomy, particularly if we can detail each type of error, might have three social consequences. At the least it would provide a checklist by which we could self-consciously run through our own measurement procedures. Second, I think it would provide a goad to methodological research. We are very short on tinkers and instrument makers, and we have a pressing need not only for standardized operations and instruments but for clear estimates of error magnitude. Third, I think an error checklist would serve in the review of research by highlighting the substantive implications of reiterating the same errors of measurement (cf. Ehrlich, 1964; Ehrlich and Rinehart, 1965; Stricker, 1967).

Sociology of Sociology

To understand the research behavior of American sociologists it is necessary to understand the social organization of sociology as it relates to research. Few investigations in this area have been systematic, but in the context of this symposium I think we should explore what little accumulated information there is.

Sociologists appear to be recruited from white collar families by a ratio of 3 to 2. Of the 3 white collar recruits, 2 are from upper status white collar homes. Recruits have been drawn mainly from medium-sized and small communities. They come primarily from Protestant homes, in proportion to the population, with recruits from Catholic homes underrepresented and those from non-Christian homes overrepresented. Working sociologists retain their religious preferences to a striking degree (Turner, Spaulding, and McClintock, 1963; Palmore, 1962).

Through the late 1920's to date (Sibley, 1963), the annual number of Ph.D.'s in sociology has comprised 2 per cent of the total number in all academic fields. The most recent figures indicate that sociology is growing more slowly than the composite of all academic fields (Sibley, 1963). Sociology accounts for approximately 8 per cent of social science Ph.D.'s (Gurr, 1964).

From a cross-sectional study, 1958–59, it appears that for every 44 B.A.'s granted in sociology, only 1 person goes on to a Ph.D. This ratio is 3 to 4 times higher than for the physical sciences (Sibley, 1963). Furthermore, sociology doctorates include a smaller proportion of sociology B.A.'s than is true of any other social science with respect to its baccalaureates (Ferris, 1965). From the B.A., it has taken a sociologist a mean of 11.1 years to obtain the doctorate. This time-lag has been higher than for any other of the social sciences (Gurr, 1964).

Although women received 55 per cent of the sociology baccalaureates, they received only 14 per cent of the doctorates (Sibley, 1963). The per cent of women majoring in sociology, 1956–64, appears to be increasing, while no change has occurred in the percentage receiving advanced degrees (U.S. Department of Labor, 1965).

Graduate Record Examination scores of applicants to graduate school indicate a low rank for sociology, fourth from the bottom in verbal and second from the bottom in quantitative aptitude. However, applying these data to doctorates, the ratio of the sociology to physical science Ph.D. scores is 0.91. The difference between recruits and finalists appears to be rather enormous.

In 1968 there were approximately 4,700 fellows and active members of the American Sociological Association. The National Science Foundation manpower reports indicate that 80 per cent are employed in educational institutions where they are paid, on the average, less than most other scientists.

This set of limited data I have just presented is doubtless open to varied interpretations. They suggest to me a discipline closely tied to the middle-class society it serves (although not particularly valued), unclear about its educational responsibilities, and even uncertain of its professional requirements.

Approximately 100 schools have granted doctorates in sociology in the 1960's although there may be twice that number offering the degree. The production of Ph.D.'s appears highly concentrated. Chicago, Columbia, and Harvard conferred 25 per cent of the total doctorates in sociology, 1950–60. Add the next 6 schools (Cornell, North Carolina, Wisconsin,

Ohio State. Minnesota, New York University) and you have 50 per cent. I would guess that one-fifth of all sociology departments grant four-fifths of the doctorates.

Crane's (1965) analysis of biologists, political scientists, and psychologists provides three findings which I think may be generalizable to sociology: (1) graduates of major universities are more likely to be highly productive than those from minor universities; (2) having attended a major university has a greater effect on a scientist's later productivity than a current location at a major university; and (3) former students of eminent sponsors were more likely to be highly productive than students of other scientists.

Wanderer (1966) provides data for sociology supportive of Crane's materials. Studying the academic origins of contributors to the *American Sociological Review,* 1955–65, he rank ordered the 21 schools which appeared in the top ten rankings for any of the 11 years covered. Top rank went to the University of Chicago whose Ph.D.'s contributed 106 articles in that period. At the bottom, rank 21, was the only non-American school, Hebrew University, whose doctorates had contributed 4 articles. The range was extreme. The top 4 schools — Chicago, Columbia, Harvard, and Michigan — contributed through their doctorates 41 per cent of all articles, although they apparently accounted for 28 per cent of all Ph.D.'s, 1920–61.

Two studies (Price, 1963; Platz, 1965) demonstrate that approximately 10 per cent of scientists account for 50 per cent of the published research. Of particular importance is the finding that only 10 per cent of the articles published account for 40 per cent of the citations to the research literature.

Thus we have a relatively small cohort of scientists publishing materials with only a small fraction of what they publish being cited. The relation between productivity and citation frequency is difficult to fully disentangle. If productivity was not related to citation frequency, this would point to serious pathologies in the scientific enterprise. Specifically it implies that some scientists doing important research were not very productive, and/or that many people are prolifically publishing trivial materials. (It might also imply that people who publish are poor scholars, but I presume that this would only be a minor occurrence.)

The data from physics suggest that quantity and citation frequency are related (Price, 1963). Cole and Cole (1967, 1968) demonstrate that quantity is a more important determinant of visibility than quality. Fortunately, quality and quantity display a moderately strong positive correlation. However, Platz's (1965) data support the hypothesis that for psychology, quality and quantity are not strongly related. I suspect that the case of psychology is more generalizable to sociology.

Even if we concede, as the data for physics indicate, that approximately one-quarter of quality scientists are not very productive, we must still probe the basis for the low citation frequency of the publications of other scientists. Two possibilities worth exploring for us are that the gatekeepers of sociological publication represent a biased set of readers and/or that editorial standards (i.e., criteria of quality) are vague. The two possibilities are, of course, complementary.

There are a number of operations that might be used as an indicator of editorial bias. One simple one I would like to present here is a straightforward count of editors (e.g., managing, assistant, advisory, consultant) of major journals. As part of a larger study of scientific communication, I enumerated the number of editorial positions, number of editors, and the number of overlapping editor-positions for three journals, 1960–68. The journals selected had relatively distinct substantive concerns: *American Sociological Review, Sociometry* (social psychology), and *Social Problems.* In the nine years studied, there were 664 positions and these were filled by 251 editors. Nineteen per cent of the editors served in only one position in the nine-year period, while 16 per cent served in 5 to 8 positions. The most important finding of the analysis is that 25 per cent of the editors occupied two or three editorial positions concurrently. For the purposes of illustration here, I take this to be an adequate demonstration of the potential of editorial bias.

Our second concern is the criteria of quality. In 1958 the ASA Committee on Research reported a pilot study attempt at devising a standardized rating form for sociological reports (Noland, 1958). Reports were rated on 3 criteria for 4 areas — *statement of problem* (clarity, significance, documentation), *description of method* (appropriateness, adequacy, replicability), *presentation of results* (completeness, comprehensibility, yield), and *interpretation* (accuracy, bias, usefulness). Using 17 articles (from the *American Sociological Review* and the *American Journal of Sociology*) and 8 raters, all senior sociologists, the Committee reported a series of almost uninterpretable tables. The report seemed to be saying that on articles of intermediate quality, the achievement of consensus was unlikely.

Seeman (1966), in his report as editor of *Sociometry*, presented the distribution of editor evaluations for manuscripts submitted from June 1, 1965 to May 31, 1966. The manuscripts were evaluated by two independent readers on a 5-point rating scale ranging from "major contribution" through "does not warrant publication." For the aggregate of judges and manuscripts, Seeman presents two 5 × 5 tables: one for rejected manuscripts and one for those accepted. Of the 103 manuscripts reviewed, 25 received opposite evaluations (rated 4 or 5 by one editor and 1 or 2 by the second editor). To determine the overall level of consensus, I calculated *Tau-c* coefficients for both tables. For rejected manuscripts, the correlation across editors was —.014. For accepted manuscripts, the correlation was —.061.

It is possible that the vagueness of editorial standards and the concentration of gatekeepers are not cumulative biases, that is, that they work in different directions. I think not. I suggest that concentration of publications by university (of doctorate) spotlights a more subtle bias — perhaps one of subject matter or methodological or stylistic bias. (Crane, 1967, explores matters of bias relating to the academic origins of editors and contributors to the *Review* and to *Sociometry*.) Neither my cursory review, nor any of the available data, can provide any definitive answer. Sociologists concerned with the organization, management, and tactics of research, however, ought to be concerned with who does what research and how it comes to be published.

REFERENCES

COLE, S., and J. R. COLE
   1967   "Scientific output and recognition: A study in the operation of the reward system in science." *American Sociological Review*, **32** (June): 377–390.

COLE, S., and J. R. COLE
   1968   "Visibility and the structural bases of awareness of scientific research." *American Sociological Review*, **33** (June): 397–413.

CRANE, D.
   1967   "The gatekeepers of science: Some factors affecting the selection of articles for scientific journals." *American Sociologist*, **2** (November): 195–201.

CRANE, D.
   1965   "Scientists at major and minor universities: A study of productivity and recognition." *American Sociological Review*, **30** (October): 699–714.

EHRLICH, H. J.
   1964   "Instrument error and the study of prejudice." *Social Forces*, **43** (December): 197–206.

EHRLICH, H. J., and J. W. RINEHART
   1965   "A brief report on the methodology of stereotype research." *Social Forces*, **43** (May): 564–575.

FERRISS, A. L.
    1965   "Educational interrelations among social sciences." *American Sociologist*, **1** (November): 15–23.
GURR, T.
    1964   "Doctorates in the social sciences, 1920–1962." *The American Behavioral Scientist*, **7** (April): 23–24.
NOLAND, E. W.
    1958   "Report of the committee on research." *American Sociological Review*, **23** (December): 704–711.
PALMORE, E.
    1962   "Sociologists' class origins and political ideologies." *Sociology and Social Research*, **47** (October): 45–50.
PLATZ, A.
    1965   "Psychology of the scientist: XI. Lotka's law and research visibility." *Psychological Reports*, **16** (April): 566–568.
PRICE, D.
    1963   *Little Science, Big Science.* New York: Columbia University Press.
SEEMAN, M.
    1966   "Report of the editor of Sociometry." *American Sociologist*, **1** (August): 284–285.
SIBLEY, E.
    1963   *The Education of Sociologists in the United States.* New York: Russell Sage Foundation.
STRICKER, L. J.
    1967   "The true deceiver." *Psychological Bulletin*, **68** (July): 13–20.
TURNER, H. A., C. E. SPAULDING, and C. G. McCLINTOCK
    1963   "Political orientations of academically affiliated sociologists." *Sociology and Social Research*, **47** (April): 273–289.
UNITED STATES DEPARTMENT OF LABOR
    1966   **1965** *Handbook on Women Workers.* Washington, D.C.: Government Printing Office.
WANDERER, J. J.
    1966   "Academic origins of contributors to the American Sociological Review 1955–65." *American Sociologist*, **1** (November): 241–243.

THEORY AND
THEORY BUILDING

CHAPTER THREE

Theory and Research

ROBERT DUBIN

The purpose of this chapter is to show what theory can and cannot do for the practitioner. In particular, I shall examine the general structure of theoretical models in the behavioral sciences. From that base I will then examine the special problems that the researcher faces which are distinct from those of the practitioner. There will then follow a discussion of the problems peculiar to the practitioner that the theorist-researcher does not often, if ever, take into account. Finally, the gulf between theory and practice will be examined as a set of dilemmas.

The burden of my observations will be to point out that there are significant differences in the work of theorists–researchers, on the one hand, and practitioners, on the other hand. These differences relate to their respective goals and social functions. It resolves no problems simply to assert that knowledge of these differences will lead automatically to their resolution. Indeed, knowledge of why the theorist-researcher and the practitioner sometimes fail to communicate could well lead to the pessimistic conclusion that they may never communicate effectively. I will take the optimistic stand that this conclusion need not result, and try to indicate why.

Theory

I have recently published a volume called *Theory Building* (Dubin, 1969). This volume sets forth the structure of theories, their components and their sources, and their empirical tests through research. I will here simply summarize some of the more important considerations on the presumption that those readers with a more detailed interest may pursue it in the volume itself.

A theory is the attempt of a man to model some aspect of the empirical world. The underlying motive for this modelling is that either (1) the real world is so complex that it needs to be conceptually simplified in order to understand it, or (2) that observation by itself does not reveal ordered relationships among empirically detected entities. A theory tries to make sense out of the observable world by ordering the relationships among "things" that constitute the theorist's focus of attention in the world "out there."

The process of building a theory requires hard work and ingenuity. 1. There is, first of all, involved a focus of attention, that is essentially concerned with choosing the elements or "things" whose relationships are of interest. These "things" out of which theories are built are usually called variables, although I prefer the more neutral term "unit." It should be emphasized that the "things" or units out of which theories are built constitute an arbitrary list selected by the theorist as being of particular interest to him (Ashby, 1966). The theorist may, if his imagination is vigorous enough, invent imaginary units, or units that have not yet been apprehended empirically, and build them into his model. Freud did this, for example, with the sub-conscious and the Id.

It may seem strange, if a theory is supposed to model some portion of the empirical world, that the theorist would ever think of using units in his model that themselves are not empirically apprehended. This apparent idiocy is not difficult to comprehend when it is recognized that the predictions made on the basis of a theoretical model need not all be tested in research. More about this point later. The theorist starts with a selection of things or units regarding which he is curious about their interrelationships in the real world.

2. The next step in building a theory is to suggest how the selected units are related to each other. It is at this point that two things emerge that are essential features of a theory. (1) A mode of relationship among the units needs to be specified in detail. (2) A simple test becomes evident for determining the domain of the theory for it will include within its scope only those units that are linked to at least one other unit within the model. The specification of modes of interaction among the units is, therefore, one very important step in determining the boundaries of the model.

The modes of interaction among the units of a theory are what I have called its "laws of interaction." The lawful statement in any theory is the statement of how two or more of its units are concretely related. While the statement of the law, must, of course, specify the units interacting, the lawful part of the statement is the specification of the mode of interaction. Thus, for example, in occupational choice, one may build a theory of the individual's behavior of choosing in at least two alternative, and mutually exclusive forms. The first law of interaction would be: an individual ranks known occupations on a preference scale from high to low and then proceeds to choose from the top, or most preferred occupation downward. The alternative law of interaction would be: an individual ranks known occupations on a preference scale from high to low and then proceeds to make his choice be progressive elimination of the least preferred occupations. These two laws of interaction have identical units — (1) a choosing individual, (2) an individual preference scale, and (3) occupations known to him.

They differ by the manner in which individuals and their knowledge of occupations are related to each other by the alternative processes of choosing a preferred occupation. Most decision theorists prefer the first law of interaction. To them choosing always goes from the most to the least preferred alternative. The empirical research on the choice process among children (Tyler, 1955) as well as the occupational aspirations of the working class parents for their children (Chinoy, 1955) suggests that the second law of interaction is viable, and may actually be the more prevalent method of choosing.

The process of putting things or units together in lawful relation to each other establishes the fundamental building blocks out of which a theory is constructed. However, there are additional features of a model that need to be specified if the model is to be completed.

3. Theories have a domain over which they are expected to mirror the empirical world. Beyond that domain it may be problematic as to whether the theory holds. What separates the domain of a theory from the "beyond," is a boundary. Every theoretical model, if it is complete, must specify the boundary within which the units interact lawfully. Beyond that boundary it may not be at all clear that the units will continue to interact by the specified law; or that all units will remain in the system; or even that the system will remain intact. Thus, for example, if occupational choice is one area of decision making, the units involved are obviously not the same and the law of interaction in choice behavior may be quite different from what would be true in the domain of mate selection, and both decision domains might be modelled quite differently from the

decisional process of picking a winner in the sixth race at Hollywood Park. There are clear-cut boundaries that distinguish the occupational choice decision from the mate selection and the winning horse decision, although all three are forms of decision making. We, therefore, expect theorists dealing with these respective areas of decision to develop separate theories of occupational choice, mate selection, and choice of racing winners. Whether there is an underlying commonality among these three domains of decision, giving rise to a grand decision theory, is an issue that needs to be explored independently.

In the social sciences particularly, there is a strange incapacity to recognize the boundaries of a theoretical model. This is partly true because in dealing with human behavior we are prone to believe that there is a commonality among the units involved and the laws by which they interact. We also operate with simplistic laws of interaction that are viewed as universal for all situations of human interaction. Finally, social theorists have an almost religious belief in the unity of the human personality and psyche, leading to the assumption that any individual actor will behave the same, in keeping with his personality style, regardless of the situation of action. For these three reasons we often assume we can safely ignore the boundary conditions surrounding a given theoretical model, or even apply the model indiscriminately to all realms of human interaction. This is an unfortunate intellectual habit we employ as theorists and practitioners. The sooner we follow the lead of our colleagues in psychology (who have rediscovered individual differences among individuals and within single life histories) and recognize that the human actor may be different in different action situations, the more realistic will be the boundaries of the theoretical models we create.

4 . We now come to the final feature of a theoretical model involved in its construction. This is the specification of the states in which the model or theoretical system operates. A system state is a condition of the system as a whole. When the integrity of the system is maintained, but its condition is markedly different from what it was previously, we describe the alteration as a change of system state. A steady state, or a change of state of a system, are important to specify for they call attention to the fact that while the integrity of the system remains intact, the operation of the system may change from one state to another.

It will be noted that I have changed terms from "theoretical model" or "theory," substituting the term "system." These three terms are used interchangeably. The terms serve to designate that unity representing man's picture of some segment of the real world "out there."

It is perfectly simple to illustrate the idea of a system state, and through the example, to suggest the importance of the notion. We can think, for instance, of an audience in a theatre as constituting a focused crowd, a group that can be moved to a state of panic with the shout of "Fire." We have no difficulty in understanding, for example, the theoretical model that an individual in a state of frustration will move to a new state called "aggression." Indeed, it is one of the common features of social science models, as used in guiding practice, that we have focused attention almost exclusively on system states whose persistence, or the oscillation among which are the prime subject matters of theoretical predictions. This is particularly true in the area of vocational choice and rehabilitation for there is involved in both realms of human behavior the same individuals changing from one state to another: from vocational indecision to vocational commitment; or from occupational failure or obsolescence to retraining and reemployment. Much of social science theory is concerned with changes within persons and groups through time. The theoretical models we build to mirror these longitudinal changes are typically models describing successions of system states, whether the system be an individual or a social group.

Given the units, their laws of interaction, the boundaries within which the units interact lawfully, and the states through which the system may move, we have the necessary and sufficient components out of which to build a complete theoretical model. When these features are exhibited, we may properly say we have a theory, a model, or a theoretical system. A warning, however, is necessary for there are many theorist-labelled products bearing the title "theory," that in fact are not. They may lack a set of laws relating the units within the system, or some laws necessary to relate some units to the system; there may be a failure to specify the boundaries within which the system operates; or the author may not have envisioned states through which the system moves. Any of these omissions requires correction before we may properly speak of a theoretical model.

ction of a theoretical model =

1) **Prediction**

We may now turn to a general consideration of what we do with a proper theoretical model. It is a schoolboy maxim that science predicts. We may, therefore, assume that one function of a theoretical model is to predict something.

In the social sciences particularly it is generally believed that a scientific model will also provide opportunity for developing understanding and insight about some empirical phenomenon. We will examine this second product of building a theory after an analysis of prediction and its consequences.

Prediction from a scientific model is a simple and straightforward operation. What is *always* and *only* predicted is the value that may be taken by one or more units in the theoretical model, measured on some empirical scale. I want to repeat that because it is so simple and often ignored or misunderstood. The only thing that is ever predicted from a scientific model is a value of one or more of the units in that model.

It will be noted that since the task of prediction is to declare what the values are on one or more of the units contained in the scientific model, the test of a prediction is always a test of values taken by one or more units. Put another way, the empirical test of a scientific model is never a test of its laws directly, but only a test of the values taken by one or more of the units that may be predicted from the lawful relationships among the units of the system. Thus, a prediction never succeeds in directly testing the laws built into a model.

This conclusion should not prove surprising for one can never test a relationship, the test being only of the consequences of a relationship. Putting this into the context of common experience, if we said, for example, that two people are linked together by a relationship of love, we would then predict that each would behave toward the other in certain ways; would not behave in other ways; and would act in concert in particular ways in relation to third parties in their environment. Thus, we do *not* test the lawful relationship by which two people interact when we declare that "they are in love." We *do* test the consequences of this law of inter-action by measuring the behaviors between the individuals, and together with respect to other individuals. In short, we measure values on some scales of behavior for the two people connected by a love relationship.

This suggests for us one of the very important limitations on the empirical test of any theoretical model. We never test directly the laws of interaction of the model. We only test the values predicted for one or more of the units by the law or laws relating the units within the system. It is a common language usage to speak of the laws of science and to view their construction as the important element in scientific thinking. The central importance of laws of interaction in all scientific models is not to be gain-said. Nevertheless, we must fully understand that we never test these laws directly but only through their consequences for the values of the units in the models that are related by the laws.

The task of empirical testing of a prediction is made easy precisely because the scientist is required to develop empirical indicators of only the units built into his scientific model, and not of the laws of interaction. Thus, in our previous example, I would have to develop empirical indicators only of the behaviors of a person in relation to one other individual, and empirical indicators of the behaviors of such pairs in relation to other people. It seems obvious that it is much easier to develop empirical indicators of such behaviors than it would be to construct an empirical indicator of "being in a love relationship."

Prediction is a major goal of science. Scientific models should, if they are complete and adequate, result in reasonably accurate predictions. We should now clearly recognize that what we are predicting is always the value of some characteristic of the units interacting, and not characteristics of the laws by which they interact.

A special case of prediction is one in which the boundary of the model is involved. A general prediction is that the value taken by two or more units in a model are determinant up to some limiting set of values, but beyond that are no longer determinant by the laws relating those units. Thus, the boundary of a model may come to be defined in terms of critical values of the units composing the model. There are technical features of system boundaries, and boundary determining criteria that need not concern us here since they have been elaborated elsewhere (Dubin, 1969, ch. 5).

Another class of predictions made from a scientific model is about the oscillation among the states of the system. The condition of no change of state in the system is what is normally called a "steady state." That is to say, the system remains in the same condition through a period of time. This steady state may be characterized by a fixed set of values or a fixed range of values for all the units composing the system.

When a system oscillates from one state to another, this will be signalled by changes in the values of all units composing the system. The prediction problem with respect to system states is: (1) to predict the length of time a steady state will endure; and/or (2) to predict the succeeding state to which the system will move, knowing the present state in which it operates. Simple systems having only two or three systems states in which they can exist make possible oscillation predictions with a high level of certainty. For example, if a system can exist in only two states, then there is 100 per cent certainty in the prediction that, knowing its present state, one can absolutely predict that it will move to its other state, whenever it changes state. This, of course, is a beguiling feature of social science theory for the theorist wins the game before he starts if he specifies only a two state system and then predicts to which state the system will go, knowing its present state. The Marxian prediction of the inevitability of socialism following capitalism is a forecast of this order. Even in a system having three possible states there is a 50/50 chance of predicting correctly on the basis of guessing that the system will move from its present state to one or the other of its possible states.

From the standpoint of sheer utility a theoretical model is best judged by the accuracy of the predictions generated by it. These are always predictions of the values taken by single units, combinations of units, or all the units composing the system. For the practitioner, these are the features of a scientific model that turn out to be the useable outcome of theoretical models.

2) *Understanding*

If accurate prediction is the practical outcome of utilizing scientific models, then the intellectual outcome is the understanding they provide of the characteristics of the empirical domain they model. What is gained in understanding through the use of a scientific model to portray a portion of the real world is achieved by comprehending the law or laws built into the model. The locus of understanding in a scientific model is to be found in its laws of interaction. To say that two things (units) are inversely related is to provide us with understanding of the nature of their relationship. The prediction we would make from such a statement is: As the values of "thing A" increase, the values of "thing B" decrease. But the lawful part of the statement — that there is an inverse relationship — is the heart of our understanding of how "thing A" and "thing B" interact.

In the more elaborate exposition of the difference between understanding and prediction I have suggested that the former is knowledge of *process* while the latter is knowledge of *outcomes* (Dubin, 1969, ch. 1). The statement of the inverse relationship in the preceding example, is a statement of the process of interaction. The statement that if the values of "thing A" are large, the values of "thing B" are small, is a statement of outcomes. The first is our understanding of the relationship; the second is the prediction of the values of the "things" related when they are linked in a single system.

Understanding is an intellectual and/or esthetic product of a theoretical model. Accurate prediction is the practical product of the theory. From the standpoint of the practitioners, what is important about a theoretical model is the accuracy of its predictions, and not the understanding that it may contribute. Thus, the structural engineer may forego the joys of intellectual comprehension of the laws of stress of materials if he is given formulas that are accurate in predicting the reaction of structural material to given kinds and levels of stress. We can design structures on the basis of the latter knowledge without partaking of the understanding knowledge. In exactly the same way the practitioner in any discipline can forego the understanding knowledge (not that it is desirable, only that it is possible) if the theory with which he operates provides accurate or reasonably accurate predictions.

The great advantage of depending upon theories only for their predictive accuracy lies in the fact that the practitioner need not be committed to any given theory if an alternative one is more accurate in its predictions. The practitioner can operate with a simple pragmatic test that he makes of any theory in his practice: Is it more or less accurate in its predictions than an alternative theory? A scientist, on the other hand, may relish a particular theory because of the understanding it contributes to his knowledge and may be only mildly disturbed by the fact that its predictions are either untested or inaccurate.

Research

From this point on I will use the term "theory-research" or "theorist-researcher" to indicate what seems to me to be the proper designation of theory building. Research, except when it is confined to pure description, is concerned with testing theory, just as theory, when it is differentiated from theology, is concerned with being tested through research. It is literally impossible to separate theory and research since the function of each is dependent upon the realization of the other.

I have made a strong case for description as providing the stuff out of which the theorist-researcher builds models (Dubin, 1969, pp. 85:226–228). Good description is essentially good reporting of what may be apprehended and observed systematically in the empirical world. The habits and skills involved in accurate reporting are not confined to those functionaries carrying the designation of "researcher." Indeed, it is often true that practitioners are more knowledgeable about, and more capable of accurately describing the domain of their practice than are researchers. There may, however, be important instances when the trained observer can see what the man on the job overlooks, partly because of habituation to the experience. Thus, it is not possible to draw a strict line between the ability of practitioners and theorist-researchers uniquely to perform the functions of descriptive analysis. This is one of the important areas in which there is significant joint contribution to the scientific enterprise by the practitioner and the theorist-researcher.

In contrast to their joint contribution of descriptive accuracy about the domain being modelled by theory, there is a very real disjunction between theorist-researcher and practitioner regarding the purposes of research. As indicated above, the research is performed to test a theory. The practitioner may be interested in knowing if a theory has been tested in order to determine the degree of confidence he will accord its predictions. Beyond that, the practitioner has little if any interest in the theory-testing operations. The theorist-researcher has a much different orientation which needs to be examined in order to appreciate a significant source of non-overlap in outlook between theorist-researchers and practitioners.

There are two possible research stances toward a theoretical model:

1. The researcher may set as his task the proof of the adequacy of his theoretical model.

2. The researcher may set as his task to *improve* the starting theoretical model.

If the purpose is to prove the adequacy of the theoretical model, then important limitations are placed upon the research operations. If, on the other hand, the purpose is to improve the theoretical model, then some of these limitations may be set aside.

The limitations of the proof orientation are the following:

1. Data are likely to be collected for values on only those units incorporated in the theoretical model. This usually means that, either experimentally or by discarding data, attention in the empirical research is focused solely upon values measured on units incorporated in the theory.

2. In very much the same fashion, either experimentally or by discarding data, values on any given unit incorporated in the study beyond the predicted range may also be excluded from attention. In this manner, important data on the units that have been incorporated in the theoretical model are ignored because the model does not predict values in the empirical range of values.

We may conclude now that the orientation of seeking to prove the empirical truth of a theoretical model is wholly legitimate and important in establishing the initial linkage between a theoretical model and its empirical domain. Furthermore, it is psychologically important in establishing that the theorist have some certitude that his theoretical model does indeed link up with the empirical world.

At the same time, it should be recognized that the knowledge added by an empirical test to prove the accuracy of a model is limited only to that fact, namely, that the model does link in some useful way with an empirical domain. The knowledge of the phenomenon being modelled is contained in the theory, not in the empirical world. Furthermore, so long as subsequent tests continue to prove the theory, the theory remains static and unchanged.

The alternative approach of improving a theory is one that does not contain the limitations of the proof orientation. Consequently, it is likely to give rise to a constant reevaluation and reformulation of the theoretical models of a discipline as the empirical knowledge requires such modifications. The essential operations involved in a research approach to theory oriented toward improving it is to give particular attention and prominence to deviant cases and nonfitting data that feed back immediately onto the theory building process by resulting in theory modifications. None of the advantages of the theory-proving orientation are lost. But, in addition, the opportunities exist for theory modification and, therefore, for growth and improvement in the theoretical structure of a discipline. It seems sensible to conclude that the more viable orientation, but not necessarily the only right one, is to seek improvement of a theory when an empirical test is made, rather than only proof of it.

Practice

The practitioner in the field of human enterprise is concerned with making something work. He may be an industrialist trying to make a work organization effective; he may be a government official concerned with adequate performance of civic functions; he may be a school executive trying to maintain an adequate educational environment; or he may be a social worker concerned with improving the adjustment of individuals to their environment. The emphasis upon doing something that has observable consequences has important implications for the distinction between a practitioner and a theorist-researcher. This distinction can be appreciated by examining the concerns of the practitioner.

1. The practitioner has to know the present conditions with which he is dealing and which he is intent upon either preserving or changing;

2. The practitioner has to have a grounded purpose or goal for preserving or changing the present situation;

3. Where change is the decision, the practitioner has to have some preferred direction in which the change should go; and

4. Normally the practitioner wants to evaluate whether the subsequent state of affairs achieves the goal set for it.

It is evident that the scientist building a theory and testing it, and the practitioner directing or intervening in the practical affairs of men share only one of these four concerns, namely, an interest in accurate knowledge of the present conditions of the situation. The scientist is interested in good description of present conditions because this provides the stuff out of which he builds his theories. The practitioner is interested in the same kind of descriptive knowledge because in order to make changes he must have accurate knowledge of what is to be changed.

Beyond this commonality, however, their interests diverge. The theorist-researcher is interested in testing and improving his models. The predictions that he makes from the models are intensely practical from the standpoint of the practitioner. The theorist-researcher is not interested in the normative decisions as to whether the present state of affairs is to be continued or changed, the direction in which the change is to be oriented, or the evaluation of whether the change has been attained successfully. Thus, in the end the practitioner is left on his own resources to solve these three problems and shares with the theorist-researcher only a concern with having an accurate description of the present state or condition of the domain of his interest.

This limited articulation between theory and practice has its obvious consequences for the respective functions of, and relations between, the two spheres of intellectual activity. The theorist-researcher presents the practitioner with models of an empirical domain on which they can sometimes reach accord and then says: "If my model accurately reflects the characteristics of this domain, then I predict the following things to happen should any of the elements of this domain change their values." If the model is a reasonably accurate depiction of the real world, these predictions may be very useful in suggesting to the practitioner what the most probable outcomes are if he changes the values of one or more units in the system. Such a prediction is useful, however, only providing the practitioner is willing to accept the theorist-researcher's modelling of the empirical domain.

Suppose, however, the practitioner is confronted with two or more models that together purport to represent the same empirical domain. The fact that they are different models means that they will generate different predictions about the system being modelled, should the values of its units be changed. The practitioner now has to ask: "Which of these models do I want to utilize?" The answer may be grounded in some normative consideration that can vary widely among practitioners. This is by no means an easy choice, and I shall point out presently that there is a dilemma relating to the education of practitioners that leads them to become attached to certain models and prefer them over others.

The theorist-researcher is in no position to be more knowledgeable than the practitioner about the desirability of change, the goals of change, or the successful achievement of a chosen change. It is at precisely this point that we find one of the major structural reasons for failure of theorist-researchers and practitioners to become effective cooperators in problems of social policies, and their realization.

The theorest-researcher is normatively neutral, not because this makes his product more "objective," but is normatively neutral because what he is doing does not require normative considerations in formulating or carrying out his scientific functions. The situation is reversed for the practitioner for he is centrally concerned with normative issues in deciding if a system should be changed, the direction change should take, and the success with which it has been attained.

Furthermore, the goals of research in the theory-research realm, as we have already seen, are not the goals of the practitioner, and indeed, are in important ways antithetical to what the practitioner is doing. The practitioner needs a fixed and stable theoretical model whose predictions guide his normative conclusions at least with regard to the desirability of change, and its goals. The scientist is bored almost literally with a fixed theory and has no interest in it precisely to the degree that it is fixed or "established." Thus, on the grounds of orientation toward theory the theorist-researcher has a very distinctive point of view having little if anything in common with the equally distinctive point of view of the practitioner.

Some Dilemmas

One of the important dilemmas with which practitioners are faced when confronted with theorist-researchers is the disjunction between contemporary theory, on the one hand, and the kind of theory the practitioner is likely to have learned through his formal education, on the other hand. If it is true that social theorists are working constantly to improve their theory, and if it is true that they are sometimes successful, then there is a high probability that the kind of theory about human behavior that practitioners have learned in their own schooling is likely to be supplanted during the period of their active practice. To the extent that practitioners use theory in their work, they are likely to be using an outmoded theory, or one that has been significantly modified since they learned it. There is thereby created a further disjunction between the work of the theorist-researcher and his contemporaneous colleagues in practice. This phenomenon is characteristic of the field of medicine and the medical practitioners have learned the desirability of insisting upon regular in-service training for doctors in the field to bring them up to date about medical theory. Doctors even use closed circuit television to bring the experts from medical centers to the locale of the practice of medicine. Professional conventions also serve this same function by bringing the practitioners into contact with theorists, thereby disseminating the newest theories to the field.

The practice of in-service training has perhaps been less developed in the applied areas of social science with the result that there is a high probability that practitioners using social science theory will be significantly behind the current theoretical developments of the social science disciplines. There is probably a lag of 5 to 10 years between the time a theoretical model becomes fashionable in a discipline and its utilization by practitioners in areas of social behavior. In this connection, journals have been established solely to provide liaison between theory and practice as with *Trans-Action* in the United States and *New Society* in Great Britain.

Another dilemma in linking theory with practice rests on the messianic stance that is sometimes adopted by theorist-researchers. This is the tendency to assume that the skills of the theorist-researcher automatically and maybe uniquely qualify him to solve the problems of the practitioner, regardless of the theorist's competence or knowledge about the areas of practice under question. There is a very unfortunate tendency for social science theorist-researchers to lack the modesty essential to a scientific community. If, for example, I know something about industrial relations in a scientific way, I may indulge my vanity by assuming I can translate this knowledge and the theory making sense out of industrial behavior to the fields of race relations or international relations. This is made easier if I can trade upon a general reputation in my discipline to provide entrée as an "expert" into an area of practical concern about which I do not possess any scientific knowledge. Needless to add, it is a responsibility of the practitioner to guard himself and his colleagues against being influenced by such ignorant theorist-researchers.

Theory, Research, and Practice

I have so far indicated that there is significant discontinuity between theory-research and practice. This disjunction is the product of the manner in which theory is developed, its purposes, and its research test, on the one hand, and the purposes of practice, on the other hand. Theorists and practitioners alike would be comforted if they knew some magical way to link interests in order to achieve a higher level of accomplishment on each side. Having said that there are good reasons why theory and practice do not readily articulate, I want now to point out that cooperation is nevertheless possible.

I have already indicated that the contribution of theory to practice is to provide reliable predictions about what will happen to the system on which the practitioner is working. This is surely a significant contribution from theory to practice that requires no further amplification.

The practitioner makes a significant contribution to the theorist-researcher by providing the knowledge of the real world that comes from constant experience with it. This knowledge based upon experience has two important ways in which it influences the theorist-researcher.

1. Knowledge of the "real" situation may lead to the selection of the units built into a model different from what would have been chosen had the theorist simply thought about the problem by contemplating his navel.

2. Knowledge of the "real" situation may influence the choice of empirical indicators utilized in testing a theoretical model.

In the domain of human behavior the varieties of possible actions far exceed the ability of any individual to derive them logically. For example, I have shown that there are 1,048,586 distinctive ways in which two persons can interact if we employ Parsons' model of social behavior (Dubin, 1960). As theorists we have a much greater chance of dealing with real actions in their many guises if we listen to the practitioners whose daily work is focused upon human interaction. I can, perhaps, best illustrate this by calling your attention to the theory and research in the field of social power. You will recall that the theory of what is popularly called "power structures" derived from an analysis of the reputations of individuals in a community for their ability to determine, or influence, social decisions. This reputational approach is based upon a belief that if knowledgeable individuals in a community are asked to specify others known to them who exercise social influence, these respondents can give accurate answers that reflect the real world of social power. The theory of how large or small, how homogeneous or mixed, how old or young is the population of the power elite is inductively derived from the knowledge-able responses of the practitioner's wielding power. It took Floyd Hunter, with his interest in developing a "realistic" model of community power structure, to turn to those who lived with and in local power structures in order to find out their composition (Hunter, 1953). The contribution made by Hunter was a product of his wisdom in turning to the practitioners to learn more about the subject of his attention.

In a similar fashion, the practitioner in a field may contribute to the development of better empirical indicators for measuring the values on the units employed in theoretical models. To cite a personal example, I once had a lengthy conversation with a knowledgeable industrial relations executive who described an interesting member of his company work force. This was a man in his late 30's who was a good worker but lacked commitment to his job or company. The executive declared that he was puzzled by this apparent incongruity until he accidentally learned that the man was a lay preacher in a minor religious denomination with working class members. This one case immediately set me thinking about measuring what I had long since incorporated into my own models of industrial behavior, namely, the compartmentalization of actions into separate institutional realms. From that one example came the suggestion of how I might measure compartmentalization, and as a result developed the Central Life Interest instrument (Dubin, 1956). Although it was unwitting, the practitioner made a very important contribution to my research by pointing out a solution to a vexing problem of measurement.

You will note that in both of the examples cited, the practitioner is not conscious of the contribution he is making to the theorist-researcher. Although the contribution is real enough, it is not self-consciously made. This raises the problem of what is it that the practitioner can do that will deliberately contribute to the scientific enterprise.

The starting point of a self-conscious contribution is to overcome a feeling of awe in the presence of theory. There is some tendency for the theorist to be accorded unwarranted respect by the practitioner. To the extent that this overrides the objective judgement of the utility of the predictions derivable from theoretical models, the respect is misplaced and can be positively dysfunctional for it may suppress the practitioner's critical evaluation of the efficacy of the model.

The practitioner has a genuine responsibility to maintain a skepticism about theoretical models, which has as its affirmative outcome a willingness to improve upon them. The skills of a theorist are not so esoteric that they remain beyond the reach of practitioners. At least in the two ways I have suggested above the practitioner can become a working member of the theory-research team.

It has already been indicated that the theorist-researcher and the practitioner have differing goals that lead to differing viewpoints about a theoretical model. It is precisely the difference in viewpoints that makes it difficult for the two roles to be combined in one person. Should this happen, then the theoretical models are likely to become nothing more than *ad hoc* collections of variables whose values are most likely to predict values on variables of special interest. Thus, if one is interested in predicting movements of the business cycle some of the best predictors are statistical series whose upward or downward movement early signal the more general movement of business activity. It is not necessary, nor is it often possible to give a theoretical reason why particular indicators give better signals than others of the cyclical fluctuations in business activity. In the same way the prediction of success on parole depended solely upon finding some demographic or personality indicators that correlated highly with actual success on parole and then using these indicators to make predictions about future parole applicants. In a comparable fashion the profile of interests of successful men in an occupation or profession is used as a basis for matching the interests of persons being given vocational guidance when the Strong vocational interest test is utilized as a tool for prediction. Trade tests employed in rehabilitation counseling use the same technique of extrapolating past correlations to future situations. In every instance there may be a good prediction without any model or theory upon which it is based. The simple analytical tool employed is to extrapolate from existing relations future conditions that are believed to have high probability of obtaining.

Most theorists would recoil from such predictions as being non-theoretical. However accurate the predictions may be in given instances, there exists no model within which the lawful relationship among the variables correlated can be found. The practitioner can accept the adequacy of the predictions without knowing how they obtain. The theorist will feel compelled to build a model that tells him how the predicted outcome results from the interaction among the variables incorporated in the model. In the process of doing so he may generate predictions different from those obtained by extrapolation, and perhaps not as good. Nevertheless the theorist will hold to his theory because it provides him with some understanding of how variables are related to each other while the extrapolation may not yield such understanding.

It is generally unlikely that good theorists make good practitioners, or *vice versa*. The practitioner can contribute most to the theory building enterprise by maintaining the critical appraisal that his contact with the real world entitles him to make. If the theoretical model does not correspond with its purported empirical domain it should be the practitioner who is first to note and announce this. If the predictions made from a theoretical model are imprecise, then the practitioner, who has to live with such predictions, should be firm in proclaiming this inadequacy. Constant pressure should be exerted by the practitioner upon the theorist to do better. Certainly the theorist should be expected to do better than the folk wisdom of the average practitioner. But the folk wisdom should not be abandoned, willy nilly, simply because some theorist has declared his product to be better. The utility of the theory must ultimately meet the test of application by the practitioner. When it does we have the fruitful interplay between practitioner and theorist.

REFERENCES

ASHBY, W. ROSS
    1966   *Design for a Brain*. London: Chapman and Hall. 2nd edition.
CHINOY, ELI
    1955   *Automobile Workers and the American Dream*. New York: Doubleday & Co.
DUBIN, ROBERT
    1956   "Industrial workers' worlds: a study of the 'central life interests' of industrial workers." *Social Problems*, **3** (January): 131–142.
    1960   "Parsons' actor: continuities in social theory." *American Sociological Review*, **25** (August): 457–466.
    1969   *Theory Building*. New York: The Free Press.
HUNTER, FLOYD
    1953   *Community Power Structure*. Chapel Hill: University of North Carolina Press.
TYLER, LEONA E.
    1955   "The development of 'vocational' interest: 1: The organization of likes and dislikes in ten-year-old children." *Journal of Genetic Psychology*, **86**: 33–44.

CHAPTER FOUR

Theory, Meta-Theory, and Scientific Research

POWHATAN J. WOOLDRIDGE

There is still considerable divergence among scientists in their conceptions of theory and explications of its functions. In part, this may be due to the casual attitude that many empirical researchers in the social sciences take towards theory building. Meta-theoretical discussions of the relative merits of different kinds of theories are likely to be dismissed as largely irrelevant to the solution of the problems the researcher faces in his day-to-day activities. Yet, insofar as the ultimate purpose of scientific research is to formulate and test theory, then definition of the nature of theory is a logical prerequisite to discussion of strategies for designing and organizing such research.

To argue the relative merits of research techniques and procedures out of the context of their potential contribution to the development of cumulative bodies of theory implicitly results in re-defining the goals of research in terms of what C. Wright Mills termed "abstracted empiricism" (1959). Such research is designed to describe empirical relationships and it can, of course, have theoretical implications. But research which is not explicitly designed to make a theoretical contribution is likely to have ambiguous results. Nor is the research likely to be reported in a way which makes its theoretical implications clear. In making "secondary" theoretical interpretations from such research, one often commits errors which the original researcher could have avoided due to his qualitative knowledge of the research setting. It is therefore essential for the social sciences and the social practice professions to develop researcher-theorists, or even practitioner-researcher-theorists. Such individuals would combine research know-how and practical experience with a commitment to the building of general theory.

This paper proposes a meta-theoretical focus for the social sciences, and for the social practice professions. It then discusses some of the implications of this position for research and theory building. Finally, it explores the interrelations between "basic" social science theory and social practice theory.

The Nature of Theory

The component elements of any theory are undefined or elemental terms, definitions of complex terms based on the elemental terms, basic statements (axioms or laws) about the relationships between terms, rules of logic for drawing inferences, and derived propositions.[1] Theories can be more or less well integrated, articulated, complete, self-consistent, etc. But they need not make any predictions about the nature of the real world. (The theories of mathematics, for example, make no such predictions.) Of theories that do make statements about the real world, some are subject to empirical verification, and others are not. For example, theological explanations make statements about the real world which are not subject to empirical verification).[2]

To call a theory scientific implies that it is empirically testable and that such tests are the ultimate criteria of the theory's validity or invalidity. Scientific theories must therefore contain measurement propositions linking the theoretical variables to empirical phenomena under specific circumstances. Such measurement propositions, in contrast to theoretical propositions, may be of severely restricted generality. When the sole purpose of a theory is to make statements modeling reality with a maximum of precision, generality, and parsimony, then it is completely scientific. This criterion demands that there be no other value commitments to keeping a scientific theory or any of its propositions. If we find a theory that is more useful in describing, predicting, or manipulating the real world, then the new theory must replace the old. For example, the acceptance of the Copernican theory of motion of the planets in preference to the Ptolemaic theory was justified in terms of its greater simplicity. The replacement of Copernicus' model by Kepler's mathematical formulations was justified in terms of greater precision and simplicity, and the final explanation of the motion of the planets in terms of Newton's laws of universal gravitational attraction was preferred due to its much greater generality.

This is not to argue that theory building in science is value-free, but, rather, that it is subject to a particular set of values or criteria. In practice, scientists are often under pressure to use other values in determining the truth or falsity of a theory. In the above example, theories of planetary motion came to have important ideological significance, and the astronomers who tried to change them for scientific reasons encountered a great deal of opposition from ecclesiastical sources. To the extent that a theory becomes part of non-scientific ideology, to precisely that extent it becomes non-scientific. The scientific or non-scientific nature of a theory is therefore determined by its uses and its logic of validation, rather than by its subject matter. And the scientific nature of a theory is a matter of degree rather than kind.

This way of classifying and examining theories stems from the philosophical position of pragmatism. As Kaplan puts it, the pragmatic viewpoint asserts that the meaning of a theoretical statement lies not in answering the logical positivist question "What would the world be like if it were true?", or the operationist question "What would we have to do to come to believe it?", but rather in answering the question "What would we do if we *did* believe it?". The "action" to be taken on the basis of belief must be thought of in the broadest possible context — including such actions as making a predication, reformulating a theory, or performing an experiment (1964, pp. 43–44).

The criteria of validity for a scientific theory depend upon the purposes specified by the kind of theory under consideration. This conception leads directly to two conclusions of some interest. First, that the boundaries between different kinds of theories (e.g., psychological theories, sociological theories, biological theories, nursing practice theories, rehabilitation counseling theories, etc.) can be determined according to the differences in purpose of the theories. Second, the purpose of the theory in turn determines the context in which the validity of theoretical laws and propositions is to be evaluated. Thus, while the validation of a scientific theory depends on empirical phenomena, the significance of any given set of phenomena for the validation of theory depends on the extent to which any discrepancies noted between theoretical predictions and data have consequences which are important from the perspective of the theory in question. These points enter implicitly into much of the discussion below.

Causation and Theory

Scientific theories commonly assume that all events are inherently predictable from other events. The contrary notion, that all or some events are not subject to such prediction, is known as *emergence*. A closely related doctrine is *relative emergence*, which holds that certain phenomena are at present non-predictable because of technical limitation or other considerations though they may not be inherently non-predictable (Rudner, 1966, p. 71).

Whatever the validity of the doctrine of emergence in logical positivist terms, its validity in pragmatist terms is essentially nil. The assumption that phenomena are unpredictable would be of utility if all attempts to predict the phenomena would fail completely. But the history of science shows a multitude of such assumptions of unpredictability to have been proved wrong in the past, and it is logically groundless to assert that no such assumptions will be proved wrong in the future. Even the doctrine of relative emergence is heuristically sterile, and it tends to discourage the research necessary to invalidate its presuppositions.

A doctrine that has gained some popularity in the social sciences might be termed the doctrine of *non-causal emergence*. In this view, some phenomena are held to be predictable, but essentially non-manipulable. Variables may be systematically correlated with one another, the argument goes, but this in no way implies that the correlation is the product of some casual process or processes.[3] This doctrine, in both its relative and absolute forms, suffers from the same heuristic sterility as the doctrine of "predictive" emergence. A more fruitful research strategy is to assume that *all* variation in observed variables is causally produced. This leads to the corollary that whenever the variation in any two variables is not statistically independent, whatever lack of independence exists is produced by some causal process or processes. This does not imply, however, that the causal genesis of the relationship could be fruitfully analyzed from any given theoretical perspective. (The relationship might be due to observer bias, to a biased index, or to some other process irrelevant to the theory under study. Or it might be due to a combination of complex processes which existing theory and technology are inadequate to unravel.) The popularity of non-causal emergence in the behavioral sciences is probably due to the frequency with which systematic relationships between variables go beyond the capacities of our current research technology and behavioral theory causally to explain phenomena.

As used by many social scientists today, the statement X is a cause of Y means essentially "if I manipulate X, then *ceteris paribus*, I will affect the probability that Y will assume some value or values at some later time." Phrased thus broadly, the concept of causation is freed from the notion that effects are equivalent to observed changes. (Instead, the effect of the manipulation is defined as the difference between the probability distribution after the manipulation of X and the probability distribution as it would have been without the manipulation of X.) Strictly speaking, this definition assumes that the process used to manipulate X does not have an independent, direct effect on Y. For example, the proposition that "unit increases in X tend to cause three unit increases in Y" implies that *increases in X which are produced by factors which have no direct effects on Y* will be associated with increases in Y (at the average rate of a three unit increase in Y for each unit increase in X).[4] If the factor manipulated to produce a unit increase in X also produced a four unit decrease in Y (besides its indirect effects through X), then 1 unit increases in X would tend to be *associated* with 1 unit decreases in Y for that population and that particular manipulation. This biased association would not be generalizable to other populations and manipulation procedures however. The general law-like statement relating X and Y would remain "unit increases in X tend to produce three unit increases in Y."

To the practitioner, the need for causal theories to guide his practice will be particularly apparent. It is not enough for the practitioner to predict that his client is likely to experience certain difficulties. He must also know how to intervene to produce (cause) changes in these prognostications, such that his client's chances of avoiding the difficulties will be improved. To the practitioner, prediction without power to manipulate and influence is a dubious gift, indeed! Nor should the practitioner trust predictions that are not based on knowledge of the causal processes producing the co-variation between variables. Such predictions are a notoriously chancy affair, as innumerable stock market speculators and roulette players have learned to their dismay.

Even assuming the stability of the observed relationships, there is another reason why the practitioner who seeks to apply behavioral science by using observed relationships between variables to predict the future is likely to be disappointed. As Freeman (1969) points out, measures of most behavioral science variables are low in reliability. This low reliability attenuates even relationships based on relatively strong causal processes, to the point that the prediction of one variable from another is likely to be grossly inaccurate. While this is a severe limitation for using behavioral science to predict, there are circumstances under which the causal implications of an observed relationship between variables will nevertheless be relatively clearcut. Under such circumstances, it is often possible to draw inferences about the underlying causal processes behind the relationship, even when the measurement of an effect is unreliable, *if* the measure is "valid."

In this respect I disagree with Freeman's ordering of the importance of reliability and validity (1969). If the focus of the research is on testing a given causal theoretical proposition, then the validity of the measure — i.e., the extent to which it has the assumed causal relationship to the variable which one is attempting to measure — is all important. The reliability of the measure — i.e., the extent to which there is a relatively low amount of error variance produced by other causes of the measure — is of lesser importance in testing a theory, whenever the error variance can be assumed to act solely to attenuate the relationship rather than to bias it.[5] Thus even low correlations between variables can sometimes be used to test an hypothesized underlying causal relationship important to the improvement of client welfare.

For example, there have been a number of experimental studies in which various somatic variables, such as post operative vomiting rates, blood pressures, pulse rates, temperatures, etc., have been used to measure stress (Leonard, *et al.*, 1967). The fact that these somatic variables are not highly reliable measures of stress does not make the sharp decreases in these indicators produced by expressive interaction less interpretable. Since unreliable measurement would tend to attenuate (reduce) the correlations, it may even be inferred that the changes in stress must have been particularly large to have produced correlations of the magnitude obtained.

Abstraction and Theory

A controversy has raged in the behavioral and social sciences for a number of years over the issue of operationalism. Operationists have claimed primacy for operationally *defined* elements as the basic building blocks of theory. The alternative is to see theoretical variables as elements whose meanings lie not solely in any given operation or set of operations, but also in their relationships to other theoretical variables. In this view, the meaning of a theoretical term must be considered in the total theoretical context of which it is a part. (This is referred to as the horizontal or *systematic* component of meaning, by Kaplan (1964), as opposed to the vertical component of meaning specified by an abstract concept's relationship to the less abstract variables used to measure it.) In this view, the term operational *definition* is a misnomer, since no set of operations exhausts the meaning of a theoretical concept. (cf. Rudner, 1966, p. 20: Kaplan, 1964, p. 56). In this paper, the relationship between operational variables and the theoretical variables measured by them will be taken as associational rather than definitional, and the genesis of the association will be taken to be causal.[6]

Philosophers of science often regard the purpose of abstraction as description. Any concrete event represents an overwhelmingly complex collection of characteristics. Abstraction selects aspects of phenomena which will be usable in attempts to gain power over the world through manipulations guided by theory. This view of abstraction, which might be termed "descriptive abstraction," works well in considering the process by which observables are used to define variables whose meaning lies primarily in a "vertical" link to direct observation (i.e. operational variables). And the testing of theories demands that we use such operational variables as "stand-ins" for theoretical variables. But in a given research context, operational variables are usually linked to their theoretical counterparts through their presumed empirical (*not* definitional) association with the theoretical variables over the samples and circumstances studied. Such a link assumes the existence of a causal process (or processes) which produces the association. And it becomes important to analyze not only the relationship between theoretical variable and operational counterpart, but the causal process presumed to produce it as well.

In conducting behavioral research, the causal linkage between theoretical variables and their operational counterparts is used in order to test the underlying theory, not for the purposes of explaining the operational variables. And the external validity (generality beyond the sample) of the relationship between a theoretical variables and its operational counterpart is not at issue. What is at issue is the utility of the operational variable chosen for the research purpose, which is to investigate a given set of theoretical relationships with a minimum of ambiguity. Furthermore, the operational variable is not always an effect of its theoretical counterpart. In some instances it may be a cause of the theoretical variable; in other instances the linkage may be through a third variable which produces variation in both; or some combination of these processes may be specified. This argument — that variation in operational variables can be analyzed according to their proposed causal relationships to theoretical variables — could well be termed "causal abstraction."

The relating of theoretical variables to operational variables in cause-effect terms is often decried as "reification." Such a criticism is often justified by denying the real world existence of the theoretical *terms*, since conceptual inventions can not reasonably be said to have causal efficacy. Yet, in many respects it does make sense to refer to such factors as "intelligence," "prejudice," or "norms" as having causal efficacy in the production of empirical phenomena.[7] In logical positivist terms, the counter argument is to assert the real world existence of something serving as a *referent* for such terms which has causal efficacy. In pragmatist terms, it seems possible to avoid the real-or-not-real problem entirely. Where thinking of the relationship between theoretical variables and their operationalized counterparts as causal helps the theory-builder to avoid mistakes in building useful theories, he is free to do so. Where such arguments are not helpful, they should be abjured.

It is not useful, for example, to *define* a theoretical term by a set of empirical manifestations and then to propose the theoretical term as a useful explanation of the empirical manifestations which define it. If we *define* intelligence as that which is measured by a given I.Q. test, then it would not help to explain differences between test scores by saying that they were produced (caused by) differences in I.Q. It is essentially in this context that philosophers of science argue against reification. But when the relationship between an operational variable and its theoretical counterpart is treated as propositional rather than definitional, then the horizontal (systemic) meaning of the theoretical variable can be used to test the validity of the operational variable as a measure of the theoretical variable for any given sample of cases. It is even possible to regard the causal relationship as an explanation of the phenomena which are typically used to measure it. For example, insofar as not all refusals to employ a physically handicapped person are due to prejudice, then the assertion that a particular refusal was due to prejudice is by no means tautological. Such an assertion connects the genesis of the behavior to theoretical processes which would not apply if the refusal was interpreted as due to a purely rational evaluation that the applicant was unqualified, for example.

To sum up, the use of variables defined by descriptive abstraction in explaining the phenomena used to define them is tautological, and dysfunctional to theoretical development. But the use of variables defined by causal abstraction in the explanation of empirical phenomena is legitimate whenever there is sufficient surplus meaning to make the statement non-tautological. This implies that there can be no one-to-one isomorphism between such theoretical variables and any given set of empirical phenomena.

Theory and Research

We have already discussed one major point relevant to the relationship between theory and research that stems from the above discussion — that it may make sense under certain circumstances to make inferences about the causal relationship between theoretical variables on the basis of data gathered using unreliable measures of one or both variables. In fact, if we can make the strong assumption of no correlated measurement error, then, for a given level of association between variables, the less the measurement reliability, the more the evidence implies a particularly strong relationship between the theoretical variables measured. The argument is as follows — if X and Y are correlated, and if X and Y are measured by effects of X and Y (say X' and Y') that are also subject to considerable variation from other factors, then the correlation between X' and Y' will be attenuated by an amount equal to $1/\sqrt{r_{xx} \, r_{yy}}$ where r_{xx} and r_{yy} are the relative reliability coefficients for X' and Y', respectively.[8]

It follows that for a given magnitude of observed relationship between X' and Y', the correlation between X and Y can be inferred to be stronger when unreliable measures were used than when reliable measures were used. Of course, this does *not* imply that unreliable measures are to be preferred, but simply that it is possible under some circumstances to make inferences about the correlation between the underlying theoretical variables being measured. Now, inferring what the underlying statistical relationship between X and Y *would be* if you had reliable measures does not help one to predict, assuming that no better measures are available. However, if we can argue from theoretical considerations that the only reason that X and Y are correlated is that X is a cause of Y, then the relationship between X and Y becomes the major focus of practical interest whenever prediction of the effects on Y of a *manipulation* of X is important. And it is precisely this kind of information which is of the greatest value to the practitioner who wants to help his client.

Let us now consider how we can assert that there is no correlated measurement error between X' as a measure of X and Y' as a measure of Y. In causal terms, this boils down to the statement that X' is not a direct cause of variation in Y or Y', that Y' is not a cause of variation in X', and that no third factor exists (other than X) which is a cause of variation in both X' and Y'. This assertion depends on our knowledge of the causes of variation in X' and Y'. And such knowledge depends on the existence of causal propositions based on past empirical investigations which we are willing to generalize to the present circumstances.

In the discussion (above) of the significance of expressive behavior to stress reduction, the author interpreted observed reductions in post-operative vomiting, blood pressure, pulse rate, etc., as evidence that certain kinds of expressive interaction tend to reduce psychological stress. There are many factors other than reduced psychological stress that are capable of producing decreases in blood pressure and pulse rate, or in vomiting behavior. Yet the inference that systematic differences in the experimental and control groups were due to stress reduction is reasonably secure, since there were strong theoretical grounds for asserting that the variables *systematically* manipulated by the experiment could not have produced such effects except through the reduction of psychological stress. Since the host of other factors affecting these unreliable indicators had been randomized by the assignment procedure, it is reasonable to assert that the statistically significant differences in the indicators used must have been due to the variables systematically manipulated by the experimental procedure, and hence to reduced stress. It is not so much the *amount* of measurement error that should concern the researcher who wishes to test a causal proposition, but the theoretical plausibility that the measurement error will systematically bias the test.

As stated above, measurement propositions need not be a part of the primary body of theory defined by the theoretical focus — nor need they be broadly generalizable. For example, propositions about the factors that tend to cause variation in responses to a given questionnaire are often not generalizable to certain categories of subjects, times, places, etc. But these limitations do not necessarily lead us to modify our measurement procedures to make them more general. Instead, we may be willing to use different operations to measure the same theoretical variable under different circumstances, if we have a theory that predicts that the switch in operational variables won't be misleading. (For example, the translation of questionnaires for persons who speak different languages, the use of modified I.Q. tests for certain sub-populations, etc.)

The above discussion suggests that it is partly through theoretical considerations of causality that we support the validity of the assumptions we make in interpreting any given research result. This is true whether or not the theoretical propositions we are trying to test are causal. For example, we assume that the asking of a question tends to produce (cause) an answer, and that the content of the question interacts with the characteristic of the individual whose attitude we are trying to measure in affecting the probability of a given answer. This causal model then provides the theoretical justification for asserting that we have measured the individual's attitude — i.e., that there will be a known statistical relationship (however attenuated) between the responses of individuals and their attitudes. It is not difficult explicitly to consider the assumed causal processes which operate to produce the data we analyze. And such conscious consideration is a necessary step in increasing the validity of our research designs.

In order to be most helpful, the analysis of measurement error should be structured to emphasize the context in which the measurement process occurs. The importance of error in the measurement of a variable, X, by an operational variable, X', depends on (1) the other variables in the design which are to be studied in relation to X, and (2) on the way that these other variables are to be measured. Whenever the source of the measurement error is not causally linked to the other variables of interest, or directly to their operational counterparts (measures), then the error variance is random and the effect of the error is only to reduce the magnitude of the relationships. But if the measurement error is causally linked to other variables in the study, or directly to their measures, then the theoretical inferences drawn from the study may be systematically misleading. While the long range goal of the social sciences should be to achieve measures of as great an absolute validity and reliability as possible, the continued use of measures which are highly unreliable demands at a minimum the careful analysis of sources of error variance in the context of the study design.

The developer of a new body of theory is faced with an apparent paradox. If the correct interpretation of research results depends on the adequacy of existing theory to rule out alternative explanations, and if theory can only be arrived at through the correct interpretation of research results, then how does one begin?

The conventional answer is to see research and theory-building as a continual interchange between inductive formulations and deductive tests. This interchange produces increasingly better fits between data and theory, initially through a more or less trial-and-error process (guided by logic and "insight" to be sure). While this answer may be correct in one sense, it is not very helpful to the researcher who wants to do theoretically relevant work in an "underdeveloped" theoretical area.

Such a researcher should look first to the resources that exist in the cumulative products of man's past theory building in other areas. These can be used to reject some logically conceivable interpretations of data as theoretically improbable. And "common sense" knowledge of what is going on is often very helpful in getting started, whether or not such knowledge is accorded the status of theory. Glaser and Strauss (1967) suggest the particular importance of immediate experience with the empirical realm of concern when theories are to be built in new areas. Their suggestion seems well taken. They also imply that the logic of verification is not useful in such theory building efforts. However, the general logic of verification discussed in this paper — careful consideration of alternative explanations and the cross checking of deductions — is as useful in building "grounded" theory from direct experience as in evaluating the validity of a research design.

There is at least one research tool that is not often given its proper importance in the early phases of theory building — the randomization experiment. While the stereotype of experimental design is of a highly structured procedure designed to permit inferences about the effects of some rigorously operationalized stimulus, randomization experiments can also be used in an exploratory fashion that approximates the freedom of trial-and-error approaches. (Wooldridge, *et al.*, 1968; Leonard *et al.*, 1967). Used this way, the ability of randomization experiments to rule out alternative explanations can be very helpful to the researcher-theorist, when theory proves an inadequate guide to the identification of those variables which it is necessary to control. Such designs are particularly appropriate to practice settings, where the practitioner-researcher is directly investigating the results of his own practice. Under such circumstances, theory built on the basis of loosely structured randomization experiments can provide full grounding in direct experience, and can at the same time effectively rule out the possibility of mistaken interpretations due to spuriousness.[9]

Social Practice Theory

It is a common misconception that scholars from the so-called "basic" sciences (i.e., physics, chemistry, biology, psychology, sociology, etc.) have a monopoly on the construction of scientific theory. This impression is quite common in sociology — perhaps because of the lack of any well defined "clinical sociology" involving specific responsibilities for services to clients through a socially defined set of legitimate means. (Presumably, for the discipline to be labeled clinical *sociology* the "clients" would have to be social-structural, i.e., societies, organizations, or other groups). Since we have defined the domain of a theory in functionalist terms, it makes sense to talk about the "practice theory" of a given profession as a distinct area of theory with its own defining focus.

The purpose of a practice theory is to improve the efficacy of actions taken by a given kind of practitioner which have the purpose of serving his client in ways relevant to the practitioner's professional responsibilities (Wooldridge, *et al.*, 1968). This purpose defines a functional context in which a given practice theory focuses on (1) socially permissible means which the practitioner has autonomy in manipulating, (2) goals which are part of the professional responsibility of that kind of practitioner in serving his client, and (3) contingent conditions specifying the relationship between means and goals which are typically encountered in that kind of practice. This is quite different from the defining focus of sociological theory or psychological theory. From the frame of reference of sociology, the question "So what?" means "Now that I know this, how do I modify my notions of how a social system functions to describe, explain, or predict more accurately?" From a practice theory frame of reference, the question "So what?" means "Now that I know this, what can I do to provide more effective services for clients?" In other words, the "basic sciences" define their theoretical domains in terms of the general kind of system the theory deals with — be it societies, complex organizations, small groups or personality systems. The practice disciplines define their theoretical domains according to the kinds of means judged to be within the practitioner's legitimate scope of influence, the kinds of ends judged to be within the practitioner's area of professional responsibility, and the kinds of contingencies often encountered in practice.

Practice theories can be fully as abstract as theories of the "basic" sciences. It is in some respects a mistake to view the theories of sociology, psychology, biology, and physics as general theoretical foci from which practice theories may be unambiguously derived. This is a relative rather than absolute limitation, which stems more from current theoretical weakness in the basic sciences than from the ultimate impossibility of articulating basic theory and practice theory.

First, all theories must inevitably involve discrepancies between predictions based on theory and real world observations. One major problem is that the defining criteria of the importance of a discrepancy differ according to whether the theoretical focus is that of a basic science or a practice discipline. Second, the general theories of such basic sciences as sociology and psychology are as yet crude, and largely unsuccessful in predicting the effects of variation in one variable on another variable in terms which can be safely generalized to diverse circumstances. Third, even if reliable general theories did exist, this would not solve all the technical problems of effectively manipulating a given theoretical variable in the given set of circumstances likely to be encountered by the practitioner.[10] Fourth, all the relevant side effects of a given manipulation are unlikely to be predictable from basic scientific theories.

Once discovered, all the propositions relevant to a practice theory might be classified as sociological, psychological, biological, or sometimes all three (e.g., socio-psycho-somatic causal chains). But it would surely be groundless optimism to expect all these propositions to be explicit or implicit in existing basic science theories — or to be able to derive them and anticipate their practical importance even if they were. In short, whether or not practice theory is a body of theory technically separable from "basic" theory, practitioners are well advised to act as if it were.

It would be easy to mis-read the implications of the above discussion for building practice theory. The point is not that efforts to articulate practice theories with "basic" theories are a waste of time, or doomed to failure. On the contrary, such efforts are often useful. Practitioners should think of basic theories as providing insights which can often be used to strengthen practice theory. But they should *not* neglect the development of their own brand of practice theory in the mistaken belief that basic theory "says it all."

The development of the practice theory of a given area is ultimately the responsibility of the professional practitioners in that area.[11] While basic scientists may study a given practice, they seldom do so for the primary purpose of advancing practice theory. They are more likely to be interested in developing theories *about* social practice then developing practice theory *per se*. For example, a theory explaining why a given kind of professional practitioner and client typically interact the way they do or why particular kinds of persons become practitioners, would not necessarily be part of the theory of that profession. Its relevance would be established only if such a theory led to propositions about how and why some kinds of permissible manipulations by the practitioner are likely to be more effective than others.

Even when a theory presents causes of the problems the practitioner wishes to solve, it is not necessarily a part of the practice theory of that profession *per se*. Such theories contribute to practice theory only when their implications for practice are made explicit. Usually this means that the theory must suggest something about the relative efficacy of various possible means *available to the practitioner* in dealing with the problem. For example, to argue that prejudice against the handicapped often interferes with their job adjustment would be an incomplete proposition from the perspective of vocational counseling theory as given here. But it could *lead to* propositions which would be within the theoretical domain of vocational counseling theory. For example, a proposition stating that certain kinds of psychological preparation, which could be given by rehabilitation counselors, would make it easier for the handicapped to adapt to encounters with prejudiced people. Or a proposition showing how the rehabilitation counselor could measure and match the ability of a handicapped person to handle prejudice with the probability of his encountering prejudice in a given kind of job situation. Or any other kind of proposition which states *both* a relevant problem *and* some way that a rehabilitation counselor can do something about it.

Descriptions of the existence of a phenomenon, or of its statistical relationship to other phenomena (*sans* causal implications) are useful to the practitioner only insofar as they have implications for goal-directed activity. This usually means that they must describe the contingent conditions specifying which kind of means will be most effective in achieving practice goals. Or, on occasion, they may call attention to neglected needs of clients which existing practice theory is adequate to treat and which the practitioner recognizes as his responsibility. But, for a descriptive study to have clear cut practice implications, the description must have focused on those aspects of the situation most important to practice theories of diagnosis and treatment. This is seldom the case when the study is conducted by a "basic" scientist. And, unfortunately, it is often not the case even when the study is conducted by a practitioner. Suchman's comment that evaluation studies are often undertaken with the attitude "let's do the evaluation and then decide what to do with the results" is all too characteristic of studies by basic scientists and practitioners alike. Reconceptualization of the research hypotheses to be tested in practice theory terms is one way of assuring the relevance of the research.[12]

Summary

This paper has proposed a general meta-theoretical orientation and some middle range meta-theoretical guidelines for increasing the relevance of research to theory and of theory to research. The general orientation is that social scientists should evaluate research procedures in terms of their utility in testing and generating theory in the given research context. In order to accomplish this, the researcher should: (1) be explicit about the causal assumptions implicit in his data gathering and measurement techniques, (2) be willing to present and analyze general abstract theoretical interpretations of his research results, and (3) explicitly define the theoretical focus from which the research results are to be evaluated.

Causal analyses were seen to be of particular importance in practice theories, where the intent of the practitioner is to intervene in order to produce (cause) a difference in the clients' situation. But in order to use causal analyses in building practice theory it is first necessary to understand the very general sense in which the term "cause" is to be used. A variable (X) is usefully viewed as a cause of another variable (Y), if (on the average) changes would be produced in Y by manipulating X.

Defining cause thus broadly, it makes sense to use hypothetical constructs developed by a process of "causal abstraction" in building general theories. Such constructs are theoretical variables such as "prejudice," "anxiety," "intelligence," "status discrepancy," etc., which are seen as producing variation in observable phenomena without being isomorphic to such phenomena.

This general approach also leads to some interesting implications for theory testing. It suggests, for example, why research which discovers only weak relationships between variables can have important theoretical implications. It also suggests that the *amount* of error in a measurement procedure is of less importance than whether or not that error is systematic with respect to other variables whose relationships to the measured variable are under examination. Finally, it suggests the importance of randomization experiments in the exploratory stages of research, where existing theoretical knowledge is inadequate to control possible sources of spuriousness.

The definition of the focus of the practice theory of a given profession also stems from the general approach used here. In essence, a proposition lies within the theoretical domain of a given practice theory if it predicts the effects of *actions* which the practitioner can employ, on *goals* for which the practitioner assumes responsibility, under *circumstances* which the practitioner is likely to encounter. One problem in the development of practice theory is a tendency to see any proposition related to *either* means *or* goals *or* circumstances as a high priority subject for research. Much of such research has little or no direct implications for practice, though it may lead to research designed to have such implications.

Discussions of theory and meta-theory always seem somehow removed from the practical world of daily activities such as conducting studies or attempting to meet the needs of clients. Yet, the development of a cumulative body of useful theoretical knowledge in an area is in a way the most practical of activities. Without adequate theory, we are faced with the prospect that our best efforts towards effective research or practice may fail to accomplish their objectives, or even worse may have contrary effects (i.e., worsen client welfare or produce misleading research results). Without the development of appropriate meta-theories to guide theoretical formulations, and appropriate methodologies to guide research efforts, social scientists and social practitioners alike will waste much of their efforts on the development of inherently feeble theories and the collection of data whose relevance to theory is obscure.

NOTES TO THE CHAPTER

1. In many respects this definition resembles the conceptualization of theory provided in Rudner (1966).
2. Dubin, however, seems to exclude both formal theories (such as mathematics) and ideological theories as "non-theoretical" (1969b, pp. 8–9).
3. Dubin seems to take essentially this position (cf. 1969b, pp. 89–95, *passim*). Possibly the difference is that Dubin defines cause differently than it is defined here (see below). While he presents no specific definition of cause he presents examples of "non-causal laws" — e.g.: Marriotte's law (Boyle's law) which would be classified as causal by the criteria presented in this paper.
4. For a discussion of some common misconceptions of the modern implications of causal terminology, see Hirshi and Selvin (1967).
5. Part of the problem lies in the definition of terms. Validity can be defined as "the extent to which a measurement procedure produces scores which lead to the same statistical expectancies as the variable measured" or as "a correlation between a criterion variable and an indicator." And reliability can be defined as "the variance of the scores produced by the measurement procedure around their statistical expectancies" or as "a correlation of one measure with another measure of the same thing." In each case, the first definition is methodological-theoretical and the second is an operational definition commonly used in research. Freeman seems to be implicitly using the operational meanings, whereas my own discussion is couched in terms of the methodological-theoretical meanings. Ambiguities in the conceptualization and operationalization of validity and reliability are conceded to be a major problem in psychology, but this problem has received relatively little attention in sociology (Coombs, 1950; Guttman, 1955; Tryon, 1957).
6. This position is essentially similar to the position taken in Blalock, 1968a.
7. For a relevant discussion, see MacCorquodale and Meehl (1948).
8. See Guilford, 1965, p. 486. While the argument is presented here for the case of a linear regression model, similar considerations of attenuation apply to any model.
9. Experimental designs are not, however, a safeguard against mistaken interpretations resulting from biasing manipulation of the independent variable or due to a biased measure of the dependent variable (Wooldridge *et al.*, 1968, pp. 64–65).
10. See Suchman's (1969) discussion of the "evaluation of 'technique'."

11. An interesting implication of defining practice theory in this way was brought to my attention by William Form. Whenever the responsibilities and roles of occupational specialties with different designations are sufficiently similar to result in essentially identical definitions of their domain of practice theory, then one could argue that these specialties do not qualify as distinct professions. This sort of distinction could provide a useful theoretical tool for discovering underlying unities beneath the proliferation of occupational sub-specialties with divergent titles, but similar technical content.

12. Note that this criterion of relevant research includes the possibility of *basic* research designed to have implications for practice theory, but not directly evaluating an action program. Indeed, from the perspective presented in this paper, the usual distinction between "basic" and "applied" research is replaced with a distinction based on the kind of theoretical focus used to guide the research.

REFERENCES

BLALOCK, HUBERT M., JR.
  1968   "The measurement problem: a gap between the languages of theory and research. Pp. 5–27 in Hubert M. Blalock, Jr., and Ann B. Blalock, *Methodology in Social Research*. New York: McGraw-Hill.

COOMBS, C. H.
  1950   "The concepts of reliability and homogeneity." *Educational and Psychological Measurement*, **10** (Spring): 43–56.

DUBIN, ROBERT
  1969a   "Theory and Research." In Richard O'Toole (ed.), *The Organization, Management, and Tactics of Research*.
  1969b   *Theory Building*. New York: The Free Press.

GLASER, BARNEY G., and ANSELM L. STRAUSS
  1967   *The Discovery of Grounded Theory: Strategies for Qualitative Research*. Chicago: Aldine.

GUILFORD, J. P.
  1965   *Fundamental Statistics in Psychology and Education*. New York: McGraw-Hill.

GUTTMAN, L.
  1955   "An outline of some new methodology for social research." *Public Opinion Quarterly*, **18** (Winter): 395–404.

FREEMAN, HOWARD E.
  1969   "The implementation of research investigations." In Richard O'Toole (ed.), *The Organization, Management, and Tactics of Research*.

HIRSCHI, TRAVIS, and HANAN C. SELVIN
  1967   *Delinquency Research: An Appraisal of Analytic Methods*. New York: The Free Press.

KAPLAN, ABRAHAM
  1964   *The Conduct of Inquiry*. San Francisco: Chandler.

LEONARD, ROBERT C., JAMES K. SKIPPER, and POWHATAN J. WOOLDRIDGE
    1967   "Small sample field experiments for evaluating patient care." *Health Services Research*, 2 (Spring): 46–58.

MacCORQUODALE, KENNETH, and PAUL MEEHL
    1948   "On a distinction between hypothetical constructs and intervening variables." *Psychological Review*, 55 (March): 95–107.

MILLS, C. WRIGHT
    1959   *The Sociological Imagination*. New York: Oxford University Press.

✓ RUDNER, RICHARD S.
    1966   *Philosophy of Social Science*. Englewood Cliffs: Prentice-Hall.

SUCHMAN, EDWARD A.
    1969   "Action for what? A critique of evaluative research." In Richard O'Toole (ed.), *The Organization, Management, and Tactics of Research*.

TRYON, R. C.
    1957   "Reliability and behavior domain validity; reformulation and historical critique." *Psychological Bulletin*, 54: 229–249.

WOOLDRIDGE, POWHATAN J., JAMES K. SKIPPER, JR., and ROBERT C. LEONARD
    1968   *Behavioral Science, Social Practice, and the Nursing Profession*. Cleveland: The Press of Case Western Reserve University.

DEMONSTRATION AND APPLIED RESEARCH

CHAPTER FIVE

Action for What? A Critique of Evaluative Research

EDWARD A. SUCHMAN

One generation ago, Robert S. Lynd published his classical challenge to research scientists — *Knowledge for What?* (Lynd, 1939). In the midst of a period of breathtaking advances in all of the physical and social sciences, he proposed a time for stock-taking to evaluate the purposes and utility of such rapidly accumulating knowledge. Basic or "pure" research, he argued, had an objective beyond that of expanding disciplinary knowledge. The scientist, as a member of society whose research was supported by society, had an obligation to concern himself with the possible application of his discoveries to the needs of society.

While this proposition may have given rise to a great debate in the 1940's, it has become largely academic in The Great Society of the 1960's. The explosion of the first atomic bomb destroyed forever the detachment of the physical scientist. For better or worse, he found himself unavoidably in the center of the arena of national affairs. It wasn't long before he was joined there by the social scientist. If the physical sciences could produce such a shattering impact upon the world of nature, why shouldn't the behavioral sciences have an equally telling effect upon the world of man? Why couldn't man's knowledge of the forces governing himself and the societies he had created be applied to the remedying of the defects within those societies?

Lynd's challenge of "Knowledge for What?" has been answered one generation later by the resounding battle cry of, "Knowledge for action!"

The emphasis today is clearly upon the application of knowledge to the amelioration of social problems. The same scientific methodology that had been so successful in discovering knowledge was now to be brought to bear upon the utilization of that knowledge. Social change could be planned and implemented by scientific research upon the causes of society's ills and by the development of intervention programs to meet these causes. Man, it seems, had now entered a period of widespread planned social change or innovation. Action programs in all areas of health, education, and welfare have become the watchword of the day (Bennis, 1960; Fairweather, 1967).

But action for what? Just as Lynd had challenged the purpose of knowledge in an era of new discoveries, we might today challenge the purpose of action in an era of frenzied and ever-increasing activity on an international, national, and local scale. What are we trying to accomplish with these action programs? Is knowledge for knowledge's sake to be replaced by action for action's sake?

Evaluation — the Study of Planned Social Change

To answer this question of action for what, social scientists are developing methods for studying planned social change in an attempt to evaluate the purposes and effectiveness of such change. These evaluative research studies attempt to apply the methods of science to service and action programs in order to obtain objective and valid measures of what such programs are accomplishing. Underlying these efforts are three implicit assumptions: (1) that man can change his social environment; (2) that change is good; and (3) that such change is measurable. Thus, social problems are viewed as amenable to deliberate intervention, while the success or failure of such intervention is subject to demonstration through scientific, evaluative research studies (Suchman, 1967).

From the point of view of this report, evaluation connotes some judgment concerning the effects of planned social change. The target or object of the evaluation is usually some program or activity which is deliberately intended to produce some desired result. The evaluation itself attempts to determine the degree of success or failure of the action in attaining this result. Thus, evaluation represents a measurement of effectiveness in reaching some predetermined goal.

The key elements in this definition of evaluation are: (1) an objective or goal which is considered desirable or has some positive value; (2) a planned program of deliberate intervention which one hypothesizes is capable of achieving the desired goal; and (3) a method for determining the degree to which the desired objective is attained *as a result of* the planned program. All three must be present before evaluation can take place.

These three elements can be recognized in Riecken's definition of evaluation as "the measurement of desirable and undesirable consequences of an action that has been taken in order to forward some goal that we value" (Riecken, 1952: 4). The emphasis upon the study of change is clearly seen in the four questions posed by Herzog for "a satisfactory evaluation of effort": (1) what kind of change is desired?; (2) by what means is change to be brought about?; (3) what is the evidence that the changes observed are due to the means employed?; and (4) what is the meaning of the changes found? (Herzog, 1959: 2). Unless one can visualize an *objective* involving change from some less desirable to some more desirable state, an *activity* or program designed to produce this change, and *criteria* by which one can judge that change has taken or is taking place, one cannot formulate the necessary evaluative hypothesis, viz., "Activities A, B, C will achieve objectives X, Y, Z."

The Need for Evaluation

To some extent, all programs of planned social change, whether educational, economic, medical, political, or religious, are required to provide "proof" of their legitimacy and effectiveness in order to justify public support. The demand for "proofs of work" will vary depending upon such factors as degree of faith in authority and competition between opposing programs or objectives. The current proliferation of new types of social intervention which challenge traditional approaches to health, education, and welfare and which compete for both public and financial support are under constant pressure to show that they are better than established programs and deserve a larger proportion of available resources. There probably comes a time in the development of any new approach to a social problem when, after an initial outburst of enthusiastic activity, a breathing period of evaluation sets in.

The need for evaluation rarely occurs in an atmosphere of complacency. Dissatisfaction and puzzlement lie behind most demands for evaluation. The natural tendency of an entrenched program is to resist change. Only when the public voices its displeasure at the way a social problem is being met or a public service is being rendered, or when professional conscience becomes too uneasy about its efforts at correcting social conditions or

providing public services does talk of evaluation begin. The same factors that create public concern about the social problem to begin with also underlie the demand for evaluation: (1) a "perceived discrepancy" between what exists and what is desired, (2) a feeling of a "need for adjustive activity" to resolve this discrepancy, and (3) an "awareness of ignorance or doubt" about what should be done (Merton and Devereaux, 1964). As stated by Borgatta: "When conditions are bad enough and social conscience is brought into play, both the need and the potential for improvement may lead to the development of a program designed to be corrective. Most programs that receive systematic attention for evaluation occur in the context of correcting an existing situation" (Borgatta, 1966).

Before an evaluation is undertaken, it is important that the sources of "dissatisfaction and puzzlement" be identified as clearly as possible. Unless this is done, it becomes difficult to formulate the study in such a way as to provide the answers that will be needed to remedy the dissatisfaction or dispell the puzzlement. Thus, an evaluation study should be a problem-solving enterprise with a clear cut relationship to some decision-making function. Perhaps the most crucial question to be asked before an evaluation is undertaken is, "What decisions about the program or its objectives will be affected by the results of the evaluation?" Further development of this question would force consideration of why the evaluation was being done, what alternative courses of action were being considered, who was in favor of or opposed to the evaluation, how much weight the results of the evaluation would carry, and what resources existed or could be marshalled to support the recommendations of the evaluation. A good exercise is to "suppose" positive or negative results and then to predict what would be done as a result of either outcome.

The answers to questions such as the above will increase the likelihood that the results of an evaluation will be utilized and help to forestall unnecessary and unproductive studies. Unless a reasonable assumption can be made that the results of the evaluation will be utilized, there is probably little need for the evaluation. Much too often evaluation studies are undertaken when there is very little likelihood that anything will change regardless of how the evaluation comes out. The attitude seems to be "let's do the evaluation and then decide what to do with the results." In such a case, the evaluation is probably unnecessary and certainly inadequately conceived.

One further consideration has to do with the appropriate and desirable time for evaluation. An evaluation study should not be undertaken until an activity or program has had enough time to prove its possible effective-

ness. Obviously, the program has to have become operational before it
can be evaluated. To some extent an evaluation can be limited to determining whether or not a program has succeeded in establishing itself;
but, as we shall see later, this is a limited evaluation that has little to do
with the actual effectiveness of the program.

However, while a program should not be evaluated too soon, neither
should it be evaluated too late. The evaluation should occur while there
is still time to apply the results to the operation of the program. This
means before the activity has become so entrenched that change is no
longer possible or can only be made with great difficulty and disruption.
It is well known that evaluation has its greatest success with new, experimental activities and its least success with established, traditional
programs. In the case of newly developed programs, it may be possible to
"build-in" evaluative research in such a way as to feed back information
to the program. Such built-in evaluation can also serve the purpose of
"quality control" and redirection for an on-going program.

Evaluation is most productive when it can become a continuous process
of program assessment and improvement. Too often the need for evaluation is narrowly defined in terms of a one-shot, "pass-fail" decision. Not
only is this unrealistic, since very seldom are the results of an evaluation
study so definitive as to "prove" a program a complete failure, nor are the
administrative considerations usually such as to permit the total termina-
tion of a program, but also an important function of the evaluation should
be to improve shortcomings of the program in order to increase its
effectiveness. Evaluative research is best viewed as a learning process
with the focus of interest being an analysis of *why* a program is failing or
succeeding.

The answer to this question "why" might encompass an analysis of:
(1) the attributes of the program itself that make it more or less successful;
(2) the population exposed to the program in terms of which sub-groups
are reached and which affected; (3) the situational context within which
the program takes place, such as auspices, locale, competing programs, and
community support; and (4) the different kinds of effects produced by the
program, such as cognitive, attitudinal, or behavioral, long or short-term,
unitary or multiple, including special attention to any negative side-
effects. Information on the above aspects of program operation represents
the research contribution which evaluation can make to any programmatic activity (Suchman, in press). In this sense evaluation involves more
than judging; it also includes an understanding of process and a constant
feedback of information for program revision.

Functions and Types of Evaluation

Evaluation is an important component of administration, whether such evaluation be formal or informal. If we view the administrative process as a "cycle" which includes the following special activities: (a) decision-making, (b) programming, (c) communicating, (d) controlling, (e) reappraising (Litchfield, 1956: 12), it becomes apparent that evaluation is an essential tool of management. Since the major focus of administration is the organization of resources and activities so as to achieve some desired objective, and since we have defined evaluative research as the study of the relationship of planned activities to desired objectives, we place evaluative research at the heart of the administrative process. In fact, we would argue that evaluative research constitutes the methodological and empirical backbone of any attempt to build a field of administrative science or practice theory.

From this point of view, evaluation becomes programmatic research whose major function is to aid administrators or program operators to plan and adjust their activities in an attempt to increase the probability of achieving the desired action or service goals. Evaluation is, thus, an integral part of any operating system. It is present at all stages of the system and not confined, as is commonly thought, to the terminal effects of a program. This conception of evaluation as a self-contained, one-shot study of the effectiveness of a disembodied, clearly defined program or activity stems, in part, from the model of experimental research which calls for before and after comparisons of the results of some single "stimulus." Overwhelmingly, action and service programs are continuous, on-going events, however, which cannot be meaningful segmented and disengaged from the entire operational process. As we shall see, the design of evaluative research becomes strongly influenced by this important consideration.

We may identify a sequence of development which relates four major aspects of programmatic activity. While these stand in a logical progression as diagrammed below, it is important to visualize a constant interaction among them with success at one stage moving the process forward to the next stage, but with failure at any stage leading to a "recycling" to some earlier stage. This sequence is as follows:

This process model has been applied by Guba and Clark to educational programs in terms of the following series of steps; *research* leads to two stages of *development* (invention and design) which is followed by two stages of *diffusion* (dissemination and demonstration) which, in turn, leads to three steps of *adoption* (trial, installation, and institutionalization) (Guba and Clark, p. 8). Each step has its own objectives and its own appropriate criteria of success or failure and, thus, is subject to separate evaluation. In turn, the evaluation is also subject to an evaluation of its effectiveness.

In discussing this model, Gideonse points out that innovation or change does not necessarily begin with research, but that the initiative for different actions can occur at any point in the continuum and may originate from sources not directly involved in the program process itself. He proposes an output model based on a separation of research, development, and operation each with its own rather distinct objectives and unique orientation. Research has a *knowledge* orientation with the objective being the testing of a "non-action" hypothesis. Development has a process orientation aimed at formulating organizational formats, materials, and techniques of operations. Operations has a *production* orientation whose objective is to install and administer programs designed to achieve the desired change or output (Gideonse, 1968). However, Gideonse also points out that, while they are distinct, there is a constant flow backwards and forwards between the various steps of the model.

Evaluation may occur at each stage of the above sequence, since each of these processes may be viewed as a series of purposive activities designed to achieve its own specified goal. Thus, we may evaluate research in terms of its ability to provide the necessary knowledge-base for planning; in turn, planning may be evaluated according to its success or failure in developing a program which can be tried out on a demonstration basis. Similarly, the demonstration program can be evaluated in terms of its utility for the establishment of an operating program, while the operating program becomes evaluated according to its effectiveness in achieving the desired objective.

From the point of view of this progression, we may view the objective of any earlier stage as being one of providing the *means* towards the achievement of some objective at a later stage. Thus, the objective of research is to provide knowledge as the means for planning, whose objective, in turn, is to provide a plan which becomes the means for setting up a demonstration project, whose objective now becomes the development and testing of procedures which becomes a means toward establishing the desired operational program — whose objective, to push the process further, becomes the means of achieving the desired goal. At each point in the above flow from research to operation, evaluation provides the necessary information to determine whether one should move ahead to the next stage or perhaps back to a previous stage. For example, a demonstration program which fails to produce the desired effects may require the planning of a new approach, which, in turn, may call for more research. This is why we have stressed evaluation as a continuous process.

In general, the major emphasis of most evaluation studies will be upon the demonstration and operation stages, although there is no reason, as we have formulated the process above, why research and planning cannot also be evaluated. This becomes obvious when the major function of the organization is research or planning *per se* and where the administration of such an organization is evaluated in terms of its own specific research or planning objectives. In a similar sense, evaluation itself is subject to evaluation as a form of administrative enterprise. In other words, any program of activities designed for some specified purpose may be evaluated in terms of its degree of success or failure in achieving those purposes. This rather all-encompassing statement underscores the emphasis of the previous section on the importance of determining as clearly as possible *why* any particular evaluation is needed.

Demonstration Programs

The demonstration program occupies a strategic and central place in the scheme of evaluative research. Its major purpose is the development of an "experimental" program which will permit an evaluation of probable success or failure on a "laboratory" or trial basis. The administrator has greater flexibility in designing and carrying out the program, while the evaluator has an opportunity to apply more methodological controls than he could in an operating situation. As described in the above systems model, the demonstration project is the product of research and planning and the precursor of program operations.

It is important to distinguish clearly between the objectives and research designs for the evaluation of demonstration as opposed to operational programs. The objective of a demonstration program is to develop a model or prototype for future operational programs or to test on a small scale the effectiveness of some large-scale program. First and foremost, it has an evaluative research objective; demonstration without evaluation is meaningless. The goal of an operational program, on the other hand, is to attempt to meet some existing need by means of whatever programs can be realistically established. Its primary orientation is that of immediate service. Confusion of the two may find the administrator attempting to meet a service need with a demonstration project or a research need by means of an operating program — usually with little success. To be sure, there may be an element of service in a demonstration program and of research in an operating program, but the differing *primary* foci must be kept clear.

This confusion may carry over into the types of evaluation designs used. A demonstration project is usually set up as a one-shot trial while an operating program is an on-going affair. The purpose of developing a demonstration program is to permit one to have greater control over both the "stimulus" and its administration, to offer the possibility of matching experimental with control populations, and to make before and after measurements. Obviously, an evaluation of this type of program calls for an experimental research design. And yet many demonstration projects are carried out as miniature operating programs with little or no attempt at methodological rigor. On the other hand, a service program is a continuous, on-going operation in which there is usually little possibility of withholding services from a matched control group or of making before and after measures. This type of program requires a systems research model which accentuates the feedback of information and constant revision of the program. And yet many program evaluators attempt to apply a rigorous experimental design to such operating programs, and wonder why they have failed, or blame the program administrator for not cooperating with them. As we shall see, this distinction between demonstration and operational programs has many highly significant implications for both the methodology and the administrative aspects of evaluative research.

There are several types of demonstration projects which have different purposes and require somewhat different evaluation designs. These variations are related to the state of existing knowledge about the objectives and the means for achieving these objectives, as well as to the resources and opportunities available for carrying out the evaluation. In a general way, we may classify demonstration projects as: (1) pilot programs, (2) model programs, and (3) prototype programs. To some extent, these variations are related in time, with the pilot program coming first, followed by the development of a model program, and then the prototype program. We look at each briefly.

The *pilot program* represents a trial-and-error period during which new approaches and new organizational structures or procedures can be tried out on a rather flexible and easily revisable basis. James stresses the importance of this type of program as an opportunity for doing program research and for learning from experience. He recommends that in this type of project, "Great stress should be laid upon selection of objectives, exploration of the strategic factors involved, building evaluation into the project, and retaining enough flexibility to keep the demonstration useful during its entire development. Instead of stressing only the services to be achieved, careful attention must be given in program development to the elements of failure and what can be done about them. Rather than be annoyed at the problems which arise, their appearance should be welcomed as learning opportunities" (James, 1961: 133).

The emphasis of pilot programs should be upon variation — variation in the way the program is organized, in how and by whom it is carried out, where it is located, whom it reaches, etc. Flexibility, innovation, redirection, reorganization are all desirable, and attempts to structure or "freeze" a program at this stage are premature. Obviously, the pilot project requires "quick-and-easy" evaluation with primary emphasis upon the "feedback" of results for program changes. This does not mean that success or failure are not to be judged, but that the basis for such judgments need not depend upon rigorous experimental designs. This pilot stage is one of exploratory research and the main objective is to learn enough to be able to move ahead to the development of a program which can then be evaluated in a more systematic manner.

The *model program* represents the end result of a series of productive pilot projects. Based on what has been learned in the pilot projects, a program can be designed which stands the greatest chance of success. In one sense, the administrator who sets up a model project is still feeling his way. He believes that he can achieve the desired objectives given the proper circumstances, but he is not certain enough to want to try out the program under regular operating conditions. He is seeking to demonstrate that success is possible, not that it is practicably achievable. In a way he is now ready to design a definitive experiment as a test of his hypothesis that activities A, B, C can achieve objectives X, Y, Z, but wishes to assure himself that activities A, B, C have really been put into effect under the most desirable circumstances.

The evaluative design for a model program is almost the exact opposite of that of a pilot project. Now, more than anywhere else, a carefully controlled experiment is in order. The program input must be highly structured and well-defined. Any variations of input must be controlled and keyed to expected variations in output. Extraneous "stimuli" must be eliminated insofar as possible. Experimental and control groups need to be closely matched. Criteria of effectiveness have to be defined, and valid, reliable instruments of sufficient precision constructed. Before and after measurements with these instruments need to be made. This is when the experimental design for evaluative research is most appropriate.

Caution must be exercised in the evaluation of model programs not to generalize the conclusions to standard programs. The temptation is to feel that if the model program has been proven to be effective, it may now be put into effect on a broad scale. This is justified only if the same exemplary program can be translated into a routine operating program — which is rarely, if ever, the case. Perhaps one of the most common disappointments in evaluative research is to prove that, given the right circumstances, a program can be successful and then find that programs set up without control of these circumstances turn out to be failures.

To develop and test programs as operationally feasible, it is necessary to utilize the third type of demonstration program — the *prototype*. This is probably what most people have in mind when they think of demonstration projects. As defined by the Office of Vocational Rehabilitation, these demonstration projects have as their objective, "the application in a practical setting of results, derived from either fundamental research or from experience in life situations, for the purpose of determining whether these knowledges or experiences are actually appliable in the practical setting chosen" (Criswell, 1962: 1).

Most important for prototype programs is that the program be practical and realistic in terms of what can be done on a large scale with available resources. The evaluation design can attempt to approximate the experimental approach and should compare the new prototype program with traditional programs as controls. But, since the prototype and traditional programs must be carried out under normal operating conditions if one is to be able to generalize the findings, rigorous controls over matched experimental and control groups may not be readily obtainable. It is absolutely essential for the prototype program to be evaluated under conditions as similar as possible to the proposed operational program for the results to be applicable to these programs. A research dimension can profitably be added, however, in order to determine how and why the prototype program was a success or failure and to specify what aspects of the program were relatively more successful than others, and among which population sub-groups.

If we view the evaluative process as a double test of: (1) the validity of a particular approach as a means toward the achievement of some desired change or objective, and (2) the ability to institute a workable program based on that approach, then we see that the model demonstration program evaluates the first condition, while the prototype demonstration program is aimed at the second condition. The failure of an operational program may, thus, be due to either the use of a wrong or invalid approach (which could be tested by a model program) or to the unfeasibility of the approach, even though valid, as a viable means of operationalizing the approach (which could be tested by a prototype program).

Operational Programs

Once a program is already in operation — as is the case in the vast majority of instances — a different form of evaluation is required than that which we have been discussing for demonstration programs. The continuous nature of an on-going service, by and large neither requires nor permits the use of an experimental design. The focus of interest is more upon the improvement of services than upon evaluating whether or not a service is worth keeping. Health, education, and welfare programs will continue to operate regardless of the results of any evaluation study and the key question is not so much "Are they any good?" as "How can they be made better?"

This latter question requires the development of an evaluation model which stresses the feedback of a continuous stream of information into the on-going program. Such models have been called process models and have had their major development in the field of operations research. While it is beyond the scope of this paper to discuss operations research as a whole, we can look at some of its more evaluative aspects.

Underlying the operations approach to program or organizational analysis is the belief that modern complex organizations are characterized by "the study of relations rather than 'entities' with an emphasis on process and transition probabilities as the basis of a flexible structure with many degrees of freedom" (Buckley, 1967: 39). An intricate net of information and communication furnishes the basis for constant feedback and readjustment of activities. The emphasis of this model is upon an adaptive system, as opposed to equilibrium or homeostatic models, consisting of, "a complex of elements or components directly or indirectly related in a causal network, such that each component is related to at least some others in a more or less stable way within any particular period of time" (Buckley, 1967). The process is continually in operation and constantly changing in response to external as well as internal pressures.

It is clear that evaluative research within such a system cannot meaningfully carve out a single segment of the process for evaluation as a self-contained unit. The separate component *per se* is not as important as its relationship to other components and can best be evaluated as an inherent part of the on-going system. The parts of a total system, i.e., health, education, welfare, are not independent. stable, permanent structures, but rather interrelated, alterable, and temporary, subject to the workings of the system as a whole with changes in any part of the system influencing other parts of the system.

"Operations research" constitutes an attempt to formalize on-going program or organizational evaluation. More generally, it represents the entire process of program development and management with the focus of evaluation being upon the day-to-day operation of the system as a whole (Rivett, 1968). The results of this type of evaluative research become applicable to decision-making at all stages of program planning, development, and operation. One of the best developed of these systems approaches to evaluation is that of PERT — Program Evaluation and Review Technique (Cook, 1966). This plan requires the development of a network of interrelated work paths showing the intermediate steps or events and time estimates for their achievement. The various events are linked together by the activities that constrain the completion of these events. Critical paths are evaluated in terms of time and cost estimates related to the attainment of desired goals. A crucial element is the use of continuous evaluation for correcting and revising program plans.

The experimental design for the evaluation of demonstration projects becomes rather contrived and inapplicable to the evaluation of operational systems. Both its logic and practicality are questionable. Instead of the "before-after" design, we have what might be called, a "during-during-during" design. The major objective is no longer the proof or disproof of the single S-R hypothesis of experimental research, but the feedback of information about progress along a never-ending continuum of action. The model of the "definitive" experiment is an anachronism for this type of programmatic research. The evaluation must accordingly be developed in terms of its value for direction and redirection, under determinable probabilities of relative success or failure for various stages of the process, with a key emphasis upon decisions to recycle, terminate or progress from one stage to another. The evaluative problem, accordingly, must be formulated not as one of success or failure, but rather of stop, go back, revise, or continue. The objective of such an evaluation is one of constant program assessment and improvement where there is no question that programs must and will continue, i.e., education, health, welfare, and where the emphasis of the evaluation is upon increasing program effectiveness.

The Design of Evaluative Research

The input → process → output model of planned social change described above has highly significant implications for evaluative research methodology. Basically it implies some hypothesis about the ability of a program activity (the input) to influence the "causal" factors (the process) which promote or inhibit the desired objective (the output). The evaluative hypothesis reads, "Activities A, B, C will achieve objectives X, Y, Z because they are able to influence the process producing X, Y, Z" (Suchman, 1967). This statement of the problem underscores three major methodological requirements in evaluative research: (1) a description and analysis of input which identifies as clearly as possible the "active" components or change stimuli in the program or service and how these may vary; (2) an understanding of the "cause/effect" process which underlies the occurrence of the desired objective and which is capable of being influenced by the program input; and (3) a definition of the objective or desired goal in terms of criteria which permit valid and reliable measurements of attainment.

Various research designs have been proposed for testing the evaluative hypothesis as stated above (Campbell, 1967; Campbell, 1957; and Chapin, 1957). Basically these designs represent some adaptation of either the experimental or systems model. We have already discussed these models and some of their methodological implications elsewhere. Further elaboration of research designs would require more detail than would be appropriate in this paper. We would only like to emphasize, once again, the need to relate the type of design to the type of program or service being evaluated.

In this connection, it is worthwhile to note that evaluation can occur on several levels and use different research designs which vary in their approximation to the ideal scientific experiment. A necessary requirement, therefore, of any evaluation project is recognition of the level of its evaluation and a clear statement of what adaptations of the ideal design, and the consequent limitations of "proof," have taken place. A common error in evaluation is to claim more than the research design permits one to show.

	Before	After	
Experimental	X_1	X_2	$d = X_2 - X_1$
Control	X_1^1	X_2^1	$d^1 = X_2^1 - X_1^1$

The logical requirements of an evaluation study can be represented by the familiar model of the laboratory experiment (Stouffer, 1950).

Before a program begins, two equivalent groups are selected at random or by matching from the target population. A "before" measurement is made to determine the base line from which change is to be evaluated. One of the groups (the experimental group) is exposed to the program or activity being evaluated while the other (the control group) is either not exposed at all, given a placebo, or exposed to some alternative program. Where possible, neither the experimenter nor the subject should know which is the experimental or control program (to control suggestibility and unconscious bias). At the conclusion of the evaluation (or at appropriate time intervals), an "after" measure is made which is compared for change from the "before" measure (d vs d^1) for both the experimental and control groups.

The logic of this design is largely infallible. As we have pointed out, however, only rarely can it be put into practice outside the laboratory. Instead, in field research, we use various adaptations of this design. The most important of these for evaluative research are:

1. *The case study.* Individuals or groups are observed or measured for the desired change only after exposure to the program being evaluated (cell X_2 in above table). There is no base-line measurement and no unexposed control group. This is obviously the weakest, if most common, of evaluation designs. The program administrator, clinician, or therapist may be reassured if his subject shows improvement, and he may solicit testimonials to this effect, but he has no way of really knowing whether such improvement was due to his intervention, or for that matter, whether greater improvement might not have occurred without his intervention.

2. *The survey design.* After a program has been put into operation, a survey is made to determine who in the population was exposed to the program and what changes, if any, have taken place in them as compared to those who were not exposed (cells X_2 and X_2^1 in above table). This represents an improvement over the previous design in that a control group is present. However, its major weakness is the absence of any "before" measure to compare the equivalence of the experimental and control group and to provide a check on the self-selection bias of the exposed group (e.g., those individuals who expose themselves may be more favorable or susceptible to the program to begin with). To some extent, this bias can be treated statistically by *ex-post-facto* matching of exposed and non-exposed groups on relevant characteristics (e.g., those

which might produce an exposure bias). However, the "proof" is still based on correlational analysis, rather than controlled exposure.

3. *The panel or prospective study design.* "Before" measures are made of an unexposed target population. The program is initiated and "after" measures of the desired effect are made to compare changes that have taken place in those who became exposed with those who did not. If the program is an on-going one, these measures can be repeated periodically in a "during–during–during" design. Information can be fed back to the program which can then undergo a series of revisions with the effects of various changes being measured at different points in time.

This field study design comes closest to satisfying the methodological requirements of the experimental model and offers perhaps the most acceptable compromise for evaluative research. It still lacks the requirement of a random assignment of experimental and control groups before exposure, but as in the case of the survey design, such matching can be done to some extent by equating exposed and non-exposed groups on various relevant characteristics. A great deal has been written about this prospective or panel design and it is well worth the careful attention of the evaluator (Glock, 1967).

There can be little question from a methodological point of view that, insofar as possible, the evaluator should strive for as close an approximation to the experimental model as possible. It will probably be more productive to use some realistic alternative program for the control rather than a placebo or no treatment at all. A comparison with alternative programs provides more powerful evidence than showing that one's program is better than nothing at all. If the program to be evaluated is being conducted on a wide scale, it is also necessary to take into account the problem of sampling programs for evaluation. For example, the findings of an evaluation of a single rehabilitation workshop cannot automatically be generalized to all such workshops. Selecting a sample of workshops also permits an analysis of the effect of variations in the operation of the workshop.

In line with our previous discussion of demonstration programs, the rigorousness of an evaluation study design needs to be related to the type of program being evaluated, as well as to reality. Model programs are most demanding of the best experimental design that can be developed. Pilot projects, on the other hand, may make-do with case study or survey evaluation designs. Prototype and operational projects can probably have their needs best satisfied by a panel design which permits continuous evaluation and feedback for program assessment and improvement. In any case, the decision about what design to use should stem as much as possible from the requirements of the type of program being evaluated and while reality factors may necessitate compromises, these should not be made too easily or quickly and always with an awareness of the limitations they inevitably impose upon the validity of one's findings.

Evaluative Objectives and Criteria

The crucial element in any evaluation study is the presence of some valued goal or objective. Evaluation cannot exist in a vacuum — one must always ask "evaluation of what?" Unless a program can specify what value its activities are seeking to further, whether this be the amelioration of some specific social problem or the advancement of some broad humanistic goal, evaluation becomes meaningless (Gruenberg (ed.), 1966). To evaluate means to assess value, and before the assessment can take place, the desired value must be understood.

This problem of defining the values underlying a program or activity is perhaps the most subjective and difficult aspect of evaluative research. For one thing, values differ for different people. The values of program personnel may differ from those of their clients or the public. Furthermore, different program personnel and different segments of the public may have conflicting values among themselves, as witness the current controversy over "middle-class" professional values as opposed to the "lower-class" values of the poverty class. The desirability of planned social change or intervention is itself a value judgment. Social values in general define what will be called a social problem, what the acceptable and appropriate means will be to meet this problem, and who shall be given the power and resources to do so.

The statement of specific program objectives combines the value judgments discussed above with the theoretical assumptions of the "cause/effect" process. These assumptions concern the validity of the means being used for achieving the desired objective. Such assumptions underlie all forms of purposive action. We may refer to the assumptions underlying the desirability of objectives as "value" assumptions, while the assumptions as to means or process of attaining the objectives constitute "validity" assumptions. The former are largely a matter of subjective belief, while the latter are subject to empirical verification.

Objectives are commonly classified according to three different levels of generality ranging from immediate to intermediate to ultimate. In principle, one may visualize an unlimited universe of possible objectives and sub-objectives corresponding to the various levels that make up a total program and arranged according to some organizational hierarchy. On the bottom of this hierarchy, we usually find the field personnel whose objectives are largely those of delivery of services and whose success or failure is measured against the *immediate* criteria of effort expended and quantity and quality of services delivered. On the next higher level, we may find the supervisory or administrative personnel whose objectives are those of program direction where effectiveness is evaluated on an *intermediate* level according to the accomplishments or results of the efforts of the service personnel. At the top of the hierarchy is the central staff whose major function is that of program planning and development and whose policy decisions guide the performance goals of the field personnel and are evaluated on the *ultimate* level of success in meeting the social problem under attack.

A similar division of labor is implied by the distinction between "objectives," "activities," and "practices" arranged in a descending order. Policy *objectives* are formulated and evaluated at the highest level of administration, while program *activities* are designed and evaluated at the intermediate level as the means toward achieving the higher level policy objectives. In turn, personnel *practices* are developed as the means of operationalizing the program activities and are evaluated at the immediate level of worker performance. Each of the lower level steps denotes an action taken to implement an upper level objective. Thus, evaluation objectives can be conceived as making up an ordered series of means-ends relationships.

This interdependence is reflected in organizational structure and function, with the organization and techniques of work at an upper level becoming the objectives of the immediately lower level, with the objectives at any level being derived from the methods of the immediately higher level. Thus, any program can be subdivided into a continuous chain of actions in which each action is the result of the one that comes before it and a necessary condition to the one that comes after it. Evaluation then proceeds to validate the means-ends relationships between each adjacent pair comprising the program.

In terms of our previous discussion of the relationship of input to process to output, immediate goals are evaluated according to the degree to which services can be delivered (effort) while intermediate goals are evaluated according to the degree of intervention in the "causal" process that takes place as a result of these services (accomplishment). Whether such intervention results in the subsequent attainment of the ultimate goal will depend largely upon the validity of the underlying theory relating process to objective. Perhaps this formulation of the problem will help to explain why most evaluations are limited to immediate and intermediate objectives, and to dispel some of the heated controversy over whether such limited goals constitute legitimate objectives for evaluation in and of themselves (MacMahon, Pugh, and Hutchison, 1961). They do so to the extent that the "causal" process linking performance to ultimate objectives is valid.

Evaluation, in the above sense, may be divided into two parts. An evaluation of *"technique"* which tests the ability of a particular program to change the "causal" process and an evaluation of *"theory"* which tests the ability of the change in "causal" process to produce the desired objective. This latter function is more properly the province of basic or "non-evaluative" research, but it does indicate how evaluative research may also contribute to basic knowledge, and how dependent any intervention program is upon a valid theory of change. For example, an educational program designed to get people to stop smoking may be evaluated on the immediate level in terms of its success in organizing a program in such a way that people are reached with the educational materials (effort), and on the intermediate level in terms of how many people actually stop smoking (accomplishment), but whether or not the ultimate goal of a decrease in the incidence of lung cancer occurs (outcome) will depend upon the validity of the "cause/effect" theory that links smoking to lung cancer.

As one moves from immediate to intermediate to ultimate objectives, one encounters greater complexity in the number and type of factors influencing each. On the immediate level, the factors affecting the performance of personnel are relatively limited and can be more or less directly controlled. Specific effort criteria are relatively easy to develop, i.e., many-days of teaching, cases treated, literature distributed. On the intermediate level, the number of factors affecting program operation and accomplishment becomes increasingly complex, including external influences over which one can have little control. Measures of achievement reflect this complexity and often cannot be directly related to effort expended. On the ultimate level, the particular program becomes only one part of a vast array of factors which influence high-level policy goals and, not only is the magnitude of its effects diminished, but the causal links become greatly attenuated. Rossi cautions against expecting any great effects at the ultimate level. He warns, "We cannot ordinarily expect that the new treatments we can devise will produce massive results. . . . The problem of evaluation in this historical period is that new treatments can be expected to yield marginal improvements over present treatments and the cost-to-benefit ratio can be expected to rise dramatically" (Rossi, 1966).

Institutional objectives: Evaluations on the ultimate level deal almost entirely with societal indicators, such as incidence of illness, rather than measures of individual change (Sheldon and Moore, 1968). As such, these evaluations very rarely study the effects of specific programs. More appropriately they may be viewed as institutional evaluations and reflect the impact of a broad spectrum of events. Objectives are defined for the society in general and reflect social goals such as "an informed citizenry." In education, for example, such institutional evaluations have become increasingly important as the American educational system as a whole has come under critical review (Perkins, 1966). We may refer to evaluations on this level as "policy" evaluations which are system oriented.

Organizational objectives: The evaluation of complex organizations, such as a school system, hospital, or large industrial concern, requires the formulation of objectives and criteria of accomplishment on a much broader scale than program evaluation. The need for assessment on this level, however, is perhaps even greater than on the program level. Planned social change will, in the long run, be much more affected by organizational or system changes than by specific program innovations. The latter have often been referred to as "tinkering," as opposed to any meaningful intervention on a policy level involving the restructuring of an entire organizational approach.

In a general way, we may contrast two broad organizational objectives: (1) *maximizing*, or seeking the maximum attainment of objectives for any given amount of resources, and (2) *sufficing*, or seeking the attainment of acceptable or desirable states (Simon, 1957). These notions of maximizing and sufficing reflect two rather different approaches to complex organizations. The first views such organizations as rational systems which can be evaluated according to criteria of maximum output and is usually associated with the private sector, i.e., profit, efficiency. The second treats organizations as natural systems and evaluates them according to social criteria, i.e., service, amelioration, and is most applicable to the public sector. Obviously, these two differing objectives play a major role in determining the type of criteria for the assessment of success or failure in organizations.

Maximizing criteria probably attain their greatest utility in evaluations of cost-effectiveness. Few programs can be justified at any cost and effort — cost ratios are required to measure comparative efficiency. Cost-effectiveness is, thus, becoming an increasingly important tool in management. Briefly described, cost refers to the value of the resources expended to achieve a certain goal, while effectiveness refers to the quality or level of achievement. A cost-effectiveness analysis attempts to strike a balance between these two factors or a ratio of input to output. The goal is to maximize results for a given cost — to obtain the most optimal use of available resources for achieving the desired objective. This evaluation design requires a comparison of alternative courses of action in terms of their costs and their effectiveness. For example, a comparison of individualized instruction with closed circuit television would have to balance the two in terms of their cost-effectiveness ratio. The specific techniques for a cost-effectiveness analysis are rather specialized, requiring the development of special models and criteria for weighing cost against effectiveness (Morse, 1967). Such evaluations are largely limited to highly standardized and well-established programs. They rarely make sense until prior evaluations have shown program effectiveness and therefore represent the most advanced stage of evaluation.

Thompson has developed an interesting set of propositions about the evaluation of organizations based upon the completeness of knowledge about "cause/effect" relationships and the degree of crystallization of the standards of desirability (Thompson, 1967: 83–100). Where "cause/effect" understanding is fairly complete and the standards of desirability have become crystallized, an organization would tend to employ a maximizing approach to evaluation with a major emphasis upon *efficiency*. Lacking knowledge of cause and effect, but possessing well-formulated standards, the criteria of success are apt to be instrumental in terms of the desired state of affairs, with the emphasis being on sufficing rather than maximizing. Where knowledge is incomplete and standards ambiguous, *social* criteria involving the approval or disapproval of appropriate reference groups will become substituted for efficiency or instrumental tests of achievement. We recognize this to be the case in many, if not most, social action programs.

Evaluative Criteria

The problem of criteria in evaluative research has traditionally been discussed in the literature as one of finding reliable and valid operational indices for measuring the attainment of some objective. The emphasis has been technical, rather than conceptual. The result has been a long history of methodological disputation to the neglect of conceptual definition and clarification.

Conceptually, evaluative criteria represent the basis upon which decisions are made about means towards ends. We may divide this decision-making process into the following three components each of which requires different criteria of effectiveness:[1]

1. *An information component* — A reference system, model, process, or standard according to which information may be selected, collected, and evaluated. This represents a criterion of relevance — but relevance to action, and not simply construct relevance.

2. *An interpretation component* — A value position or preference system representing the desirable, the appropriate, the acceptable means and ends for making decisions. This represents a *weighting* process or decision rule by which alternatives may be assigned priorities.

3. *An action component* — A risk-taking approach to problem-solving in which criteria function to set the limits of acceptable error. This represents an *operational* process or an administrative rule by which error costs are matched against potential outcomes.

Each of the above components involves a different type of analysis; the first concerns information retrieval and utilization systems, the second, decision-making systems, and the third, risk-taking choice situations. Each of these is a key element in "operations research" and reflects the intimate relationship between evaluative research and these program management processes as discussed previously. The central role of criteria in all three underscores our concern with a more adequate conceptualization of this measure.

Given the above classification, criteria become linked to an action process. The model is that of an on-going system which at any moment is in a state of equilibrium, but which contains within it conflictual elements pushing toward resolution by means of a new equilibrium. These conflictual elements represent "discrepancies" between desired objectives and current attainments — "what is" vs. "what should be." The discovery and description of such discrepancies depends upon feedback informational criteria, while the resolution, either in terms of changed objectives or changed operations, depends upon interpretative criteria of decision-making, followed by action criteria of risk-taking. Evaluation and the use of criteria within this model is obviously not a one-shot affair, but becomes a continuous chain of discrepancy determinations and resolutions for the on-going system. Criteria, in this sense, are ever-lasting and ever-changing, and not static measures that become standardized and routinized.

In terms of the above model, evaluative hypotheses may be derived by relating a series of activities at some point in the action process to a series of objectives for this same stage. Since deliberate intervention in the on-going process is being contemplated, a theory of "causation" is usually implied. The criteria are derived from the evaluative hypothesis and reflect this "cause/effect" process. Information criteria must be relevant to the independent variable (Activities A, B, C) and interpretive of the dependent variable (Effects X, Y, Z). Action criteria must be linked to the process which underlies the relationship of the information to the interpretive criteria, or else we may attempt to change a "spurious cause" (i.e., the Hawthorne effect).

Tied in as they are to decision-making and risk-taking, the criteria of evaluative research strongly reflect the professional value-system of the program personnel in relation to the value system of significant-others, i.e., the public, the clients, the "official" governmental body, and other professionals in and out of the program. Criteria will therefore tend to be selected from the virtually unlimited universe of possible criteria on the basis of their relevance to value-laden objectives and results and then defined in terms which permit relative weighting for determining a balance among the inevitable value conflicts in any action program. Competing values constitute one of the most important elements of criteria selection and definition. Such values underlie all criteria.

A more technical aspect of criteria selection and definition concerns its "operationalism" — both in terms of its measurability and its manipulability. Ease and refinement of measurement become important technical aspects in addition to the usual scientific standard of reliability. (Validity, we have already seen, is determined by answering the all-important question, "Validity for what?" in terms of validity for information, interpretation, and action.) Criteria, to have utility in evaluative research, must be practical enough to provide measures which do not interfere too greatly with program routines and which produce answers in time enough for them to permit program changes. Refinement is determined by that level of precision which permits meaningful distinctions of success or failure to be made in terms of decisions to revise or proceed, rather than some absolute judgment of instrument precision. The old adage of not using a scalpel in a butcher shop is highly appliable to evaluative research.

Similarly, degree of manipulability becomes extremely important for the selection of evaluative variables for which criteria are to be developed. Criteria which refer to variables which permit little deliberate intervention are not too useful for program change. While such variables may have high explanatory power, they offer little leeway for administrative action; i.e., heredity or sex. In effect, the evaluator needs to look for criteria of those variables which permit interference with the "causal process" or change in the social system.

Thus, it can be seen that evaluative criteria may be used:

1. To monitor a steady state so as to determine when a correction is necessary (as in an automated system involving servomechanisms).
2. To identify alternatives in a problem (non-steady) situation and provide relevant information (as in a changing curriculum).
3. To weigh alternative courses of decision-making in terms of relative gains and losses.
4. To determine corrective action and the error-risks involved in various approaches to change.

These four uses may be viewed as "validity" indices for evaluative criteria. Technically they function as predictive criteria and are judged in terms of their ability to achieve certain desirable ends and/or to forestall undesirable consequences. They represent validity for action rather than validity for measurement or description. They are prospective predictions rather than *ex-post-facto* explanations and involve making predictions about the outcomes of induced change and matching those predictions against actual outcomes.

The above approach to the criterion problem requires further conceptual development and, even more important, empirical testing. It does seem to re-open a classical problem of scientific measurement to new formulations that make more sense for evaluative as compared to non-evaluative research. A challenging approach to this problem is offered by Etzioni and Lehman in terms of the possible dysfunctional aspects of utilizing invalid criteria in evaluative research. In general, they point out two broad classes of dysfunctions: (1) arriving at invalid conclusions which become the bases for erroneous policy decisions, and (2) ignoring those dimensions and indicators of a concept that are most susceptible to social manipulation (Etzioni and Lehman, 1967). This paper offers a convincing argument for increased attention to "social validity" as opposed to "methodological validity."

Administrative Considerations in Evaluative Research

Evaluative research is applied research and, as such, it encounters all of the problems of research management in general and of applied research in particular. Other papers in this conference are specifically aimed at these problems and there would be little point in discussing them in detail in the present paper. Instead we will focus upon some of those aspects of research administration which we feel are of special importance for evaluative research.

Evaluative research is judgmental — its major function is to determine whether certain activities are attaining their objectives. As such, it inevitably constitutes a threat to those individuals whose responsibility it is to see that the activities do achieve their objectives. No matter what is done to lessen this feeling of threat, few administrators or program personnel can be expected to view an evaluation of their efforts with detached objectivity. Since the evaluation usually is undertaken only when some dissatisfaction or puzzlement is present, the evaluation is in itself a challenge of their effectiveness. Program administrators and especially program personnel have to operate under assumptions of success and an evaluation constitutes a questioning of these assumptions. Furthermore, the conduct of the evaluation itself produces demands upon the operation of the program which may interfere with the routine administration of the program. As described by Wright and Hyman, "The staff . . . have invested considerable time, effort, and sentiment in their programs. They may be ego-involved in their activities. They may be sensitive to the cold-blooded objective probing of the scientific researcher. Even under favorable circumstances, it is common to find that action-oriented and dedicated persons are unreceptive to social science . . . how much more likely a hostile reaction may be if such measurements threaten to reveal unfavorable information" (Wright and Hyman, 1964: 23). It is a rare practitioner who welcomes an evaluation study.

There can be no denying that the basic relationship between evaluator and practitioner is one of the former evaluating the work of the latter. As Wilensky and Lebeaux have stated, "What the social scientist thinks of as 'objective investigation' the practitioner often takes as 'hostile attack'" (Wilensky and Lebeaux, 1958: 20). Evaluative research seeks change while most of the natural tendencies of program operation are to resist change. This difference in focus gives rise to a host of administrative problems and conflicts between the evaluator and the practitioner. These interpersonnel problems, perhaps more than anything else, make evaluative research unattractive to research workers and account for the reluctance of many social scientists to become involved in program evaluation.

In general, the administrative problems of evaluative research will vary according to the type of evaluation being attempted. In terms of their implications for the conduct of evaluative research, we may classify evaluation studies as follows, ranging from general to specific objectives and from large-scale to small-scale activities:

A. *System-oriented evaluations*
   1. Institutional or social sub-systems (i.e., health, education, or welfare systems).
   2. Complex organizations (i.e., hospitals, public schools, welfare agencies).
B. *Program-oriented evaluations*
   1. Simple organizations (i.e., clinics, classrooms, employment offices).
   2. Simple programs (i.e., immunization program, reading improvement, enrollment campaign).

The conduct of evaluation in the above four types of settings will create somewhat different problems in the formulation of the evaluation study, in the structure of the evaluation unit and its relationship to other units, in the personal interrelationships of evaluation and program staff, and in the utilization of evaluative research findings.

System or institution-oriented evaluations are more likely to be concerned with broad objectives and policy questions. Strangely enough this type of evaluation, basic as it is, may not constitute a serious threat to the administrator. While the institution as a whole may be under attack, and the administrator may be called upon to defend the "establishment," the threat is likely to be impersonal and his own position in the institutional system is not too much at stake.

Similarly, systems-oriented evaluations of complex organizations will tend to stress adjustive recommendations rather than judgments of success or failure. Since the major function of the evaluator is to help the administrator run his organization in a more effective manner, much of the personal threat is removed. In such cases of system-oriented evaluation, the integration of the evaluation unit into the system itself becomes quite natural. In fact, it is on this level of evaluation that one is most likely to encounter the organization of an evaluation unit within the institution or complex organization itself. Since policy decisions are usually involved, such evaluation units tend to be located in the upper echelons and to have high-prestige and status. Whatever conflicts occur between evaluator and program staff tend to be quite similar to those that occur between the administrative staff and the operating staff in general. One possible shortcoming of this type of arrangement would be the tendency to work within the system and to take for granted its general legitimacy. Thus the evaluation would be corrective rather than challenging to the existing structure or operation. While the system may become more efficient as a result of such evaluation efforts, it is not likely to undergo any basic changes.

On the other hand, program-oriented evaluations directly challenge the worthwhileness of specific activities or the performance of specific individuals. Since they attempt directly to relate activities to outcomes, the conclusions are apt to focus around the success or failure of some specific organization or program to the extent that such judgments may well determine the future existence of the organization or program. Under such circumstances, the program staff may be expected to be highly anxious about the evaluation.

Sources of conflict between the evaluator and staff on the program evaluation level may begin as early as the statement of program objectives. The program staff has a strong, vested interest in the program as it is now operating. In many cases, professional identity as well as employment is at stake. Behind any program lies a host of untested assumptions, not only in regard to basic theory but also in relation to techniques of operation. The first task of the evaluator often is to compile a list of program objectives and to examine their underlying assumptions. While being asked to specify one's objectives may be difficult for the program staff, being forced to justify these objectives and to defend one's beliefs in why one's program can be expected to attain them may actually be painful.

There are no easy answers to the administrative problems in evaluation. The major positive force lies in the promise of help that evaluation can give to policy-making and program effectiveness. Given a supportive climate and a program staff dedicated to program improvement, evaluative research can make a significant contribution and need not prove traumatic. Lacking such conditions, evaluative research may have to make its way against the resistances of program directors and staff, largely through the force of governmental and public demand for "proof of works."

Perhaps the most hopeful note in the above somewhat discouraging analysis of administrative problems is the increasing dissatisfaction that many of the practicing professions are experiencing with their traditional approaches to social problems. The stubborn resistance to solution of many of these problems has led to a growing willingness to challenge the basis of established programs — both theoretical and technical. The chance to experiment with new approaches has excited many practititioners to try to develop innovative programs. Government and public support and increased professional prestige are now being given to the evaluative research. As proclaimed by Hilleboe, "The age of accountability is upon us. If we strain against it, we will plunge ourselves into the obscure backwash of ceremonial duties. . . . But if we accept accountability as a way of thinking and a way of life, we can propel public health to a grand new era of achievement and acclaim" (Hilleboe, 1964: 48).

It is this atmosphere of a "brave new world" based upon carefully planned and evaluated social change that has given rise to the current interest in evaluative research. Such research makes little sense in a self-satisfied world content to do things the way they always were done. It becomes essential in a troubled world, anxious and willing to seek change. Social experimentation in health, education, and welfare has not only become acceptable, it is strongly encouraged in a host of new attempts to solve old problems. Within the evaluation of such experimentation perhaps, lies the answer to the question "Action for What?"

And yet to the evaluative researcher, such questioning is not only essential to the design of the study but also constitutes the challenge and reward of the research process. From this questioning of established procedures comes the research hypothesis and the possibility of new discoveries. His aim is not to justify an existing program but to diagnose its ills and to prescribe a course of treatment. If the program is "sick," such help may be welcome, but if it feels "well," such evaluation can only be viewed as unjustified interference.

To such differing values, goals, and perceptions of the problem is added the need for close working relationships between evaluator and operating staff in the conduct of the program evaluation study itself. These daily role relationships are apt to be quite conflicting. The evaluation study must make demands upon the operation of the program — it is foolish to think otherwise. It must ask for as much control as possible over the assignment of subjects or clients; it may require some form of change in how the program is run; it must insist upon the collection of data beyond that of routine record-keeping. And it must ask these things at the same time that it threatens the existence of the program. Little wonder that smooth working relationships are difficult!

Add to the above, the usual dearth of resources in time, money, personnel, and facilities offered the evaluator, and one can begin to understand why evaluative research today is almost universally deficient. Many of these problems exist in regard to working relationships between researcher and administrator in any applied setting, but they become magnified when the applied research is also an evaluation.

In many cases, furthermore, the evaluator is apt to be an "outsider." In fact, one of the major administrative questions concerning evaluation is whether the evaluator should be a staff member of the organization or program being evaluated or whether he should be brought in as an independent researcher or consultant. There are advantages and disadvantages to either arrangement and the decision must depend upon the particular circumstances. The advantages of an outside evaluator are increased objectivity and the ability to see and challenge what someone close to the program may have come to take for granted. The outside evaluator will have less personal involvement in the outcome of the evaluation and is, therefore, under fewer pressures to produce a favorable report. He is also more likely to be trained in evaluative research and to have had experience in evaluating other programs.

On the other hand, the outsider is less likely to understand the objectives and procedures of the program, especially if these require technical or professional competence. He is more likely to miss subtle aspects of program operation or objectives, especially possible "negative" effects. In addition, as an outsider, he is less likely to be acceptable to the operating staff, and more likely to encounter obstacles in carrying out the evaluation. As described by Metzner and Gurin, "Any attempt at evaluation, particularly from the outside, may well be conceived as a threat. It is an examination and report concerning how well people are doing. Very few people are so secure, or unaware of their own deficiencies, that an unknown with a notebook will arouse no anxieties. This is particularly true if the evaluations are not responding to local desire, but are brought in from above, and the purposes and relations are unclear" (Metzner and Gurin, 1960: 8). However, the closer personal relationships of an inside evaluator can interfere seriously with objectivity. There will be a natural tendency to stress the successes and to overlook the failures.

Regardless of whether an outsider or insider does the evaluation, it is important to recognize that complete detachment is almost impossible. Inevitably, the evaluator tends to be co-opted to a greater or lesser degree by the system. He begins to identify with the program and its goals; he forms interpersonal relationships with the program staff; he gets caught up in the daily operations of the program — in short, he becomes involved and can rarely just hit-and-run.

Probably the best solution is to recognize the inevitability of the conflict and to attempt to structure the situation so that the program staff plays an important part in developing the evaluation and in carrying out any recommendations. Early in the evaluation, the program staff should help to formulate the objectives of the program to be evaluated. This self-examination of program goals and procedures will also increase the likelihood of developing criteria of effectiveness which are meaningful and acceptable to the staff. In fact, it is probably unwise to proceed with an evaluation until some degree of consensus has been reached by program and evaluation staff.

The evaluation itself should be conducted with an obvious concern for the program staff's routine. Disruption should be kept to a minimum and where unavoidable should be carefully explained and justified. Finally, findings should be discussed thoroughly with the program staff and possible remedies of deficiencies explored. The follow-up component of the evaluation should be left as much as possible in the hands of the program staff, with the evaluator presenting his findings and making recommendations, but not being in a position to enforce change. Certainly, the findings of an evaluation are much more likely to be utilized if the program staff has played a part in the evaluation and is given direct responsibility for implementing its findings (Sadofsky, 1966).

In short, rather than attempting to find ways to keep the administrator and staff out of the evaluation, the better strategy may be to increase their commitment to the evaluation by stressing program improvement instead of pass-fail judgment. Since a primary criterion for evaluating the evaluation will be its ability to produce program change, the cooperation of program staff is extremely important. While the evaluation may be a tremendous success from a methodological point of view, unless its findings are utilized it may well be judged a failure in terms of accomplishment.

Weiss lists the following conditions as important for increasing the potential of utilization for evaluative research findings:

1. The explication of the theoretical premises underlying the program, and direction of the evaluation to analysis of these premises.
2. Specification of the "process model" of the program — the presumed sequence of linkages that lead from program input to outcome, and the tracking of the processes through which results are supposed to be obtained.
3. Analysis of the effectiveness of components of the program, or alternative approaches, rather than all-or-nothing, go or no-go assessment of the total program.

In addition to these general factors, utilization is likely to reflect: (1) early identification of potential users of evaluation results and selection of the issues of concern to them as the major focus of study; (2) involvement of administrators and program practitioners, from both inside and outside the project, in the evaluation process; (3) prompt completion of evaluation and early release of results; (4) effective methods for presentation of findings and dissemination of information (Weiss, 1966).

A brief word should be added about some of the indirect uses of evaluation. Some of these are "legitimate" by-products of an evaluation while others represent abuses of evaluative research. Among the desirable secondary benefits of an evaluation, we may list the following:

1. A clarification and re-examination on the part of program administrators of the objectives and underlying assumptions of their programs.
2. A more careful analysis of the content and operation of the program in order to specify what the essential aspects of the program are.
3. The identification and definition of the target population and the situational context of the programs.
4. A re-evaluation of the theoretical or knowledge base of the program especially in terms of how principles are translated into practices.
5. The formulation of hypotheses for further research to fill in gaps in knowledge especially as these would affect program planning.
6. The development of a more critical attitude among personnel including an opportunity to suggest ways of improving services.
7. An increase in staff morale and commitment as a consequence of a sincere attempt to improve the program — especially if the staff itself is disappointed in their accomplishments.

The following list of possible misuses of evaluation may serve as a deterrent to such "pseudo-evaluations."

1. *Eye-wash* — an attempt to justify a weak or bad program by deliberately selecting for evaluation only those aspects that "look good" on the surface. Appearance replaces reality.
2. *White-wash* — an attempt to cover up program failure or errors by avoiding any objective appraisal. Vindication replaces verification.
3. *Submarine* — an attempt to "torpedo" or destroy a program regardless of its effectiveness. Politics replaces science.
4. *Posture* — an attempt to use evaluation as a "gesture" of objectivity or professionalism. Ritual replaces research.
5. *Postponement* — an attempt to delay needed action by pretending to seek the "facts." Research replaces service.

NOTES TO THE CHAPTER

1. We are indebted to Malcolm Provus for one development of this classification.

REFERENCES

BENNIS, WARREN G., KENNETH D. BENNE, and ROBERT CHIN
   1960   *The Planning of Change.* New York: Holt, Rinehart and Winston.
BORGATTA, EDGAR F.
   1966   "Research problems in evaluation of health service demonstration."
           Milbank Memorial Fund Quarterly, **44** (October): 183–184.
BUCKLEY, WALTER
   1967   *Sociology and Modern Systems Theory.* Englewood Cliffs, New Jersey:
           Prentice-Hall, Inc.
CAMPBELL, DONALD T.
   1957   "Factors relevant to the validity of experiments in social settings."
           Psychological Bulletin, **54**: 297–312.
CAMPBELL, DONALD T.
   1963   "From description to experimentation interpreting trends in quasi-
           experiment." In Chester W. Harris (ed.), *Problems in Measuring
           Change.* Madison: University of Wisconsin Press.
CHAPIN, F. STUART
   1957   *Experimental Designs in Sociological Research.* New York: Harper and
           Brothers (revised 1955).
COOK, DESMOND L.
   1966   *Program Evaluation and Review Technique: Applications in Education.*
           Washington: U.S. Department of Health, Education, and Welfare,
           Office of Education.
CRISWELL, JOAN H.
   1962   *The Place of Demonstration Projects in the Program of the Office of Vocational
           Rehabilitation.* Washington: Office of Vocational Rehabilitation
           (August). (Mimeo.)
ETIZIONI, AMITAI, and EDWARD W. LEHMAN
   1967   "Some dangers in 'valid' social measurement." *The Annals of the
           American Academy of Political and Social Science,* (September): 1–15.
FAIRWEATHER, GEORGE W.
   1967   *Methods for Experimental Social Innovation.* New York: John Wiley and
           Sons.
GIDEONSE, HENDRICK D.
   1968   "Research development, and the improvement of education." *Science,*
           164 (November 1): 541:45.
GLOCK, CHARLES (ed.)
   1967   *Survey Research in the Social Sciences.* New York: Russell Sage Foundation.
GRUENBERG, ERNEST M. (ed.)
   1966   "Evaluating the effectiveness of mental health services." *Milbank
           Memorial Fund Quarterly,* **44**: Part 2 (January).

GUBA, E. A., and D. C. CLARK
undated "An examination of potential change roles in education." Virginia: Airlie House. (Mimeo.)

HERZOG, ELIZABETH
1959 *Some Guide Lines for Evaluative Research*. Washington: U.S. Department of Health, Education, and Welfare. Social Security Administration, Children's Bureau.

HILLEBOE, HERMAN E.
1964 "Improving performance in public health." *Public Health Reports* (January).

JAMES, GEORGE
1961 "Planning and evaluation of health programs." *Administration of Community Health Services*. Chicago: International City Managers' Association.

LITCHFIELD, EDWARD H.
1956 "Notes on a general theory of administration." *Administrative Science Quarterly* (June).

LYND, ROBERT S.
1939 *Knowledge for What?* Princeton, New Jersey: Princeton University Press.

MACMAHON, BRIAN, THOMAS F. PUGH, and GEORGE B. HUTCHISON
1961 "Principals in the evaluation of community mental health programs." *American Journal of Public Health*, (July): 963–968.

MERTON, ROBERT K., and EDWARD C. DEVEREAUX, JR.
1964 "Practical problems and the uses of social science." *Transaction*, Vol. I (July): 18–21.

METZNER, CHARLES A., and CHARLES GURIN
1960 *Personal Response and Social Organization in a Health Campaign*. Ann Arbor: University of Michigan. Bureau of Public Health Economics. Research Series No. 9.

MORSE, PHILIP M. (ed.)
1967 *Operations Research for Public Systems*. Cambridge: M.I.T. Press.

PERKINS, JAMES A.
1966 *The University in Transition*. Princeton: Princeton University Press.

RIECKEN, HENRY W.
1952 *The Volunteer Work Camp: A Psychological Evaluation*. Cambridge, Massachusetts: Addison-Wesley Press.

RIVETT, PATRICK
1968 *An Introduction to Operations Research*. New York: Basic Books.

ROSSI, PETER H.
1966 "Boobytraps and pitfalls in the evaluation of social action programs." *Proceedings of the American Statistical Association*. Social Statistics Section.

SADOFSKY, STANLEY
  1966   "Utilization of evaluation results: Feedback into the action program."
          In June L. Shmelzer, *Learning in Action*. Washington: Government
          Printing Office.
SHELDON, ELEANOR, and WILBERT E. MOORE (eds.)
  1968   *Indicators of Social Change*. New York: Russell Sage Foundation.
SIMON, HERBERT A.
  1957   *Models of Man, Social and Rational*. New York: John Wiley and Sons,
          Inc.
STOUFFER, SAMUEL A.
  1950   "Some observations on study design." *American Journal of Sociology*,
          56 (January): 355–361.
SUCHMAN, EDWARD A.
          "Evaluation as Research." *Urban Review*. In press.
SUCHMAN, EDWARD A.
  1967   *Evaluative Research: Principles and Practice in Public Service and Social
          Action Programs*. New York: Russell Sage Foundation.
SUCHMAN, EDWARD A.
  1967   "Principles and practice of evaluative research." In John T. Doby
          (ed.), *An Introduction to Social Research*, pp. 327–351. New York:
          Appleton-Century-Crofts.
THOMPSON, JAMES D.
  1967   *Organizations in Action*. New York: McGraw-Hill.
WEISS, CAROL H.
  1966   "Utilization of evaluation: Toward comparative study." Paper
          presented at the American Sociological Association Meeting. Miami
          Beach: September 1.
WILENSKY, HAROLD L., and CHARLES N. LEBEAUX
  1958   *Industrial Society and Social Welfare*. New York: Russell Sage Foundation.
WRIGHT, CHARLES R., and HERBERT H. HYMAN
  1964   "The evaluators." In Philip E. Hammond (ed.), *Sociologists at Work*.
          New York: Basic Books.

CHAPTER SIX

The Process Outcome Research Model:
An Alternative in Evaluative Research
(A Case Study)

MELVIN E. ALLERHAND

In raising the powerful question, action for what, Dr. Suchman strikes at the heart of the importance of critically and validly investigating the many-faceted action programs and efforts that surround us in our local, national, and international society. He touches on the prophetic as he suggests that action might very well be for action's sake only or at times for the spending of available dollars. Unless we can establish methodological designs that are relevant to the many-sided social actions, the process of self fulfilling prophecies will continue to be the basis for continuing many such actions. My hope is to identify more usable, relevant, and more valid results through the development of new forms of social science research on the application of knowledge.

For so long (and still in the present) many questions have been raised about the "genuine" scientific nature of applied or in this case, evaluative research. We seek a research methodology that fits the study of the application of knowledge and in that way we are increasing the body of knowledge about educational methodology as well as developing new research approaches. Unless the forms of evaluative research relate very specifically to the educational methodologies (the innovations), such innovations will gradually move to the more general decadence that surrounds us in the delivery of information in public and private institutions of higher and lower education. We need a breakthrough in "what turns people on." Some of my psychological friends refer to this area as attending behavior (A. A. Staats and C. K. Staats, 1963). When it is studied in a rat it is science; however, when we do the same with people it is questioned. Of course, this overstates the case. In fact, the "hard" scientists appropriately criticize our attempt to do a direct transplant of research strategy. As Dr. Suchman points out, we depart from the so-called laboratory experiment in human research involving interventions and he suggests (in a way) that such departures are bad or at least less scientific. As I read his work I think he was attempting to comply with tradition and retain some of the old time brethren spirit with his colleagues. Please excuse the possibly overstated case — but my position insists on a new model in social science research (especially around evaluating new educational methodologies) and builds a research methodology that is more relevant to our work — not a copy or imitation of the physical or chemical sciences. Social science research might well focus on the interaction of systems, recognition of the "n" number of variables in such human activity, the recognition of the inevitable changing of goals midstream as related to identifiable and sometimes unidentifiable circumstances, the confusion around what may be the stated goal of an intervention and the real goal or anticipated outcome, etc. Thus, this paper is an attempt to apply another shot of reality to evaluative research — one more step in the needed development of research methodology that is syntonic with social sciences.

Introduction to the Design of this Paper

There is no question that I entered into the thinking about such a paper many years ago and aspects of the thinking have been reflected in other work. Yet, the presence of the seminar certainly promoted this communication. Secondly, the reading of Dr. Suchman's paper offered me some insight as to where he and, as he reflected it, the field is. The thrust of his paper offered a very useful baseline for next steps. Thirdly, I was again struck with the need to develop a unique design for behavioral and social science research utilizing, but not limited by, more traditional research designs. Fourthly, I was again faced with the public-private issue in research. By that I mean, the workings of research and the efforts of researchers is quite a private matter until that very work gets into print. Very often we want to let our private thinking stay out of the "neat package wrapped in ribbon" approach followed in the usual scientific paper. Finally, the thought of designing a discussant's paper based on my personal change process in carrying out research reached insight level. After Dr. Suchman organized the literature so adequately I could not think of a more comfortable moment to present this rather personal case study of development of evaluative research design. Thus, the bulk of the paper will be divided into identifying a progression of evaluative studies and examining each study in terms of a sampling of relevant variables, viz., assessment of problem, basic design, research staff, techniques for data collection and reporting results.

The Problem

Development of Effective Evaluative Research Methodology
(A case study approach)

Most succinctly stated this report examines the question: How can the effectiveness of evaluative research methodology associated with action programs be increased? Suchman identifies four areas of application of research, including:

1. Monitoring of programs and intervention to determine correction.
2. Identification of alternatives and providing relevant information.
3. Helping to weigh alternatives for decision making.
4. Helping to determine corrective action considering error risks.

These areas mark a usable range of work. Another ingredient is the recognized need for such research. Does the program staff view the research as relevant to their work? Further, if the need is realized, do the methodological steps that are taken most effectively satisfy this need so that the research action is seen, ideally, as useful to the program team? As such I cannot agree too strenuously with Dr. Suchman's reference to Etzioni and Lehman's (Etzioni and Lehman, 1967: 1–15) contention that increased attention must be given to "social validity" as opposed to methodological validity.

Review of Relevant Factors

The initial set of factors I surveyed were in the form of thought continua which I felt would help open up the examination of this case study. Essentially I surveyed my thoughts and produced the following continua:

1. Individuals — Groups.
2. Self — Others.
3. Intrapersonal — Interpersonal.
4. Psychotherapy — Educational.
5. Treatment Setting — Educational Setting.

6. Abnormal — Normal.
7. Permanent System — Temporary System.
8. Adjustment — Adaptation.
9. Stasis — Change.
10. Observer Oriented Experimenter — Engagement Oriented Experimenter.
11. Professional as defined by level of academic achievement — Professional as defined by perspective, stance, attitude, dedication.
12. Statistical Design as determiner of methodology — Situation in which problem is found as determiner of methodology.
13. Technique Centered — Problem Centered.
14. Information or Knowledge building — Solution to specific problem.
15. Long Term Concerns — Contemporary or Immediate Concerns.
16. A Discipline — Interdisciplinary.
17. One Root — Multiroots.

These factors probably will stimulate some reactions from the readers and some of you may have generated similar reflections on the change that has taken place within you. Other factors in the list may be too privately related to where I am now. However, as I reflect on this review of related factors it becomes clear that evaluative research for me requires an open and responsive type of methodology which nonetheless is very clearly defined and can be viewed as relevant to the circumstances in which it is being applied.

In addition to the review of these personal factors, certain variables that are part of the evaluative research design might be listed. These include:

1. The formulation of the problem as relevant to the specific situation in which the research is being carried on.
2. The basic design.
3. Techniques of collecting data.
4. The statistical procedures.
5. The type of research staff used in the research.
6. The development of instruments to measure the change.
7. Factors that must be recognized and dealt with although they cannot be controlled within the research methodology.
8. The manner of and timing of reporting results.

The Variables

A considerable number of variables might be identified to study the problem of the development of an effective evaluation research model. A sample of the more salient variables have been selected for this purpose. The following statements may be considered the working definitions:

1. *Assessment of the problem*

Investigation of the program situation to determine the objectives of the program as well as other factors which must be dealt with that may not be easily controlled within the research methodology, e.g., an unstated belief in a certain therapeutic approach although the stated attitude about therapy is eclectic; the politics involved in a particular manpower program; the emotional tensions that are built up as groups are being evaluated. Other steps would involve the review of the relevant literature and other information sources useful in understanding the program intervention, the subjects, etc.

2. *Establishing Basic Design; Identification and Stipulation of the Research Strategy*

Considering the study situation, what form of research will both answer the central questions and have a relatively neat fit with the program and background situation?

3. *The Type of Research Staff*

Identification of the characteristics of staff that will be most effective in the collecting, organizing, and the reporting of the data.

4. *Techniques for Data Collection*

Selection and developing of approaches and specific instruments for the most effective collection of data including the richness of the data, reliability in its collection, and ease of recasting it for handling and statistical manipulation.

5. *Reporting of Results*

Determination of the methods of reporting information in written or oral form. Determination of timing of the reporting of results, i.e., regular feed back to program staff, final report, etc.

The Data

(A chronological presentation of a series of evaluative researches)

A. THE BELLEFAIRE FOLLOW-UP STUDY (Allerhand *et al.*, 1966)

1. *The Situation*

Bellefaire is an institution for treating and rehabilitating emotionally disturbed children. The results of the complicated treatment methodology at Bellefaire had been informally evaluated many times. The informal reports based on children writing or calling offered some useful feedback to the Bellefaire staff. The administrators were not satisfied. Thus, interest was generated in determining what are the factors within the treatment experience that seemed to be most effective in reaching children and generally, what was the rate of Bellefaire's "success."

2. *Approach to Variables*
   a) Assessment of Problem

The climate for research had been made more palatable by the involvement of previous researchers at Bellefaire. The Bellefaire orientation is to seek new approaches as limitations are found. I was a member of the staff for five years preceding the follow-up study. However, acceptance came from some quarters and not from others. Particular resistance came from the case work staff and consultants. In the initial phases, an attempt was made to involve them; however, their emphasis on each child as an individual and the general resistance to defining and categorizing resulted in minimal participation in the implementation of the research. The cottage personnel and administration were much more willing to participate in helping to develop the entire program. The willingness of the administration to participate seemed to be partly reflected by the climate in the child welfare field in general, to get into this type of evaluative research.

   b) Basic Design

Fifty boys were used as their own controls in comparing their degree of progress in the institution with their level of adaptation in the society to which they returned. Thus, the degree of change within the institution became a central variable to compare with the level of adaptation represented by a composite measure of success, i.e., a number of observers rating the child, including self-rating on coping effectiveness. Further, a standard referent was developed based on considerable relevant literature describing formative behavior at different stages of childhood and adolescence.

   c) Research Staff

The staff involved primarily a group of professional social workers and a psychologist. Two research assistants were employed to interpret emotional tone of the recordings made during follow-up interviews. One of these individuals was a major in drama.

   d) Techniques for Data Collection

The primary sources of data were the actual records that were kept by the caseworkers at the agency. Further, I interviewed and administered projective tests to each of the subjects in his home situation as well as interviewing at least one important adult in the subject's life. Rating scales were used to evaluate the child's performance as represented in the case records as well as in the transcripts of the tape recorded follow-up interviews. Areas to be covered in the rating scales evolved out of a series of discussions with Bellefaire treatment and research staff. As suggested above, the Bellefaire therapy staff had relatively superficial involvement. Decisions about the inclusion of variables and measurement approaches were seriously being stalled since the therapeutic staff had such basic resistance to this type of study. (After the study was in process for two years and data about specific children was collected, the therapeutic staff came around.) The child care staff offered many useful suggestions and showed continuous interest. The rating team of primarily social workers, participated actively and with interest in the selection of areas and subsequently the determination of the actual items and anchor points on the scales. A training program for the rating staff was developed. Records and transcripts of Bellefaire children not participating in the study were used in determining changes in the actual wording and steps within the scale. Thus, the research design was a team effort.

e) Reporting of Results

The study was carried out over about a five year period of time. Understandably there was considerable interest in the results. Three years passed before data on the entire group was available. Another six months was necessary to get any preliminary ideas. The Bellefaire staff were mainly fed research methodology and reports of "which kid was seen where." After three and a half years, only demographic material and hunches were available, but with some friendly pressure a presentation was made to staff and at an annual board meeting of the trustees of Bellefaire. The usual publication and professional meeting approaches to reporting were utilized (Allerhand *et al.*, 1966). When the book form became available Bellefaire distributed copies to the members of its Board of Trustees.

B. THE HEAD START FOLLOW-UP STUDY (Allerhand, 1966)

1. *The Situation*

The Head Start Program of 1965, the first offering of this form of rehabilitation, presented the opportunity for this study. Cleveland was phased into the national testing program to determine whether a seven to eight week Head Start stimulation program would have much of an impact on the experience of children as they entered kindergarten. I wanted to know more about concept attainment in children and the effect of teachers, level of poverty, etc., on certain aspects of thinking of these children after entrance into kindergarten.

2. *Approach to variables*
a) Assessment of Problem

One problem in this evaluative research was gaining entry into and cooperation from the public schools. After all, who was going to be evaluated and how much teacher time would be required? Further, it was necessary to have the agreement of the various Head Start agencies from whom the children received their initial experience. How do you build trust within large organizations? Fortunately, I had previous contact with the Cleveland Public Schools and particularly their research department. The research department afforded entry and guidance. But, there are elementary coordinators, supervising principals, principals, teachers, and children. Each have an understandable investment and thus want to be recognized. Each required an appropriate amount of interest and consideration.

The determination of the relevant variables for each type of evaluative research also enters into the assessment of the problem. If an evaluative researcher does not have a particular interest (as I did), a range of potentially relevant variables become evident. But, what is the best dependent variable in evaluating the impact of a pre-school stimulation program? The literature offers some suggestions; observing the actual pre-school situation offers others. My bias was revealed in the choosing of the variable. Actually, it was exposed by choosing Head Start as the situation for an evaluative study. Or did I bend the need for evaluation of Head Start to fit my theoretical interests?

b) Basic Design

The design involved a comparative study of concept attainment with 50 per cent of the subjects having participated in Head Start (HS group) and 50 per cent having not participated (NHS group) in the Summer Head Start program (1965). The HS and NHS subjects were observed in the same group of kindergarten classrooms in Cleveland Public Schools. Children from five different Head Start programs were included. Effect of teachers' exposure to Head Start, some family economic and social factors, etc., were also considered. An intensive study group (25 HS and 25 NHS) was observed on approximately a bi-weekly basis; while the main group (100 HS and 100 NHS) were observed about once per month.

c) Research Staff

In addition to my presence, the research staff included two members with special training in child development, five psychology graduate students and the remainder were inner city and suburban housewives who received on-the-job training. One of the child development specialists was a long term resident of a poverty area in the black community and had pre-school experience with the Head Start population. Some of the housewife-helpers were trained as parent testers during the summer of 1965 (Allerhand, 1967). We sought and had an inside view about poverty children and the school situation.

d) Techniques for Data Collection

The basic approach to data collection was the development of a series of scales to measure five areas of concept attainment. The scales were used by trained observers in the kindergarten classroom. The scales were developed through a series of open-ended observations in both Head Start and kindergarten classes to determine the source of the best data for the purpose of measuring the development of concept attainment *in situ*. A number of the staff observers formed a team to develop the rating scales. Prior to the entry into the classroom, group meetings were held with the teachers who were going to participate in the study. They examined the rating scales and were requested to help in the redesigning of them so that they could more effectively reflect the situation in which they were going to be used. Although the scales were again changed, after some direct application during the study period further revisions were necessary. Since the design of the study involved taking a series of nine measures during the kindergarten year, it was possible to eliminate some of the earlier measurements when it was clear that the research instruments were inadequate. The classroom based rater/observers would periodically discuss the group results with the teacher in the classroom. The classroom teacher knew the subjects of the study and it was quite possible that the teacher who had positive attitudes toward Head Start may have unwittingly given additional help and support to the Head Start child over the non-Head Start children. The reverse was also possible. Other ranges of other conscious and unconscious human motives could be identified which probably affected the results. We attempted some exploratory checks on such hypotheses. Such efforts raised some further questions.

e) Reporting of Results

As indicated above the observers periodically would report results to the teachers about the children in their own room. This was on an informal basis. During the data collection year, on two occasions trends were reported to subgroups of teachers and principals. Further, there was reporting of results in the four progress notes sent to the National Head

Start Research headquarters. Prior to submitting these reports, they were reviewed by the assistant director of the Cleveland Public School Research Department. (Her help was invaluable in implementing the program.) No changes in the reports were requested by Cleveland Public School personnel. There were two groups who were not involved in the reporting of the results, viz., the children themselves and their parents.

C. Aim—Jobs: A Concentrated Employment Program (CEP) (Cleveland College Technical Report, 1969)

1. *The Situation*

Aim—Jobs is an effort to reach and hopefully rehabilitate the "hard core unemployed" from the inner city. The evaluative research was initiated at the same time as the program began. The program sought to recruit, orient, and support-on-jobs a group of primarily young men. Aim—Jobs was the first of a series of such programs funded during the Spring of 1967. The organization may be defined as a combination demonstration and service organization and therefore, in Suchman's view, a hybrid that results in much confusion and mistrust. To develop a program as well as to have an in-depth evaluation, certainly increases the problem of trust between the program staff and the research staff.

2. *Approach to Variables*
   a) Assessment of Problem

Firstly, the "if you are interested, develop a proposal yesterday" problem was faced. The "yes" was a very available reply. In an attempt to assess the problem presented by such an employment/training program I became deeply engaged in the actual development of the plan for program. Prior to the advent of Aim—Jobs, I had a strong interest in the current problems of reaching and developing work for the hard core unemployed. (Again, here was an instance where participation and experience in the very content of the program may be a very significant variable in developing evaluative research.) As a further step in the assessment of the problem, contact was made with local representatives of the Department of Labor and the local CAP agency under which this manpower program was developed. As contact was initiated with administrative staff of the program, associations with members of industry who would be participating in this particular program were facilitated. This afforded an opportunity to get insight into the type of participation that industry would have, and also to gain an understanding of the varying orientations of industry in the handling of this specific hard core manpower problem.

It became very clear that one must attempt to develop a close trust relationship with the program people. Ideally the evaluative research should be viewed as relevant to their work, and not just an outside attempt to find out what was wrong and report it back to their funding agency. Finally, I was again struck with the need to develop a research approach geared to the uniqueness of the participants.

b) Basic Design

The design of this evaluation program was extremely complex. It was divided into three areas, viz., measuring participants' attitudes and change in these attitudes over time, the organizational structure as it changed over time and the response of industry to the manpower program. The identification of the ideal research team enters into the basic design as we attempted to relate research methodology to program and program participants. (Some details will be described later under the research staff section but as I reflect on these issues it is difficult to even retain the categories just created for this paper.) The approach was primarily a series of three measurements of various attitudinal changes, viz., one at the beginning and another at the end of orientation, and finally after the participant was in the work situation for a period of time. There were a number of comparison groups, including dropouts versus non-dropouts and AIM—JOBS participants with similar folks who entered other types of manpower programs. The AIM—JOBS organization was examined as a moving process. The variables included the degree of collaboration, perceptions of the participants, attitudes about welfare, etc. The impact on industry design was primarily to gain the perceptions about AIM—JOBS, its participants, etc., by various members of the industrial organizations that employed this group of hard core unemployed. Some comparisons based on size of company, pay schedules, etc., were included.

c) The Research Staff

Needless to say relevant research talent for such a study is as rare as finding a real militant black for a New Look Chamber of Commerce. Staff must relate to the range of poor and the range of rich. Also, some orientation to team research must be built in. Of the four researchers, two had some in depth exposure to all of the relevant manpower and community systems. None of these were black. A black research administrator was sought and found. He had most of his experience in medical-animal research. Research assistants initially were mainly white. We brought in black consultants from the inner city. Finally, we were able to employ and train some black, hard core type of research aides. Still — we had a white research methodology. Again, it was partly the problem of fitting the evaluative research design into the program and program situation. We attempted to relate our work to the black–white man's world, but we were an overly trained finger of the white, middle-class world.

d) Techniques for Data Collection

The information for the attitudinal study of participants was primarily a series of administrations of various measures initially in groups of twenty, finally reduced to five in a group. These were administered in the beginning and end of orientation and then after the employee was working in an organization. Although words and sentence structure were reviewed for relevance and pictorial approaches were included, much revision was necessary as negative feedback came from the participants. Questions were presented about the appropriateness of the items or the manner in which the questionnaire was presented. There was a fast move from an available graduate assistant, white, who was administering these measures in a group to the utilization of black research aides as administrators. As a result of the change we had more completed questionnaires with seemingly more thought given to the replies. At one point, the items were read to the respondents so that the problem of language might be reduced. We were looking for the most valid responses. True, our consistency in collecting data was a bit shoddy. To keep the comparisons over time consistent, we did attempt to use the same approach on repeat testing of the same participants. Also, we destroyed a lot of data.

In examining the AIM—JOBS organization, the data was collected through panel interviews and a series of questionnaires administered to all staff. Further examination of the collaborative nature of the organization was carried out through an action research methodology where the group process researchers worked with individuals and with groups trying to facilitate linkages among sub-groups of AIM—JOBS employees. Debriefing of the group process-researchers was established with regularity to examine the movement toward more collaborative approaches within the organization.

Data about the industrial organizations was acquired through direct interviews with supervisory personnel in the organizations as well as from some of the data that was being collected by AIM—JOBS staff. Finally a chronology of the organization was compiled through interview of internal and external observers and a review of relevant and available private and public documents.

e) Reporting of Results

One of the critical problems in handling results in this study was just the exchange of data among the participating research team members. Regular staff meetings, individual contacts with the research administrative team, exchanging memos, the requirement of various types of Department of Labor progress reports — all could not satisfactorily keep Humpty Dumpty together. (The life of collaborative research.) Feedback to the program staff was attempted and actually achieved. The principal investigator and the director of the program or his associate met on a bi-weekly basis during most of the first program year. In addition there was the submitting of all reports to the program staff prior to forwarding them to the Department of Labor. Different feedback approaches to the total staff of the organization were attempted. In addition, the research staff made itself available to carry out specific administrative research requested by the AIM—JOBS project director. This was important as a method of keeping a close collaborative orientation between the research and the program groups. I might add with all of the efforts to build feedback relationships and also to increase the trust, the orientation of the program staff for the greater part was extremely negative. Suspicion (a reality when someone is looking over your shoulder, paper and pencil in hand) is by far the greatest contributor to error variance. A most profound observation!

D. FAMILY AND CHILDREN SERVICES PROJECT (a current program)

1. *The Situation*

Family and Children Services is a part of the Cuyahoga County Public Welfare Program. It focuses on direct assistance in the delivery of various rehabilitative services to children and their families who receive welfare. Foster parents within such an organization are showing much interest in becoming an integral part of the actual staff of such an organization. Such a movement presents professional, organizational, and emotional problems. The Foster Parent Training Program of Family and Children Services had been in existence for two years prior to the involvement of the research team. In the training of the foster parents, discrepancies between the foster parents and other staff members *vis-a-vis* being viewed as integral employees of the agency became more evident. The director of the agency and the director of the foster parent training recognized the need to study the training and its effects on all agency personnel. I became very concerned about the situation, particularly since child welfare had been a long term interest. This specific agency was of particular interest for about three years prior to the initiation of the evaluative research-training program.

2. *Approach to Variables*

a) Assessment of Problem

The long term contact with the agency permitted a clearer under-standing of the multiproblems that existed within the agency. The foster parent role confusion only represented what was a much broader un-clarity as far as the roles of the other members of the institutional staff regarding direct care to the agency's children and the children's families. (Public welfare is laden with such complications.) Thus, it was evident that the range of staff activities might have to be defined and worker's roles clarified to more effectively deliver the child care services to the population cared for by the agency. Both the training and the research methodology zeroed in on this central question. There was little doubt that various questions and concerns would be raised by all members of the staff. Thus, a program and research strategy was built to handle most of the anticipated reactions.

b) Basic Design

The basic design clearly brought a marriage between program and research. The project co-directors, the director of the Foster Parent Training Program and I, attempted to design and implement the total program. Any changes in the methodology for research or program had to be dealt with by individuals from both orientations. The design involved the bringing together in a planning and advisory capacity, representatives of the various aspects of the agency involved in this particular program. In addition to this advisory committee, a task committee comprised of a cross section of the steering committee was developed to focus on research methodology and revision.

A role clarification seminar was designed both to identify content for training programs and offer a baseline for evaluation of changes that might be brought about through training programs. The central training and research variable was the role of the agency as a deliverer of child care (or parenting) to its charges. Representations of all staff involved in the agency were included in these role clarification seminars. As the series of training programs were developed, instrumentation was developed to measure perceptions of staff as far as the role of deliverer of child care services. Further, a detailed chronology of the process is being accumulated to examine the range of change in individuals and agency.

c) Research-Training Staff

The staff is made up of a team of researchers and representatives of the Family and Children Services Organization, including all levels of staff. Supervisors of foster parents or child care workers are included in the research-training staff. There is a significant mix of black and white. Foster parents are used as resource persons and staff aides in all phases of instrument building and training. At this time the agency has decided that no children would be involved in the program as subjects or staff resources.

d) Techniques for Data Collection

Data collection has been a combination of observation of the process of role clarification and direct measurement through questionnaires. The questionnaires have been developed jointly through discussion with the steering committee and reaction of various members of the agency staff. Since all members of the training program, viz., supervisors, case workers, child care workers, foster parents, must also answer the questionnaires, representatives of all groups had an opportunity to review the items and help determine their relevancy. The role clarification seminars are an unusually critical locus for the collection of data. Thus, recordings of these sessions have been made. The comparisons of the change in the role understanding initially will be completed through pre- and post-testing of all participants. However, this phase of the study-training program is viewed as exploratory. A more sophisticated design of process measures is being considered and developed for the second year of the program. We anticipate that with further trust, agency children will be involved as respondents and aides.

e) Reporting of Results

The data collected on the role clarification seminars was reported broadly throughout the agency and was specifically used by the trainers in developing the curricula for the training programs. Agency administrators have examined and discussed the results and changes in agency operation being considered. The results of the pre-questionnaire administered to all participants have been organized by training groups and there has been feedback to the teacher of the group. The overall results soon will be reported at larger staff meetings. Such direct ties with the administration and staff have increased support. Such direct feedback to participants has resulted in more ownership and involvement in the actual program.

The Results in this Case Study on Evaluative Research

I seek the ideal form of a process-outcome model. Some of the glaring omissions of not including more foster parents in the planning of the foster parent study and not including hard core unemployed in the reconstruction of the Aim Research instruments indicate that the developing of a research design to fit a particular situation needs considerable attention. The factor of developing a trust relationship with the agency or program staff was evident from the start and now is underscored, as strategies for gaining entry and continued relationship with the system. The centrality of the researcher having a strong interest and/or commitment to the content or mission of the agency or program became evident. An alternative to in depth content involvement by the researcher is the researcher and program director co-directing the total program. The recognition of the need for professional and so-called non-professional exchange is heightened. The choice of non-professionals who are more indigenous to the situation and therefore can bring their special ways of sensing the situation is so critical.

A frank stance in reviewing the real programmatic objectives is a *sine qua non*. We can end up by playing a series of games pretending that we know the goal at the beginning and that we will keep on plodding along and measure the situations that should provide data on these goals. However, if we steep ourselves in the situation, we also recognize pretty quickly that the stated goals and the real goals are often different; that the starting and the midpoint goals might be very different. For evaluative research to be able to stand up with its brethren in the more traditional forms of research in the physical sciences, we must develop a respectability for the type of research that is being done. And the only way to do this is to be sure that it is relevant and honest. We are living in programs that are extremely complex and only after we can behave with the reality that these are complex situations, can we come up with the complex designs that will honestly tap the changes that are taking place in such interventions or within such organizations.

At this moment of the paper's fourth and final revision, I can identify the following useful characteristics in my process-outcome model for evaluative research:

1. Developing a trust relationship in preparation for entry into the study situation.
2. A wedding of research and program.
3. Careful selection of criteria to insure relevance to program staff.
4. Multimeasures (from different vantage points) of particularly the criterion or dependent variable.
5. Shaping evaluative research design to fit the program or agency style.

6. Utilization of research aides indigenous to the study situation.
7. Building ownership of instruments by raters or users of measuring device.
8. Periodic measurements during the life of the program.
9. Cross-sectional measurements of different aspects of the program or functional groups in the organization.
10. Periodic feedback of evaluative results to relevant others for resetting of goals.
11. Evaluative researchers who either have a wide range of interests in program contents or ease in developing a working knowledge of content and identification with mission; or theoretical researchers who can enthusiastically implement an evaluative research effort in their areas of interest.

REFERENCES

AIM-JOBS   RESEARCH PROJECT
  1969   "A study of impact and effectiveness of the comprehensive manpower project of Cleveland (AIM)." *Cleveland College Technical Report,* **1.**

ALLERHAND, MELVIN E., R. WEBER, and N. POLANSKY
  1961   "The Bellefaire follow-up study: Research objectives and methods." *Child Welfare* (September).

ALLERHAND, MELVIN E., R. WEBER, and M. HAUG
  1966   "Adaptability and adaptation: Bellefaire follow-up study." New York: Child Welfare League of America.

ALLERHAND, MELVIN E.
  1966   "Impact of Summer 1965 head start on children's concept attainment during kindergarten." *Cleveland College Technical Report.*
  1967   "Effectiveness of parents of head start children as administrators of psychological tests." *Journal of Consulting Psychology,* **31**: 286.

ETZIONI, AMITAI, and EDWARD W. LEHMAN
  1967   "Some dangers in 'valid' social measurement." *The Annals of the American Academy of Political and Social Science,* **00** (September): 1–15.

STAATS, A. A., and C. K. STAATS
  1963   "Complex human behavior." New York: Holt, Rinehart and Winston.

ORGANIZATIONAL
STRUCTURES FOR RESEARCH

CHAPTER SEVEN

Observations on the Organization of
Social Research

PETER H. ROSSI

Introduction

When social scientists think of their intellectual ancestors, they usually
conjure up an image of a man alternating between the classroom and his
study with side excursions to the library. Only a few means of production
were at his disposal — comfortable Victorian armchairs, pigeon-hole
desks, scratchy pens and stiff paper, and the reference volumes of his
extensive private library. At least, this is the nostalgic image of the
nineteenth and early twentieth century sociologist.

There is some evidence that this myth is somewhat overdrawn. Many of
our more prominent ancestors engaged in extensive first-hand data
collection: We have only to think of Booth and Le Play to conjure up
alternative images of Victorian figures interviewing the poor. However,
even those who are known today mainly for their "theoretical" work, also
engaged in some data grubbing: Max Weber played an important role
in the early social survey movement in Germany and Durkheim and his
students played similar roles in France.[1] In this country, Ward, Ross,
Giddings, and their students dabbled although not as extensively in
generating social data directly from observations "in the field."

Nevertheless, the predominant work styles of our intellectual fore-
bearers were not too far from the mythical image of nostalgic recall; or,
at least, they were closer to that image than we are today. The art and

151

practice of social science has changed. We are in a period in which empirical social research is the predominant style of sociology and social psychology. For better or for worse, we are committed to a style of social science which regards the collection and analysis of empirical data very highly. Indeed, we emphasize empirical work so strongly that it often appears that social researchers prefer to collect their *own* data even when suitable equivalent data already exist.

The shift to empirical social research as a style of scientific activity has also meant a change in the organization of scientific activity. While there are still many social scientists who are essentially solo practitioners with perhaps a few students as assistants and junior colleagues, the era of collaborative research has arrived. Teams of researchers formed for *ad hoc* purposes are very common. But even more important has been the growth of relatively permanent research organizations whose existence extends beyond the life of specific research projects and in which there may also be an extensive division of labor.

In addition, the means of production have changed and become more technically sophisticated. The typewriter has replaced the pen; the research institute's building has superseded the scholar's study; and the computer has replaced the tallysheets. The most recent technical advance, the copying machine, has had an impact on the use of written documents. Dissemination of research findings occurs more through the use of private printing means with journal publication serving more as an archive function than as a means for diffusing new knowledge.

This change in the means of production has occurred so recently that we have not yet had the time to observe its full empirical richness and to speculate on its meaning for our field and the institutions, particularly the university, to which it is closely related. In particular, we know that social research is more complexly organized now than it was even a decade ago, let alone thirty years ago, but the forms that the organization of social research have taken have yet to be cataloged or assessed. It is clear that we have borrowed from the experiences of older disciplines who went empirical earlier, and it is equally clear that we have developed new organizational forms especially adapted to our own needs and technology.

The organization of social research is the main concern of this paper. Three central questions will be raised in the pages which follow:

> First, what are the forces that foster the organization of research into centers and
> institutes and for the more informal organization of research into efforts by
> collaborating teams?

Secondly, what are forms taken by research organizations in the present period and the advantages and disadvantages of each form in relation to the functions for which organizations are apparently devised?

Thirdly, can we make some statements concerning optimal organizational forms for research purposes of different sorts?

Gains from Organized Social Research

Clearly a large part of human activity is organized in at least the minimal sense of at least two human actors jointly contributing to a shared activity. The forces which sustain organized activity are the gains to participants arising from participation in organizations as against pursuing an activity on their own. That man is a social animal is attested to by the fact that one of the major gains to participants in organized activity comes from the satisfactions arising from interaction *per se*.

These are very general formulations, applying with equal force to the most trivial and to the most critical activities. Furthermore, they do not help to understand in a specific instance either the form of organization that develops nor the degree of organization. In the broadest sense, there are no solitary scholars or researchers; indeed, even the mythical Robinson Crusoe survived on the gains from past organized human activity that he retained in his memory (let alone the help he got from Friday). The solitary sociologist scholar relies on a more organized form of memory residing in the volumes of his library, on the results obtained by censuses, surveys, etc. The critical issue, therefore, is not whether empirical research is organized, but to what extent? Furthermore, what are the benefits (and costs) to be gleaned (or suffered) from entering into relatively enduring forms of interaction with other persons in the pursuit of empirical social research?

Part of the gains from organization stem from ease in dealing with the accomplishment of research tasks. These may be called the "internal" gains from organization. There are also gains in the area of "foreign relations," that is, gains in the ability to deal effectively with exogenous elements in the environment. We will deal first with the internal gains.

Perhaps the most obvious gains from enduring collaboration among social researchers are those which flow from collegiality. To have a set of peers who share the same interests and goals and who therefore provide an engaged audience as well as a source of advice and ideas is a gain of some appreciable magnitude.

Of course, many social scientists are to be found "naturally" within environments who provide them with peers, especially those who are within academic departments of sociology.[2] What is to be gained from organization in this respect that could not be obtained from departmental colleagues? The problem lies in that departmental colleagues are bound together in a set of varied relationships some of which may inhibit collegiality. The formation of a research organization segregates out those relationships which are bound up with common interests in research and facilitates collegiality by providing a context in which those bonds of interest held in common are stressed and other relationships (which may be competitive or fraught with some conflict) are suppressed. A research organization provides each member with the legitimate right to access to the other members in a role which is task oriented and specific rather than possibly affectively oriented and diffuse. Thus, department members may and often do form a research organization whose main function it is to provide a context wherein the ordinary forms of relating to one another as departmental colleagues are suspended in favor of more task oriented relationships, at the same time reinforcing the solidarity that arises when men share some goal in common.

Collegiality is perhaps the most important gain for the most informal research organizations (for example, the "brown bag" lunch groups that some departments have organized). It is also an important gain in larger more complex organizations. Unfortunately, it is one that is easily lost as a research organization becomes more complex and develops hierarchies of seniority, titles, and statuses. Collegiality is best and most easily sustained by equal status, equal age groups and is hardest to maintain among groups with large ranges of variations in these respects. Recognizing this need some of the larger research organizations have developed several subgroups of roughly equal age and status to regain for some subgroups the sense of collegiality that is lost for the research organizations as a whole.

Another gain to organization lies in the development of equity in the distribution of resources. In some cases, the resources may be access to computational facilities; in other cases, it may be access to students that is the main resource; in still others, actual funds may be at stake.[3] In cases where resources are scarce, a research organization may help to provide at least the appearance of equity by whatever distribution may have to take place.

In some fields the distribution of resources is particularly important. For example in astronomy, time on a telescope is limited with more demand for its use than can be accommodated easily. Observatory organization takes on the function of making equitable allocations. In the social science fields, computers, social psychology laboratories, secretarial help, research space, or research assistants are the main types of resources around which organization may grow to insure adherence to a "proper" divison of resources.[4]

Perhaps the greatest gain to participation in organized research arises out of the potential efficiencies of a division of labor. At the simplest level, providing secretarial and clerical help can make the difference between easy progress in research and one which requires many side excursions into non-essential tasks. At a more complex level, a division of labor among an administrative cadre (who keep the books, hire lower level personnel and make sure that there is plenty of coffee), research assistants, technical personnel (e.g. computer programmers, sampling statisticians, machine tenders, etc.) and, as in the case of survey research, maintaining a field staff capable of running sample surveys, can make it possible for a researcher to do research on a much larger scale and with greater efficiency than would be possible were he to attempt research on his own.

In social research, the division of labor arising in connection with the conduct of sample surveys provides the basis for the development of its most complex research organizations. The conduct of sample surveys requires the coordination of various specialized experts plus the deployment and management of a large field staff. Sample surveys are labor intensive and the coordination of the labors involved leads to lines of authority, responsibility, and control which are not to be found ordinarily in connection with social research.

Research also has its "foreign relations" problems. Financing has to be obtained from outside sources. Legitimation as a responsible and competent researcher has to be established. Competition for other uses of scarce resources within a university has to be met. Research organizations help to meet the "foreign relations" needs of researchers by packaging and thereby multiplying the political and professional resources of the individual researchers involved.

The multiplier effect on political power can be seen in the formal research organizations reputedly greater ability to command the attention of university administrations, private foundations, and government agencies. It is supposed to be easier for a formal research organization to obtain a research grant than an individual researcher, just as it is easier for a research organization successfully to advance a claim for space and research budget with a university administration than it is for an individual faculty member. Whether it is *in fact* easier for formal research organizations to obtain grants than individuals is not clear,[5] although I am quite sure that university administrations pay more attention to research organizations than they do to individual researchers.

Perhaps the truth of the matter is that formal research organizations are more useful to some than to others. Research centers are probably especially helpful to young persons just starting out on their careers for whom the centers can provide the stamps of legitimacy and guarantees of competence which their names alone may not yet carry.

For senior persons with relatively well established reputations affiliation with a center may not provide more leverage with a foundation or government agency than such a person would have on his own. For example, my own university recently established an Urban Affairs Center which will eventually subsume some of my own activities, but these were started without the Center being in existence and would neither be harmed nor helped by being part of the Center. Yet the Center "package" did manage to attract a fairly sizable Ford Foundation grant and some financial support from the local business community, none of which I could have attracted on my own. To the outside world, a formal research organization is more than the sum of its parts, representing something more attractive than an individual could possibly be.

A research organization is also viewed as somehow more responsible than an individual. An individual researcher may leave to take another position, an administrator may defect to teaching, but a research organization will ordinarily carry on their commitments, recruit new personnel, and transfer the tasks involved to new people. Furthermore, a research organization has a responsibility to respond to demands and hence may be more sensitive to the needs and wishes of potential clients and benefactors. This latter point is particularly important when it comes to applied research. For example, a Center for Research on Poverty would find it harder to turn down a prospective research contract on poverty problems than an individual who is doing research in poverty.

In short, a research organization pools and magnifies the political, charismatic, technical, and responsibility potentials of its individual staff members. In this sense the position of individual staff members is thereby enhanced *vis-a-vis* their environments of universities, grant giving agencies and potential contracting agencies.

Note that both the internal and the external gains accruing from the organization of research are greater for researchers at the very top and at the bottom of the research reputation hierarchy. A man of considerable reputation, by reconstituting his activities as a research organization, enhances considerably his ability to get work done. The division of labor possible within a center means that it is possible for him to hire junior personnel in a context wherein he can tell them what to do and thereby multiply his own efforts. For the senior man of considerable reputation, a research organization reconstitutes the authority structure of the old fashioned graduate departments with its senior members directing the work of junior members in a coordinated division of labor.

For the very junior man starting out on his research career, a research organization provides funds, amenities, leverage in the world of benefactors that is not available to him on his own. In return, he has to give up some degree of independence.

In contrast, for the middling man, participation in a research organization is a maximum gain only if the organization has a minimal hierarchical structure. If he participates as a junior in a division of labor he has lost status and it is not clear that he gains that much more in his "foreign relations" with universities and with potential benefactors. For the man in the middle, research organizations with equal status and minimal division of labor are more attractive.

It should be clear from the discussion of the last few paragraphs that there are costs to participation in research organizations, as well as gains. If a social scientist who works by himself does so at a low level of efficiency, he does have greater autonomy than one who works within an organized context. His ability to say "no" or "yes" to demands on his time is greater. He has more control over the amount of access others can have to him: of course, he has less rights of access to others.

There are other potential losses as well. Large scale research organizations do not fit well within the academic grooves. The tensions that have arisen between research centers and traditional departments have not yet given rise to academic novels, although the intrigue, conflict, and tension is often high enough and complex enough to seem worthy of a C. P. Snow novel. Perhaps it is because the novelists tend to be humanists and the conflicts between research centers and traditional departments have been going on in the physical and social sciences.

Traditionally academic departments regard the large scale centers as rich imperialists. Such centers, according to this view, compete unfairly for graduate students, swallow up junior faculty members, and engage in questionable research activities, usually of an applied nature. Center directors are seen as powerful men seeking constantly to enlarge their spheres of control with many followers who would swamp the democratic processes of departmental organizations if they were allowed in too close to departments. On the other side, Center personnel see departments as concerned mainly with protecting their status, only dabbling in research rather than being totally dedicated to research activity, and being overly protective of the "organizational integrity" of their departments.

Not all research organizations engage in running battles with traditional departments. The minimum complexity organization of the "brown bag" lunch group or the *ad hoc* research project varieties do not engender conflict with departments. It is the large scale center, with its hierarchical structure, extensive division of labor, and large scale funding that produces bones for contention.

Of course, research organizations are not exclusively sources of troubles to the academic departments to which they may be affiliated. The training of graduate students in the craft lore of social research and in the technical aspects of research practice is better accomplished in the doing of research than in the classroom. The better schools have attached research institutes because they are committed to the apprenticeship mode of research training and the formal research institute is a suitable means for accomplishing this end.

Furthermore, formal research organizations may enhance the status of a department in the field and within a university. The publications of a research center add to the collective *curriculum vitae* of a department and the publicity given to such centers in the press and in professional publications make some impact on the world.

Varieties of Research Organizations

The gains and losses accruing to the organization of research reviewed in the last section implies that research organizations can take on a variety of forms depending upon which gains are being maximized and correspondingly which losses are being minimized. Not all that appears on the academic scene, the titles of "center," "institute," or "laboratory" are identical. They vary in size, amount of funding, but even more crucially in structural characteristics.

As we have indicated in the previous section perhaps the most simple of all research organizations are the solidary, equal status groups, existing in most primitive form as "brown bag lunch groups" and in most extensive form as professional associations. An appropriate name for such informal research groups is the *collegium*.

The most salient structural characteristics of such collegia are that members tend to be of equal status, and engage in few concerted research efforts. The collegium exists mainly to provide a context in which persons interested in the same area of research can meet, exchange ideas, and perhaps cooperate on an *ad hoc* basis in specific research projects. Decision making rules in such organizations tend to be democratic in character, perhaps with rotating chairman, or in the case of large scale professional associations, elected officers and legislative bodies, but with little or no power over the activities of members except the power to admit or reject applications for membership. *Collegia* are research organizations which stress collegiality as a gain for their members and may confer some degree of status upon members.[6]

The next level of complexity of research organization, the consortium,[7] is represented by perhaps a majority of the organizations that go under the names of institutes and centers. Consortia are organizations designed primarily to maximize the foreign relations gains from organizing research and have a minimum division of labor. They are essentially collections of faculty members each pursuing his own research interests using the center to provide letterheads, secretarial service, and political leverage within the university and with funding agencies. The Directors of such centers have little authority over members and the main division of labor within such centers involves the provision of minor clerical and secretarial services to members.

Almost every major university department of sociology has one or more such consortia. At Berkeley there are so many that it looks almost as if each senior member of the faculty has his own. Chicago, too, has its share. Some are co-terminous with the department or departments to which they are attached: the Laboratory of Social Relations at Harvard includes every member of the Department, as does the Institute for Social Research at North Carolina.

It is the consortium form that departments have in mind when they indicate that they wish to start a research center. Such centers are mainly regroupings of faculty members under a different name but without fundamentally altering the authority relationships among members. They are attractive regroupings because of the leverage they provide on university administrations for funds and space and on grant giving agencies for funds. Such organizations present no problems to departmental structures and have potential benefits of the "foreign relations" gains variety.

It should also be evident that there is no particular benefit to research *qua* research from the consortium form. Whether my own research is carried out under the auspices of the Group for Research on Social Policy, as my little research consortium is called, or under no title at all makes little difference to the research. As GROSP, my young graduate student associates and I have a letterhead, some claim on research space, perhaps a greater degree of solidarity, but the division of labor among us remains the same as before we adopted a name. GROSP may not live much longer than the research project to which it provides an umbrella, especially since the graduate students hopefully will get their degrees and move on to other institutions, and, when I engage in my next project, perhaps the name will not be as appropriate as some other.

The next level of complexity is represented by "*Institutes*," centers which arise around the use and maintenance and distribution of a scarce resource, access to which has to be regulated in the name of equity. Several social psychologists may band together in an Institute to regulate the use of interaction rooms and the accompanying electronic equipment. Or, in the days of punched cards, an Institute may arise around the use of a computer — sorter or IBM 101. Or, in some cases, the resources involved may be funds: R & D Centers funded by the Office of Education have sometimes taken on the Institute form. Or, a grant from Ford may foster the establishment of an Urban Affairs Center in the form of an Institute because decisions have to be made on how the funds are to be allocated.

The allocation decisions made by such organizations tend to resemble existing principles of differentiation in the host organization. Thus, the grants given by the Rockefeller Foundation in the twenties to several universities to foster the development of social research tended to be allocated among the faculty according to their rank and prestige, not necessarily according to need and merit.[8] If anything, such organizations tend therefore to end up strengthening existing arrangements; if they accomplish something above and beyond what individual members could do on their own, it is only because existing arrangements of status and authority coincided with merit and research competence.

The highest level of complexity is shown by "research firms,"[9] those research organizations which have elaborate divisions of labor, hierarchies of authority and status within their professional cadres, and whose personnel do not coincide with departmental structures. Perhaps the best examples are the Institute for Social Research at the University of Michigan, the National Opinion Research Center at the University of Chicago, and the Bureau of Applied Social Research at Columbia University.

The critical differences between the "research firms" and the centers previously considered in this paper lie in the development of separate professional staffs and a relatively stringent line of authority. The Directors of research firms have a great deal more authority, particularly over the professional staff which has no faculty status. The gains of research firms are primarily in the foreign relations area and also those which derive from the more intensive division of labor: hence, it is no accident that the best examples of research firms are those that have arisen around the research activity in the social sciences which requires the most extensive division of labor, the conduct of sample surveys. Properly to conduct a survey one needs to assemble at a minimum the following skills: sampling of human populations, questionnaire construction (an art rather than a science and hence highly dependent for its highest development on extensive practical experience), interviewing, data processing, and data analysis. All of these would be needed to conduct sample surveys of any size, but they become particularly crucial when sample surveys are to be conducted that cover more than a small neighborhood or small community. Specialization becomes absolutely essential when the surveys are to cover a large geographic area, such as a region or the nation as a whole.

It is still possible for the individual researcher or for a small group of researchers plus their acolyte graduate students to conduct sample surveys of institutionalized populations (e.g., the Freshman class at Michigan State University) or of odd at-hand types of universes (e.g., Flint, Michigan). Indeed, most of what passes for social research that gets into professional journals is based upon such odd universe research.[10]

It is no longer possible (indeed, if it ever was) for a social scientist to do anything more extensive without setting up at least an *ad hoc* bureaucratic apparatus of considerable size and complexity. The startup costs for a national survey are too great to be absorbed by a single survey alone; hence, only the specialized national survey organizations have the capability of undertaking them. For example, assembling materials and drawing an area probability of the United States would cost somewhere between $50,000 and $75,000. Hiring and training a national staff of interviewers (even if you employed persons who had previous interviewing experience) would cost somewhere around $50,000 additional. No single national survey can sustain those costs and such startup costs have to be spread out over a number of national surveys. Thus, the specialized national survey organization, in the form of research firms, has come into existence.

It is very significant that large scale survey research did not develop within universities but was grafted onto universities after it had passed through the critical periods of infancy. Thus, the National Opinion Research Center is still a separate corporation which affiliated itself to the

University of Chicago after it had become a going concern. Michigan's Survey Research Center was set up initially by a group of researchers who had worked together as a team running a survey research organization within the Department of Agriculture during World War II. Columbia's Bureau of Applied Social Research in its earlier manifestations had been the Office of Radio Research and had shuttled from Princeton to the University of Newark and occupied a very marginal status at Columbia until it was finally fully absorbed by the university in the middle fifties.

Developing a research firm — a large scale organization with an extensive division of labor — does not come naturally to a university department. Indeed, the principle of organization of a university department abhors all but the most minimal division of labor. Essentially an academic department is a collection of scholars whose work is only minimally integrated in a division of labor sense. Professors are required to teach courses, and these courses are supposed to be integrated in some sort of rational way to form a curriculum. But there is very little supervision over what is taught in courses or the way courses are taught, and most curricula remain plans which are implemented only vaguely.[11]

In American universities, departments do not engage in common scholarly enterprises in which a research task may be broken down into component tasks, each member taking a component as his contribution to a common research project.[12] Indeed, when an academician refers to the independence of academic life, he refers to the fact that once he has met his teaching obligations (over which he has a great deal of control, the amounts of which have been in a steep secular decline) he is free to pursue his own intellectual interests within the limits set by local production standards and the amount of research funds he is able to obtain from granting agencies. His presence on the campus is not taken for granted outside of teaching duties. At certain seasons of the year, when research review committees of the National Science Foundation and the National Institutes of Health are meeting in Washington D.C., a better set of academics than exists on the staff of any American university can be put together by routing visiting faculty members out of the hotels and motels in the D.C. area.

It is the independence of the academician and his reluctance to engage in an extensive division of labor which has led to the grafting onto university structures of research firms rather than attempting to impose a division of labor on existing departmental structures. Characteristically, research firms have "directors" while departments have "chairmen"[13] expressing in the titles of their chief administrative officers the greater authority of the one as compared with the other. Because of his greater authority the director is much more important to the functioning of a research firm than a chairman is to the functioning of a department, a large factor in the difficulty many departments now experience in finding someone who is willing to take over the chair.[14] A research firm functions best when its director provides both intellectual and administrative leadership, but a department functions best when its chairman knows how to sense departmental consensus, to summarize the consensus in policy and to guard the independence of individual members from encroachment by either university administration or students.

The radically different organizational principles of the research firm and the academic department lie at the root of the controversies that often characterize the relationships between such centers and the departments to which they are closely related intellectually. On the one hand, the departments regard the centers as potentially imperialist organizations, sopping up scarce resources, providing a haven for second rate personnel (no first rate person would submit himself to being part of a divison of labor), and generally accruing too much power. On the other hand, the research firm personnel often develop a stance which characterizes the academicians as amateurs and dilettantes in research, more concerned over guarding the worth of their status than with pursuing knowledge through research of the highest standards.

There is little doubt that being a professor is more prestigious than being a researcher. Tenure — that mysterious state of grace into which a professor is elected by his colleagues in ceremonies only more guarded in secrecy by the election of popes and from which he can fail only by committing crimes of the most revolting character — has not generally been extended to research firm personnel except at the highest levels. Tenure is the source of the greater institutionalized charisma of the faculty. Researchers have generally been paid more — at least as far as salary is concerned. But professors have sources of income from outside sources. One of my former colleagues used to boast (somewhat vulgarly) that he paid his income tax with his university salary. Thus it is not clear that the researchers employed by research firms have a greater income, although it does seem that their salaries are greater, especially in the early stages of career lines.

The cadre of professionals, technicians, and clerks that make up a research firm constitute an expensive apparatus with a constant if not growing appetite for funds. To keep a national survey center going at a level of activity which is a minimum for the maintenance of survey quality requires an annual budget of close to two million dollars. This level of funding would provide that there is sufficient field work to retain a sampling staff, provide work for interviewers (so that they do not drift into some other part-time activity) and keep the staff occupied. This funding exigency is a source of one of the major problems of a survey center. Large scale surveys are expensive and there are few sources of funds to which one can turn for support. In effect, unless universities allocate continuing support, survey centers tend to become more and more closely tied to the needs of potential big clients. The big client of this historical period is the federal government and the major source of funding lies in the welfare and education branches. More surveys are being conducted on the problems of the poor than on almost any other topic at the moment.

The price of having a large scale survey center is the necessity to take on "projects" in order to keep the apparatus functioning at least at minimum levels of efficiency. The intellectual quality of applied research is not necessarily lower than that of "pure" research, but its prestige is lower. Hence the attractiveness of research firm positions to professional social scientists is less than that of academic positions. Were is not for marginal types of professionals — men who do not like to teach, women who are barred from the university because of nepotism rules, individuals who are over-age in grade, etc. — it would be difficult to staff such centers with any but less than first rate personnel. Indeed, it is often the contention of the departments that institute personnel are in fact less than first-rate and hence ought to be insulated from the department by being kept out of teaching, access to graduate students, etc.[15]

In an earlier article on a related topic,[16] significantly written while I was Director of the National Opinion Research Center, I referred to the practice of "robin-hooding," a term coined to cover the practice of smuggling "pure" research interests into applied research projects, sometimes with the connivance and knowledge of the clients but more often without their knowledge and informed consent. At the time, I was overly impressed by the opportunities "robin-hooding" appeared to present. In retrospect, it seems like a very inefficient way of pursuing a line of research interests, involving making many detours and following a very crooked line towards an objective.

It appears to me to be unlikely that research firms involving extensive divisions of labor will be started at other universities. The existing research firms are being converted to the patterns congenial to traditional university forms, as in the case of the Survey Research Center at Michigan or the

Bureau of Applied Social Research at Columbia or gradually being pushed out of the university as in the case of the National Opinion Research Center at Chicago. Both SRC and BASR look more like the minimal division of labor collection of almost equal status individuals than they used to. NORC's historically strong connections with the sociology department are presently very weak and seem unlikely to get stronger.

The future will undoubtedly see sample surveys be undertaken by academic personnel through subcontracting with either commerical or non-profit institutes connected only very vaguely with universities. The tensions between the groves of academe and the business firm-like structure of the large scale institute can be solved by decomposing the activities involved in large scale surveys into those parts which are mainly intellectual in character — survey design and analysis — and those which are mainly administrative in character — sampling and data collection.

Of course, the future may see the development of new research methods which may recapitulate the history of sample surveying. One can imagine, for example, the development of techniques for extending experimental designs into applications in the field, requiring an extensive division of labor, administrative apparatus, etc. Such a development might foster the establishment of one or two research firms whose problems, in relation to the universities they may be connected with, will resemble those of the survey centers of the recent past.

Lest the impression be left with the reader that these four types of research organizations represent the only ways in which is organized the social research of today, it should be borne in mind that there are many solo researchers who work by themselves or perhaps with one or two research assistants. Indeed the actual working groups within consortia and even research firms may, on closer inspection, turn out to be such solo or small groups of researchers working on particular projects and drawing upon the resources of the consortium or the research firm just as the solo researcher would draw upon the resources of any other service organization, like the library or the computer center.

There is much to be said for the solo researcher mode of research organization, particularly for those types of research in which an extensive division of labor is neither dictated by the logic of the research activity or the scope of the task involved. Indeed, a good case can be made for the purchase of research services, e.g., interviewing, coding, etc., from either commerical firms or large academic research firms, rather than setting up new research firms in order to meet the needs of particular research projects. The weight of hyperorganization has laid heavily upon research activities. Extensive organization is not a good substitute for intelligence and creativity, and although a whole may be more than the sum of its parts, it is not a great deal more. A social researcher of recognized competence and creativity who engages upon research which requires relatively little in the way of a division of labor may lose more than he gains from participation in either a consortium or a research firm.

Although the main concern of this paper is with the social research activities that take place within the academic context or at least on the periphery of the groves of academe, it should be recognized that there are other contexts within which social research is conducted which lie outside the university entirely. Research departments of government and private agencies constitute one such non-academic mode, as well as the separate research organizations either profit or non-profit, represented by organizations like the Educational Testing Service or the Stanford Research Institute. Whether by design, imitation, or accident of history the forms of organization of such non-academic research organizations tend to follow those we have discussed above.

Thus, the collegium is represented, for example, by the research committees of health and welfare councils being informal, non-working meetings of persons interested in sets of common problems. Consortia can be found in the basic research departments of organizations like the Educational Testing Service or may be represented by organizations like the Laboratory for Socio-environmental Studies of N.I.M.H. in which essentially autonomous individuals or small groups work on their own problems supported by the services of the larger organization.

But, the preferred mode of research organization is the research firm, with a Director of Research, his own staff, and a more or less integrated program of research. The best of research firms in the non-academic world produce research of considerable importance and stature: The National Merit Scholarship Corporation's research group has a list of research publications which would do honor to any academic department of educational sociology of psychology. Similar statements could be made about the research departments of the National Academy of Science, the National Research Committee which has turned out under Lindsey Harmon such excellent monographs using data from the national roster of scientific personnel. These are examples I have taken primarily from the fields in which I have had some interest. I am sure that other social scientists can find other examples.

The problems of such social research enterprises are considerable. For one thing, although salaries may be higher in such organizations, they have considerable difficulty attracting high level personnel. Mission oriented research is not as attractive to autonomy seeking social scientists as the freedom afforded within academic departments. Hence the non-academic research organizations, when they work well, tend to be manned by good researchers who happen to be on the margins of academia, women, men with Ph.D.'s from third and fourth rank universities, persons who are wedded for some particular reason to particular local communities, persons who abhor teaching, etc.

A second main problem is how to attain and sustain a critical mass of research personnel. There are few social researchers who are completely solitary workers. At minimum they need research assistants and usually someone with whom to talk about the research and with whom to plan a research endeavour. The single man research department is more than an anomaly; it is simply unworkable.

A third main problem is how to maintain sufficient control over the setting of research problems, the conduct of research, and the publication and dissemination of research findings. In large part, this is a political problem; research has to compete with other demands on funds. Mission oriented research can hardly be allowed to raise questions which might find the total enterprise of the sponsoring organization to be fatuous. Hence the best research enterprises tend to be walled off structurally from their parent organizations. Thus the Educational Testing Service's basic research operation is totally divorced organizationally from the operational side of ETS. Or, the Laboratory for Socio-environmental Studies of N.I.M.H. has little connection with the granting or other operations of the Institute, and is physically located some miles apart from the N.I.M.H. central offices.

The successes of such "captive" social research organizations in this era of short labor supply tend to be fragile and ephemeral. They flourish for a while, and then decline as the men who made them flourish and are enticed away by offers of more money or status, or both. Research budgets are among the first items to be cut back when agency funds are cut. No matter how objective agency administrators appear at the point of hiring researchers, they are still likely to panic when the research begins to cast doubt on the efficacy of the agency's operation.

For these reasons an operating agency is perhaps best advised to contract for research with an existing research firm rather than to start its own research organization. For the same amount of resources, ordinarily, better researchers and perhaps better research could be obtained through control over the conduct of research.

Toward a Philosophy of Social Research Organization

Social research organizations yield both gains and losses to participants. I have tried to indicate what some of the major positive and negative benefit flows are. Obviously the reason we set up research organizations is to obtain potential positive benefits. Similarly, when we dismantle an organization it is because the perceived costs outweigh the benefits, although it does appear that we continue organizations often long past the point when the flow turns from positive to negative.

A research organization, then, is worthwhile when it somehow augments the activities of individuals appreciably beyond what they can do on their own and when the costs of participation are smaller than the benefits. What are the conditions under which such a positive flow can be maintained?

To begin with, let us consider the circumstance under which costs are small. This is the case for the collegium: it uses up time, but hardly any other resources and in turn affects the major part of the individual social scientist's activities very little. It also does not augment the work of individual members by very much. Some may be inspired by discussion with colleagues to do things differently than they would have on their own, and some may enter into collaborative work that might not have occurred under other circumstances. But, by and large, the actual performance of research is untouched by such an organization. Note also that the costs of maintaining such an organization are borne fairly equally by its members, although the benefits may be unequally distributed. It is perhaps for this last reason that senior members of such groups tend to drift away, ostensibly under the pressure of other commitments, and that such groups are most successful when composed of equal age and equal status members.

Consortia of the usual level of complexity, involving primarily machinery for the equitable allocation of resources, e.g., a laboratory or the provision of clerical and administrative services, have a somewhat more durable existence. The benefits are clear, although limited, and the costs are slight. It is useful to be able to hand the administration of research grants over to some competent secretary and the director is not expected to supervise in any intensive way or to "coordinate" research activities. If such a research organization manages to obtain a director without too many ambitions and with a devotion to providing administrative services, benefits will be real although not very large. Problems arise when a director attempts to "direct" or impose too many meetings, or attempts to supervise research which staff members are conducting, or otherwise departs from an essentially supportive role.

The large scale research firms which promise the greatest potentials both for yielding large positive benefits and for imposing great costs on participants and their environments. A large scale center is at its best with a director of considerable intellectual stature and leadership ability. It is only when such a director is clearly a man of first rank stature that his supervision of research does not raise the hackles of pride on staff members. It is also under such conditions that the foreign relations of the research center, particularly its relations with academic departments, can be handled properly. It is this dependency on *charisma* which makes a large scale research center such a vulnerable organization, and so difficult to institutionalize. If one could be sure that a man you appoint as director has *charisma*, then large scale research centers would mushroom on every campus. But no one is trained for the role and can only be seen as properly fulfilling the role after he has taken the position itself. By definition *charisma* is a gift that can only be received by an individual, not earned through work or study.

Large scale research centers have another disability. They are extremely difficult to dismantle. The commitments to personnel are great. A research center can exist for years on applied research contracts of low intellectual yield. The momentum of a large scale organization is great and administrators abhor putting an end to anything that has a large gross income. Large scale research institutes never die: they just wither away intellectually.

The philosophy of research organization towards which this discussion is tending argues for the consortium as a better mode. The research firms are too risky. The collegia yield too low a return. A conservative research organization policy therefore favors the middle ground, with enough organization to make things somewhat easier, but not too much dependency on either the risks deriving from non-charismatic leadership or the weight or a bureaucracy that has to be fed on a month-to-month basis.

In the social research of today the efficiency of the consortium mode is enhanced by the development of organizations like NORC or commercial survey firms who are willing to undertake through subcontracts the very onerous task of gathering data through large scale surveys.

Similar contract services exist with respect to computer soft and hardware. These contract services make it possible for the solo or the small group of researchers to expand their research capabilities considerably without expanding their immediate research organizations.

NOTES TO THE CHAPTER

1. For a fascinating account of the beginnings of empirical social research in Germany centering around the *Verein für Sozial Politik*, in which Max Weber played an important role, see Anthony Oberschall, *Empirical Social Research in Germany, 1849-1914*, Basic Books, New York, 1965. A similar account of empirical research in France can be found in the doctoral dissertation of Terry N. Clark, *Empirical Social Research in France*, Columbia University, 1966.

2. The importance of the social and intellectual support provided by a group of professional peers can be seen most dramatically in the low attractiveness of work contexts in which the individual is the sole sociologist or social psychologist in the organization. Thus, research positions in medical schools, schools of public health, health and welfare agencies, in small liberal arts colleges, etc., suffer particular disabilities in recruiting social researchers when the organizations are unable to provide an environment which contains a sufficient number of social researchers to at least have the potential to provide a congenial professional peer environment.

3. The conflicts that may arise over division of resources are among the most important of the centrifugal forces in organized research. Indeed, it is almost always possible to detect when an organized research project is going poorly because this is the point at which hostility becomes generated among project members. A project going well has lots of resources (i.e., good data and interesting findings) to go around but one which is going poorly generates intense concern in individual members whether each will have a sufficient "cut" of the research findings to recoup the investments they have made in time and money. In one such project that I know of, project members began to lock up their computer runs to prevent other members of the project from "stealing" their findings!

4. The practice of "bulk budgeting" can help to create a very strong organization with a high level of participation by members. Thus, there is at least one university which allocates monies to its departments in lump sums to be divided among professorial salaries, staff salaries, stationery, etc., by the department itself. The Dean stated to me that this practice tended to result in either strengthening the hand of the department chairman enormously or in producing a very strong democratic organization within departments. The R & D Centers and Regional laboratories supported by the Office of Education enjoy (or suffer from) a modified form of bulk budgeting with much the same effects on the position of the Director and of staff members.

5. Of course, some granting agencies take a very different view, regarding with

some suspicion applications that come in from research organizations and giving preference to those submitted by individuals. The Russell Sage Foundation, for example, argues that an individual's grant is easier to evaluate than that of a research organization because in the latter case it is not clear who has drafted the proposal, who is really the principal investigator, and who will actually carry out the research involved.

6. An interesting and somewhat pathetic example of how an organization which was formed to maximize collegiality among social scientists and remains mainly to confer status is the Sociological Research Association. The Association was formed in the 1930's by a group of young sociologists mainly to foster the development of empirical social research. For reasons which are obscure to me, it restricted membership to 100 people, a device which made the Association a prestige conferring organization. The Association persists even now when its initial aims have largely been achieved — most sociologists if they do not engage in empirical research are at least in favor of it — and its membership consists largely of aging sociologists who meet once a year to hear usually unexciting papers read by one of its members after the usual hotel banquet dinner. The Sociological Research Association no longer is in the forefront of anything but persists to administer its *numerus clausus*, conferring status by membership but offering members hardly anything more.

7. Used with apologies to the inter-university consortium on political behavior, which on an inter-institutional basis is similar to what is meant here.

8. Indeed, this is one of the major reasons why some of the private foundations, notably Rockefeller and Carnegie stopped giving grants to institutions for the institutions to allocate among faculty and moved instead to grants given for specific projects.

9. I have used this term in the full realization that in the context of academia "firm" has the negative connotations of profit seeking and commercialism. Yet the term seems quite appropriate since their structures so closely resemble the business firms we are more familiar with.

10. Because the universes samples are not terribly relevant or maximally appropriate ones, most social research leaves much to be desired as far as generalizability is concerned. The limitation of coverage gives rise to bewilderingly contradictory findings, for after all, Flint, Michigan is not the United States nor does the Freshman class at Michigan State represent college Freshmen in the United States.

11. Indeed this is part of the reason why students are demonstrating such dissatisfaction with university teaching today. The division of labor within departments has deteriorated so far under the pressure of a labor market which has made relaxation of teaching duties one of the major means for attracting faculty that students are confronted with lackadaisical teaching in poorly planned courses within anarchic curricula.

12. In contrast, some European universities have maintained an internal rank system implying a division of labor in which senior men direct the work of junior

men. Nor was faculty autonomy always the case in American universities: The design of the Social Science Research Building at the University of Chicago provided for suites of offices in which a senior man (occupying the largest office) would be surrounded by his juniors (in smaller offices) with a common foyer to be shared by secretaries and research assistants. The architect designed the building in the 1920's to facilitate the division of labor that was then current in the social sciences.

13. Chief administrative officers of academic departments were not always named "chairmen." Nor were they always elected by their departments for limited terms as is predominantly the case today. The title used frequently a few decades ago was "head" and the office was often held for indefinite terms.

14. Chairman have little authority, much responsibility, and gain few "brownie" points for pursuing their tasks well. It is a nice post in which to put someone past his prime who needs a good excuse for not producing as much as he once did.

15. This problem has been "solved" for some of the applied laboratories in the physical sciences by establishing the laboratories at some physical distance from the campus. The Hopkins Applied Physics Laboratory is fifteen miles from the main campus. Lincoln Laboratories at MIT is some thirty miles away, and the Argonne National Laboratory connected with the University of Chicago is also far enough away to make easy moving from laboratory to campus difficult.

16. "Scholars, Researchers and Policy Makers: The Politics of Large Scale Research," *Daedalus*, **93**, 4, Fall 1964.

CHAPTER EIGHT

Reflections on the Organization of Social Research

MARVIN B. SUSSMAN

Peter Rossi in his paper, "Observations on the Organization of Social Research," does exactly what the title conveys to the reader. He has made a series of observations on the organization of social research. The result is many tantalizing notions about the organization and meaning of research but not in too much detail; he gives us breadth at the expense of depth. His descriptive analyses cover most organizational forms of research. Little attention is given to why these have come into existence and what are some of the obvious and not too obvious problems of each organizational form. There is some discussion of the genesis of research organizations, but his approach almost automatically excludes a systematic in-depth analysis of each form; how it began, its structure, basic research activities, and the problems it has in maintaining its own organizational system over time.

Another difficulty, and to some extent a limitation of this paper, is that Professor Rossi poses a rational-economic model in explaining the genesis of research organizations and their operations. The rational model has an economic motif with efficiency in activities and production of data its most salient objectives. The rhetoric of the rational model as stated by Professor Rossi is, "Obviously the reason we set up research organizations is to obtain potential positive benefits." . . . "A research organization then is worthwhile when it somehow augments the activities of individuals appreciably beyond what they can do on their own and when the costs of participation are smaller than the benefits."[1] Research organizations do not necessarily come into being because of rational considerations or are judged to be worthwhile because they produce quality data. It is likely that a number of research organizations have come into existence because of the idiosyncratic, philosophical and ideological meanderings of individuals who possessed a strong urge for power in academic circles. Also, the judgment of the worthwhileness of a research organization may be less because it helps the individual academic obtain quality data beyond which he can undertake research on his own, but more because the client who pays the bill likes the product, it is a "smash" — good P.R. for the company, foundation or sponsoring government agency. Also the client "guides" the research organization in the selection of the problems to be investigated by enticing a sufficient number of entrepreneurial leaders of the research organization to go along with the co-option. The "rank and file" have to go along knowing where their bread is buttered with the hope that they can "bootleg" respectable academic research. A rational approach to organizational development does not occur universally in a world which is not completely rational.

My tasks in this paper are to add to the observations made by Peter Rossi about the organization of research groups; analyze and comment on some of his descriptions; and discuss a number of the non-rational factors which influence the origin and operations of research organizations.

Professor Rossi describes a variety of research organizations which range from the collegia — "brown bag" group — to the research firm. He provides a variety of reasons why each type of research organization has come into existence with cost, efficiency, and the needs of the academic researcher as a consequence of a division of labor the most salient ones. One variation of this perspective is that the division of labor in research as we now know it today has come about as a consequence of the general increase in the differentiation of functions in our society and not necessarily because of particular needs of academic researchers. With a continuous increase in bodies of knowledge, occupational roles and expertise in societies of progressing complexity, one could predict the division of labor in research activity as one would predict specialization in any other area of work.

Related to this perspective is the place of the research organization in the educational enterprise. What appears to be overlooked in most analyses of the beginnings and structure of research organizations in the social sciences is that interests in research stem not only from a concern to add to the body of scientific knowledge but also to improve the quality of teaching and learning through research. Educational institutions, which have been for the most part the mothers of research organizations, are in the business of education. This means students, training, courses, seminars, theses, dissertations, examinations, degrees and so forth. Given this traditional function of the university, namely, that it has students and that professors do teach, one can postulate that the varieties of research organizations that have come into existence have been equally motivated by the desire to fulfill this long-staid objective as well as the one of adding to the body of scientific knowledge.

The creation of a collegia, consortium, institute, or research firm was the consequence of making the educational enterprise more vital and perhaps, at least initially, more solvent. For reasons well stated by Professor Rossi, the educational systems which sponsor such institutes found that these could be used to attract and even keep bright faculty and become a source of major funding for research and the training of students. With the increase in graduate training facilities in the United States since World War II the research component of any budget of an educational enterprise varies from twenty to eighty per cent. Major universities like Yale and Harvard expend approximately fifty per cent of their annual budget for research and most of this money comes from government sources. Funding of today's university requires continuous sources of monies for research and training and pedagogical concepts which integrate the learning and research processes within the educational enterprise.

Research organizations to date have made no determined effort to integrate their objectives with those of the educational enterprise considering the fact that the training of new generations of students for research or other purposes is a shared aim. The economic model with its profit-and-loss principle, used by most research organizations in developing their structure and in carrying out research activities, has been the greatest deterrent to creative and integrative endeavors with the educational institution. The structural constraints imposed by this model are so severe that few eclectic and imaginative leaders of research organizations are able to undertake experiments in training or integrate in any systematic, consistent, and continuous fashion academic training in the university with their research activities. Such experiments are costly ventures and require back-up funds from university or non-research activities. Research organizations, even those which are considered respectable and quality data producing ones such as the Survey Research Center at the University of Michigan or NORC at the University of Chicago, have functioned with a profit-loss balance sheet in mind. Running in the red is not an unusual phenomenon but university "hard" money is seldom used to make up any deficit. Another grant from a benefactor, client, foundation or government agency is the temporary solution, and deficit funding becomes a way of life. For some research firms overhead charges, field costs, and data processing charges are contracted for very much like any other commercial activity such as building a battleship or a rocket that will send man into outer space. A few of these research organizations have "made it," own their building and real estate, have endowment, and send their staff to international conclaves.

Most research organizations are less fortunate. My impression is that in order to justify their formation most presented an argument of self-sufficiency as a way of obtaining the freedom to form an organization. Consequently few money, space, or staff commitments were obtained from the educational enterprise. Perhaps, an even more important deficit was the lack of integration with the objectives of the educational institution. Side by side the research organization and educational enterprise exist, and the mix which occurs is more of a consequence of fortuitous circumstances rather than planning for a learning experience.

It would be unfair to state that all forms of research organizations are unrelated to the needs and interests of the educational enterprise. Since most begin within an educational system of some kind there are generic relationships which are not easily eliminated but do become eroded in time. I suspect that any study of the history and development of research organizations in the United States would indicate an evolutionary pattern of development. Those which started out as collegia very closely related to the educational enterprise evolve through time into bureaucratic and monolithic types of structures. Today this conglomerate of research structures which vary in size, resources, and output are minimally involved with the educational enterprise even though they are structurally part of it.

One alternative explanation regarding the beginnings of research organizations is that many began unplanned, and rational explanations and procedures were imposed at a later time to meet the demands of the marketplace. I have no hard evidence to support this assumption but my familiarity with a number of research organizations and some of their functionaries provides comfort to this notion that the genesis of formalized research activity was more idiosyncratic than planned development. History will record that under the aegis of academic freedom some individuals stepped forth to build research empires which would give them· power, prestige, and status not only in the profession but within their own university. The colloquial expression "money talks" is more than an amusing mouthing. Money has guided the founding of all educational enterprises. In the 18th century the now famous college at New Haven, Connecticut, was named after a benefactor who endowed it with a few hundred English pounds. It is quite common in 1970 for a college to advertise that it would rename itself if a donor provided five million dollars.

Administrators long were knowledgeable in the language of money and the art of grantsmanship. They responded to the untapped rich source of research funding and for some academics with entrepreneural inclinations the alliance was made. It did not take very long to discover that the academic marketplace was as responsive or even more so to profit, gain, and payoff than was the garment industry of New York. Some of the new breed of researcher-developer academics were able to circumvent the normal steps of the career line to professional prominence by moving into the research-administrator role with control over funds, data sources, and publication priorities. With differentiation of functions within the research organization, it has become increasingly difficult to determine who are the scholars and the specific intellectual contribution made by each participant. Determining the individual contribution to creative scholarship and knowledge is so central to the evaluation procedures of the academic enterprise that the advent of the research organization and its "protection" of the individual through representation of the collectivity requires establishing new criteria for the character, levels, and rewards of the academic ladder.[2]

The possibilities of relating organized research activity to the learning process and the training of students is so intriguing that I have often wondered why this has never been done even as a federally financed demonstration. For example, one objective could be to train cadres of comparative cross-cultural family researchers on the doctoral level who will be able to undertake with other colleagues research on family-organizational relationships in societies at different levels of modernity and undergoing different rates of change. The specific theoretical or substantive focus of the training program is not relevant to this discussion and is used only to illustrate a number of possible training and learning experiences.

The major themes of such training are *learning by doing* and intensive *intellectual and social interaction* during the period of experience and study. Assuming that training is equally important with research, one can experiment with a number of structures which may achieve the training objective without impairing the research outcome. Three types of structures are:

1. *Peer Group Research Team*

A team of researchers, students, and theoreticians functioning as coequals organized around a conceptual problem, developing its theoretical dimensions and then pursuing all necessary steps: field operations, interpretation of data, write-up of findings, and final report.

2. *Master-Apprentices Research Team*

A research team is organized around the talents of a "great man," similar to postgraduate training in architecture or law (entering the firm). The team focuses on a single problem, from its initial conceptualization to its solution; from theoretical formulation to empirical testing, data processing and analysis, and report. The project is of limited duration and phased for each step of the process — initiation to completion. Team members are heterogeneous in skills, experience, intelligence, sex, age, and are located in a central work place.

3. *Bench Experience*

This type of training incorporates a learning-and-doing approach; it stresses a one-to-one relationship between learner and teacher. One distinguishing feature of this model is a deliberate attempt to *match* learner and teacher in relation to reciprocal interests and potential payoffs and to insist on practical experience, exposure, and study of behavioral science issues and problems. I liken this training to the craftsman's model, my own experience in becoming a skilled watchmaker. Apprenticed to a master, I learned how to turn a pivot, make teeth in a wheel, and replenish worn-out bushings — a process of learning by doing and applying theoretical knowledge.

Other types of training arrangements can be developed and tried for their efficacy in meeting the goal of a well trained research behavioral scientist without compromising the quality of the research product.

Very few academics will dissent with Professor Rossi's analysis of internal gains derived from the activities of different research organizations. These include provision of legitimate access of faculty members to one another; colleageality; equity in the distribution of resources; efficiencies in the division of labor, meeting research commitments at reasonable deadlines; and providing at very low cost an abundance of data to younger colleagues in the department who are "hell-bent on making a reputation for themselves in the field." These advantages are forthcoming where there exists a strong academic department made up mostly of doctorates pursuing a "steady" career line and located in a stable university. The structure of universities and departments is in transition; work settings are unstable and many departments because of shortages of trained personnel and community demands have made non-Ph.D. appointments; in a few instances these appointees have not even completed high school, and consequently do not have the academic preparation or interest to enjoy internal gains from research activity. Even the hard-nosed research-oriented universities and departments are bending toward social action programs and academics are increasingly taking on roles as social change agents.

Community-based research is involving non-academic personnel; safari-type research is a thing of the past. Also target populations in urban environments want some sort of payoff for the time consumed by being researched. In some sections of the country the working classes and the poor have formed into client organizations so that when research outfits want to interview individuals the base charge is $25 an hour for a standard survey questionnaire and additional charges are made if probing in depth is required. This reported Los Angeles example may be exaggerated but it typifies the growing revolt of the research client and the demand for closer integration of university practices and the needs of the populace.

Given the changing structure of the community, university, and academic departments and roles, one of the potential uses of the research organization is obtaining data for policy making and social action. The organized research outfit has the mechanisms and means to respond quickly to the information demands of community action and governing bodies. It has the promise to deliver on time facts upon which changes in policy can be based with consequential modifications in political, community, and organizational structures and programs.

The conflict between the needs and purposes of the research organization and those of the educational enterprise is left unresolved by Professor Rossi. Such a solution is not one of the major objectives of this paper. But the fact remains that this conflict does exist and few individuals have come forth with solutions for reducing the conflict by developing an organizational structure that would satisfy both parties. This development may be an impossibility. We have already indicated the research organization is based on an economic model complete with a division of labor, accountability, and some means for evaluating its product. The academic department, which is the traditional unit of organization of the university, functions more under a service than an economic orientation. Professors and, increasingly, students behave under the aegis of autonomy and there are few socially acceptable placeboes to evaluate the product, the learned man. There is a client-centered focus in academia but this is becoming distorted over time for a more visible product, publications, honoraria, consultantships, and so forth while the rhetoric is that "students are the most important product." Given these two different types of organizational structures, purposes, history, tradition, and origins, is it at all possible to develop a new work structure that would integrate and harmonize these disparities and yet serve the interests of both?

Dr. Rossi's discussion of a philosophy of social research organizations is much more one on a feasible organizational structure that will work to the benefit of the academic and the client rather than with a philosophical approach to research organization. He believes that a large-scale research organization is the one most likely to meet the needs of the majority of individual or team researchers operating in educational and other work systems. Furthermore, the large-scale research firm can function at maximum efficiency if it can obtain and hold as its director a person with charisma who is followed and obeyed and does not function as an executive director over countless board meetings. Research is learning by doing and somebody must provide the leadership for the doers. The head of the research firm has responsibility for the well being of his staff and clients, and accompanying this responsibility there must be authority. This may not be Professor Rossi's philosophy but at least this is my interpretation of it. He believes that large research firms such as NORC can provide data gathering and analysis services to individual and team researchers. Problem formulation and sophisticated theoretical analysis should not be excluded from such a repertoire if "the price is right." Clients can pool financial resources and use NORC's organizational structure for these services.

Two observations can be made regarding this philosophical posture. First, there is not too much philosophy in what Dr. Rossi presents, and second, it is highly questionable whether NORC or any other research organization can provide the multiple research services required by behavioral scientists in their study of a large variety of problems each one requiring different research designs, methodologies, and techniques.

Problems which lend themselves to a survey analysis approach may be handled very satisfactorily by large research firms. Individuals and teams of investigators will pool their financial resources and buy some time of a fielded national survey. This may be a workable solution. As a past user of such services I am concerned about the biasing effects caused by the diversity of questions employed in order to satisfy objectives of the three or four individual users who make up the usual *ad hoc* survey.

Theoretical problems requiring observations and depth analysis in order to get at processes, mechanisms, causality, change over time, and the like are not easily obtained through the standard survey approach. The training requirements for researchers on these conceptual and technical levels are so great that very few research organizations have individuals in sufficient numbers stationed around the country in sampling points to undertake a national study requiring the use of non-survey techniques.

An approach toward a philosophy of research organization would begin first by asking what are the types of problems behavioral scientists are currently researching and what is the appropriate mix of research design and methodologies required to study these problems? One would begin on the conceptual level of problem formulation and development and then see what is the required research design and methodology and the appropriate organizational structure to undertake the study. Problem analysis of this kind may lead the individual to devise new research structures other than those which exist today. One such form of research structure would be characterized by flexibility and would be time-limited for the specific purposes of undertaking investigation of a single problem. For example, if the research problem was concerned with the structure and activities of linkage systems, especially those which relate members of the family to bureaucratic organizations in societies of growing complexity, one could form a research organization of limited duration within the continental United States to study this problem in various regions and then temporary structures would be created to do comparative cross-cultural analysis involving research teams from different societies. Research operations would be locally based as they are in most national surveys conducted by research firms or academics located in educational institutions. These locales would have responsibility for the training and directing of field operations in their respective regions. If research firms like NORC or the Survey Research Center are willing to provide consultant services and help in technical areas such as sampling and computer operations, such services could be purchased by this *ad hoc* research organization. Once the research was completed the *ad hoc* organization would go out of business. The reason for forming this flexible and temporary investigative structure is that the study of linkages would require not only intensive interviewing but also observations of family members' participation in interstitial structures such as voluntary organizations. The conducting of quasi-experiments on how family members handle bureaucratic organizations may be required. Also of interest is how family members are socialized for competence in handling the normative demands of bureaucratic organizations. They may call for in-depth observations over time. The intensive data collection on socialization processes and linkage behavior requires the kind of supervision of interviewers and observers which is not normally available or necessary under ordinary survey conditions. The *ad hoc* organization which can employ a variety of skills from its repertoire at different times and under varied conditions is most likely to achieve multiple objectives of causality, descriptive analysis, and hypotheses testing.

Also an *ad hoc* organizational structure is more in harmony with the autonomy stance of the academic investigator. The professor is much more than a user of commercially bought data. There is the possibility that his involvement also will mean commitment to the theoretical development of the research problem as well as to the completion of the data processing, analysis, and report. In being an active participant in the research process he is likely to become more understanding and sensitized to the problem he is investigating and much more concerned about a successful outcome. Consequently, I can foresee the development of research organizations of this type that may have an indefinite life from a few months to twenty years. This type of organizational structure has its own problems, namely, providing comparative data and handling the problems of terminological and conceptual equivalence, priorities of investigators and overdeveloped egos. Another critical problem is getting each member to actively participate and do his share of the work. However, as with every type of research organization there are problems, advantages, and disadvantages.

In the last analysis, as Professor Rossi points out, one has to weigh the social and economic costs. I am merely suggesting that any philosophical approach to the organization of a research enterprise should take into account the nature of the problems to be studied and should shape the research structure around the problems rather than having those problems studied because of the internal maintenance needs of the research organization.

NOTES TO THE CHAPTER

1. Peter Rossi, *Observations on the Organization of Social Research.*
2. Group authorship of publications is more prevalent today than thirty years ago. Also heard more frequently in the gossip network of the professional association is the charge that the "super" or P.I. who had nothing to do with the research has taken "a piece of the action" or published it all under his name relegating the deserving to the "*et al.*" category.

THE MANAGEMENT AND
TACTICS OF RESEARCH

CHAPTER NINE

The Management and Tactics of Research

EDGAR F. BORGATTA

It is difficult to discuss the managerial and tactical problems of research without having reference to the total research process. The design of research and how it is administered is intimately associated with the problems of data collection. Indeed, the design of the research also is intimately tied to the analysis.

Research on social action programs, whether they be specific medical programs in a single institution or more general implementation of policy in every community, requires a reasonable specification of the part that the research itself has in the action program. The formal requirements for the research obviously limit what can be carried out. If the research is an afterthought when a new program is being started, and essentially may be defined as "window dressing" that is added on because it is the thing to do, then the research may have little or no potential for payoff. The researcher working under these circumstances may find that data collection for the research as he visualizes it is incompatible with the situation; he may find that he has no authority, that the research is viewed by those in authority as being disruptive and a nuisance, and that the only feasible designs possible under the circumstances may not articulate at all with the stated objectives of the evaluative research.

The above statement clearly suggests that a *pro forma* indication that evaluation will be carried out is not necessarily consistent with carrying out an evaluation. Having fixed a program of social action, a direction to carry out evaluative research may involve so many constraints as to be impossible. What can be done under the circumstances may be some descriptive work which will not permit evaluation in any direct sense. If evaluative research is to be carried out, it has to be carried out in spite of the mandate of the program and possibly in violation of it. So, a situation may be defined where there is a request for evaluation of whether or not the program is effective; then all that is permitted is to find out whether or not the agency is satisfied with the program, the clients are satisfied with the program, the public is satisfied with the program, possible comparison to other situations, and so forth. Actual evaluation may not be involved at all.

The reason emphasis is placed on such circumstances is that they are frequently encountered in evaluative research, and thus attention is directed toward management of research and collection of appropriate data under such circumstances.

The answer required appears to be the realistic one. It just cannot be done, and to attempt it is merely to fly in the face of reality. Still, it is also a matter of reality that public and private agencies will continue to request evaluative research under these circumstances, and if there is money available, organizations will contract to do the work, whatever it may turn out to be.

The management of data collection requires an intimate relationship of the research design with the program that is being evaluated. Criteria for effectiveness must be stated. There must be some criterion, a limited objective that can be specified quite directly. Or, there may be a single objective that is defined quite diffusely, with little precision, as in the types of concepts one frequently encounters in our philosophically oriented essays, such as: improving the lot of man, or enriching the life of the poor, or some similar euphemism. In the latter case, as soon as the research explorations reach a point of asking for indicators of when these global criteria would be noticeably changed, there arises a specification of subcriteria or multiple criteria. Then, there may be specification that if this improves, and this improves, and this improves, or if these improve, and other things do not worsen, then there would be an indication that improvement had occurred. From the procedure of examining the criteria of improvement the specifications of the research design are shaped. The types of controls and comparisons that are to be made can be specified and provision built into the research design. This procedure raises many questions if carried out aptly; and if the questions are properly explored in advance, the research has potential for providing interpretable results.

If the process is not carried out in advance, however, unless unusual circumstances of skill and good fortune coincide, the research may be worth about as much as the planning that went into it.

If a program has been in existence, and changes are projected, even if there are no possibilities of a direct control group design, evaluative research may be feasible. For example, the medical model of experimentation with new drugs or procedures frequently uses the baseline of previous experience as the implicit control group. So, agencies or programs may be described at a given point in time, and examination can be carried out subsequently when changes in the program have been instituted. But, the essential point is that in the description of the program both before and after the changes instituted, the research must gather information relevant to the criteria of evaluation. Indeed, looking at this model it is possible to see that the notion of a single evaluation may not be appropriate, and what may yield more information in the long run is a type of sequential contact where the criteria of effectiveness are measured successively in time. The importance of such a generalization is that the changes instituted in a program in such a design may not be the "cause" of an improvement; but merely the fact that a change has been described that is expected to improve the situation may have the consequences in the responses of the persons involved, both agency, client, and the observing public. A procedure that involves successive assessments would indicate whether or not such improvements dissipate with time, which would be a hypothesis relating to the fact of change rather than the changes themselves. Additionally, such successive assessments may also yield knowledge about other factors that are involved that may be correlated with high and low performance on the criteria. Conceivably, seasonable variations, annual variations, and other periodic phenomena may be involved that have nothing to do with the pre- and post-observation and the hypotheses related to the ameliorative input.

Thus, the effective design of research requires an intimate relationship between data collection and the management of the program itself. If the right kinds of records are kept in the agency or program, the basic descriptive research noted thus far could be automatic. It would appear that a fantastic amount of generalizable information is lost because research is not built into agency and program data collection. In fact, to the contrary, one has to marvel at the amount of relatively irrelevant information that is collected and accumulated. Consider, for example, the endless quantities of personalized caseworker notes, essentially unsystematic descriptions, that get buried each year. This production may well be compared to a relative paucity of standardized information and the frequent inaccuracy and inconsistency of even the background characteristics of clients in such agencies. More remarkable, even in publicly supported agencies where the information is supposed to be kept for control of processes, records are often in poor shape with irregular reporting. The essential point, however, is that appropriate data collection in any agency or program may have more descriptive value. While consequences of given events may not be definitively found in such data, at least some objective basis for speculation can be provided.

With regard to management of data collection in such circumstances, research objectives are only one of the values served, and so only one of the determining factors. As noted, some pieces of information may be required for the implementation of the program itself, and others may be required because administrators or others in the system think it is important. Research oriented data collection can only be maintained if the responsibility essentially resides with the designated research authority.

The last assertion leads to a question in data collection that is indeed a problem of management, or of the development of techniques to be built into a system. How do the researchers know that the data are being collected systematically, accurately, and with a high degree of completion? Obviously, check systems have to exist in order to guarantee that data are collected in a usable fashion. There is a low level but very general belief that research forms somehow get filled out adequately, even if nobody pays attention to the process. The fact of the matter as we have asserted earlier is that in general even under rigid systems of supervised data collection, incompletion is a serious problem. The management of research requires that there be an early check system to examine the completeness of forms, whether these are arbitrary background gathering forms or complex ones in the areas of social and psychological factors. If check systems are not instituted at an early point, problems tend to accumulate. Time generates many of these problems in the following ways: If incompletions are frequent in forms, attempting to correct the incompletions after many forms have accumulated may become an overwhelming job. Early attention to the problem may cause correction immediately as those administering the forms get the feedback on what things need to be checked and how instructions should be given. In other words, original data collection procedures may be modified. If forms are collected in sequence, as, for example, in weekly contact periods, if the checking does not occur between the contacts, information may be gathered that is virtually meaningless since reconstructing it extends beyond the last contact. Additionally, the seriousness of purpose in data collection comes under question if incompletions and sloppy procedures are tolerated. Assuming that the researcher has control over the processes and has participated in the planning of the research, then, there should be ample attention given to the checking of the process of data collection. Indeed, long-time observation of data collection agencies, including the survey research agencies, seems to suggest that this type of investment for the management of data collection is vital. Cost factors are always to be considered in the design of research, but the research can hardly be better than the data collection, and this is not a matter that can be left to the good will and training of the persons having the primary contact with the data source. Interviewers, clerks, and others must have supervisory completion checks built into the system, especially if there are large numbers of persons involved. Paranoia about truth in research is one of the essential canons. It may be stated as follows: never trust anyone, not the machine, and certainly not yourself; all are subject to error and inadequacy.

The comments thus far imply that systematic data collection providing descriptive but objective information about an agency or program has value. From the point of view of generalization, however, the value may be extremely limited. Is the agency or program representative of a class of programs? Unless there is some confidence that this is the case, each such research becomes a case history, often detached and uninterpretable in terms of other case histories. The question of management of research and data collection cannot be detached from the objectives of the research itself. If the research is too institutional and local to provide kinds of information that the administrators in the agency, granting agency, or others specifically request, this can be accomplished, but the ultimate appropriateness of the goals should be questioned if there is an implication that this is evaluative research. Case histories, even when data are systematically gathered, are not a substitute for more generally conceived evaluation researches; nor are they a substitute for descriptive researches, if one is attempting to generalize to a class of agencies or programs. The unit of sampling must be considered, and if the agency or program is the unit, then there must be a sufficient quantity of units in order to provide generalization to a population that is projected. Again, with the management of research as the crucial question, in order for this to be feasible, the research must dictate the sampling and data collection, and if this is not possible, for all practical purposes the research cannot be carried out. It is one thing to say that researchers have to be tactful, appreciative of local problems, able to attract support of practitioners, and so forth, and to say that they must depend entirely on the good will of cooperating agencies and persons. Cooperation by agencies on a self-selective basis just is not equivalent to a concept of sampling. While some researchers have done heroic jobs under poor circumstances, it appears improper to suggest this as a mode of operation when the inadequacy and the futility of research collected under unfavorable circumstances is so well-known. Here I may interject the personal note that I have advised a large number of agencies over the years *not* to attempt to do research because their resources were inadequate and their facilities, numerically and substantively speaking, would be insignificant for possible generalization to the field as a whole. Under these circumstances self-interest in the process involved certainly is to be lauded and encouraged, but this is different from the delusion that one is doing evaluative research with some potential for generalization.

One implication of the above is that much attention to evaluative research may be misguided, when the program or the agency as a whole is the unit to be investigated. It may be that a concept of administrative or area research will need to supplant research that is agency oriented. However, if agencies are autonomous or only loosely federated, or if agencies are participating in research programs only on a voluntary basis, very little may turn out to be feasible. Experience seems to dictate that agencies cooperate very poorly when a research requires effort on their part. They always raise questions, salient ones for the agency, about who is going to absorb the cost, what the meaningfulness of the results will be for the agency, and since data collection procedures introduced into an agency situation may alter the work patterns of professionals, even under conditions of committed research participation, coercive measures for compliance to research are rarely undertaken.

In government-type researches, similar problems exist. Administratively, conceivably, research designs running through many agencies might be developed. With what expectation would they be carried out if they involved concepts of uniform conditions of data collection? There are some government agencies that have many unit offices where the unit could be the basis of "administratively controlled" research, but I am not sure that any of these units are in the areas of interest with which we are concerned. For example, I have in mind that county ACS offices have small and well-defined personnel structures that replicate, but the concerns of these units tend to maintain rigidly defined service contact with the population, and the hierarchy of statuses of the personnel do not lend themselves to high professionalization.

It is fair to ask at this point what many of the considerations mentioned have to do with the management and tactics of research. Particularly with data collection, the point that is being emphasized is that a researcher who enters a situation where he cannot control the processes of data collection has made his first and most serious error. Practical and tactical questions that are directed toward solving the day-to-day research problems, like how to find a subject after so many calls are made, or how to make sure that the person who is collecting the data is really doing so, pale in comparison to the complete frustration which results from not being able to do the research because one cannot do so for lack of authority.

*   *   *

It is appropriate to give a little attention to a matter of tactics in data collection. Possibly here one has to suggest that the word *tactics* be given a little bit of analysis, at least by implication, in order to proceed. Here it is worth suggesting that the word tactics implies that data collection may be viewed as a battle, or at least as a manipulative situation where it might be good to have Machiavelli as an ancestor. I am inclined to think of tactics as a *post hoc* judgment that if someone tries a procedure when things seem to be going wrong and it works, then he used tactics. But, possibly more can be said than this. Let us use an example. In a recent survey which involved being on a number of college campuses, the researchers contacted the administrations of the colleges and universities and requested cooperation in data collection. The subject matter of the research was sex, sometimes judged delicate and sensitive as a topic, and for this reason cooperation was seen as important in the design. Somewhat to the surprise of the researchers, one very distinguished university refused to cooperate, and the question was, "What do we do now?" The advice given to the researchers, and this I think may be judged as a matter of tactics, was to write to the university saying that the researchers regretted that the university could not cooperate because such cooperation facilitates the carrying out of the research. For example, it makes it possible to centralize the place where interviews are held, it avoids questions and misinformation being addressed to administrators at the university that they cannot answer because they are not informed of the research going on, and it facilitates the research task because it makes it possible to avoid all the additional contacts that are required since many students want to volunteer participation in the research, and the research design is one of a probability sample. Needless to say, the research was carried out and no difficulty was encountered. The tactics here were relatively simple and involved merely the simple analysis of the power structures involved and a judgment that the university could not prevent the data collection.

The use of this example is instructive for other reasons. It is very difficult to speak of tactics in general. Frequently when one speaks of tactics, concern is directed to the nitty gritty of how one gets the data collected under circumstances that appear to be unfavorable. Tactics in a social agency with regard to data collection may focus on the professional involvement and avoidance of development of defensive reactions on the part of professional workers. This may be accomplished in many ways, and persons experienced in these areas can give much advice for a particular research project. For example, social workers have an image of what they are doing that sometimes tends to be circumscribed by a language that has developed in the profession. In certain circumstances they may be suspicious that researchers are not interested in doing research that will involve those facets of an agency program that they consider to be important. One may call it a matter of tactics for the researchers to explore in detail the concerns of the social workers and build these into the research, or one can say more simply that this is a responsibility of the researcher. The essential point is that social workers and researchers may not be at cross purposes at all, and a wrong tactic can certainly be identified of having researchers arrive with preconceived notions that social workers are incompetent to communicate what concerns them and what may be important in an agency setting. As a matter of relating the nitty gritty of research in these circumstances, a practical rule is to build into the research those things that researchers consider essential, but to also build in those that are of concern to the social workers. This may take some investment in preliminary meetings, discussion of pilot and preliminary forms, and other investments that are familiar to experienced researchers. It also may require collection of types of data that actually do not get treated for various reasons. For example, in a research in which data were collected on evaluations of case interviews, forms were devised that involved aspects of the interview that the researchers abstracted from the literature of social interaction, interviewing, and other related areas. Then, the types of information to be collected were discussed with social workers in group meetings. The forms were tested and sequentially revised in response to contacts with social workers.

Eventually, a relatively limited list of things to be evaluated after an interview was compiled. The forms were highly acceptable to the social workers and the language used was compatible with their professional language. Still, at the time an emphasis existed in the social work profession to suspect checklists of such descriptive evaluations. From the point of view of the researchers, the checklists were essential because in the nature of the research that was being conducted a constant stimulus response was required over a long series of possible contacts for the social worker. Information on each aspect had to be gotten at each contact. From the point of view of the social worker, however, the professional stance suggested that this type of summarization was simplistic and not sufficiently indicative of the processes involved, even after the social workers had involved themselves in the process of trying to abstract the essentials of the interview situation. For the researchers, the criterion of efficiency of individual data collection was a most important problem, since the researchers were not unsophisticated and knew that an appropriate design would have to anticipate the human failing of avoidance of burdensome tasks. So, the checklist part of the data collection was designed to take approximately four to five minutes for completion. Then, in order to provide for the residual concerns of the social workers, space was provided for additional comments and elaboration. The matter of tactics here is about as follows. The researchers could have insisted on not having this section of the form because it would be burdensome and time consuming. The tactical decision was to put it in, and to see what would happen. What happened was what the researchers anticipated. Virtually no social workers used the additional space and provided comments. It might be remarked further that after they had experienced the form, those few who were asked about this said that with use they felt that the forms indeed did cover the major aspects of the process they were concerned with. The data thus collected through the burdensome comment — or not collected — provided no difficulty for the researchers subsequently.

*   *   *

We may now begin to make the transition to questions of the management and tactics of research with reference to data analysis. Here an early question that must be answered is: "What kind of findings were expected from the research?" If a simple experimental design has been involved, the analysis may also be extremely simple. Indeed, the more rigorous the experimental design with regard to the ideals usually stated, the simpler the task of analysis, as it is completely dictated by the design. Data may be organized for an analysis of variance. Less than complete satisfaction of the ideal may lead to using other techniques. For example, if there is reason to suspect that in spite of application of the random sampling procedures the groups differ, and the ways in which the groups differ initially are considered important, a covariance model may be appropriate. With further weakening of the designs, the application of statistical procedures becomes less precise and interpretation becomes more speculative and loosely based. Even if "findings" occur, they must be suspect on the grounds that the ideal model of the experimental design showed weakness.

The clarity with which objectives have been set and a reasonable structure for fulfilling the objectives has been provided bears directly upon the problem of management of data analysis. The horror that often faces researchers at this stage is how to manage incomplete information on the one hand, and what to do with information gathered for which no service was specified in advance. The first set of problems deals with how the data have been collected. Here the researcher has to begin at the point of analysis with whatever data he has collected and rarely can he go back and get that which has been left out. From the point of view of completion, the obvious problem of analysis is that incompletions are not necessarily distributed randomly, and it may indeed be that there are important selective factors in non-reports. With non-report cases, at best what can be hinted at is that they may be important and that selective factors may be demonstrated, but the relationships that would have been involved cannot be produced. So, the management of data analysis is intimately tied to the management of data collection. Failure at one point leads almost inevitably to failure at another.

The problem of incomplete data is not independent of the problem of handling open-ended responses. Those who like open-ended interviews using a skeleton schedule may think they are approaching "depth" with the respondent. Others who have dealt with data analysis in attempts at generalization may feel that this is merely a system for building in imprecision in data collection. What the cynics say on this score can reasonably be summarized as follows. First, after the fact, open-ended questions must be categorized so that appropriate pretesting and development of an instrument would have provided the most frequent categories and in one concept at least the respondent could have placed his own response in a category. Second, and this refers to the less structured procedures, if respondents are not presented with equivalent stimuli by the interviewers, the possibilities of getting blatantly wrong impressions from the respondents are present. This is not the place to enter a detailed discussion on data collection, but it is clear that if one looks at the problems of data analysis and at the types of inferences to be made after the research, data analysis will influence — indeed, should influence — the data collection processes.

The above remarks emphasize the fact that data analysis problems may be those associated with the failings of data collection, rather than with the model of analysis that is chosen.

The situation that develops with data that are collected for which provision of analysis has not been anticipated is another matter. What does one do when one encounters the question: "I see what we're going to do with the data from the workers, but what are we going to do with the data from the supervisors?" This brings to memory the anecdote of how New Yorkers are to be identified. Person A asks the New Yorker: "Is it true that New Yorkers always answer a question with a question?" New Yorker: "How should I know?" Obviously, the researcher has to be a New Yorker in these circumstances and has to ask back: "Why were the data collected in the first place?" The answer for the researcher may have been appeasement of an agency that thought that this was "a good thing to do." Under these circumstances, all answers are going to be vague and difficult. On the other hand, if there was a well thought-out reason, this will also be manifest.

This focus on how the data will be treated raises additional questions focusing on the planning of the research. Essentially, this involves the conception of the research and how the research process is viewed. Very often, in the circumstances where an evaluative research is worth doing, it may also be worth examining the intrinsic value of data that can be collected in the situation. It may be that generalizable descriptive relationships can be found by the introduction of very small additional cost or time factors in the data collection; that by collecting a small amount of additional data, some alternate sets of relationships may be examined that have potentially great value for the applied discipline and the basic science as well. After the fact, it has become popular to speak of "secondary analyses." It is better to worry about secondary analyses before the researches are done than afterwards, as very small increments of data collection frequently can change the whole character of the "secondary analyses."

The notion of "secondary analyses" seems an odd one. Essentially, research should be organized to fully exploit data that are collected, and data analysis really represents such a minor cost in research that drawing the essence of "secondary analyses" out of basic data files borders on the trivial. Practical experience seems to indicate that most of the costs go into preparing the data decks, not in the machine analyses. The costs and preparation of the data decks do not reside with mistakes that IBM punchers make but in the preparation of the forms, coding, and other processes in anticipation of the punching. We have noted this emphasis above.

Another way of stating the fact that there is relatively little problem in data analysis once data decks are prepared is to note that at this point in time there are packaged programs to do virtually all the operations that any researcher would like. When a research project doing evaluative or survey research includes money for a programmer, one might well be suspicious about the researcher's knowledge of data processing. Indeed, one might even be suspicious about the researcher's knowledge about appropriate statistical procedures, as most interesting procedures and surely all the common statistical and numerical procedures are available in packaged programs.

A problem in the analysis of data that must be emphasized deals with the experience of the researchers and how well they know what they are doing. There is a response to data analysis that can be called the "candy store" response. It involves the notion of a researcher saying something like this: "We'll have three of those, four of those, two of those, and some of those." Since it is easy to call up programs and carry out analyses, sometimes these procedures are executed with little thought or rationality. Why should a factor analysis be carried out? If it is to see if there is a scale, something is wrong with the research process to begin with, since this should have been determined in pilot or earlier stages in the research. If the researcher says, "I want to do a discriminant function analysis," a fair question is: "Do you know of any circumstance where it has been done and where interpretation has been facilitated beyond other techniques?" And, if the researcher says that he wants to carry out a latent class analysis, maybe the simpler question to ask is: "What for?" All these programs should be available, but the management and tactics of data analysis require that the researcher know what he wants to do and that this makes sense from the point of view of the interpretations he wishes to carry out.

The emphasis on the researcher as a person aware of data analysis procedures and the interpretation of statistical and numerical procedures cannot be set aside. There have been many fashions and fads in data analysis and statistical procedures, some of which have been debilitating. Some emphases that have been developing are well placed, but may be regarded improperly by researchers. For example, there is much current interest in "causal inference" and "path analysis." These procedures have great merit if they can be applied. They have great merit also for their instructional value in showing the limitations of interpretation that should be known in drawing inferences with correlational data (as contrasted to experimental manipulation data). Researchers should know, however, what the limitations of application of these procedures are. The fact of the matter is that data collected for such applications may be treated in many ways, however, and have one virtue in common. Ordinarily, product moment correlation or regression analysis is involved, and this means that the emphasis in data handling is on estimation procedures rather than "hypothesis testing" in the more usual sense.

This paper has skirted rather than dealt with the topic of the management and tactics of research. In part this is necessary because it is difficult to convey experience; and experience may be the keynote to how to get a research project done. Also, a good research training is basic to getting a research project done, and it would be facetious to spend the space and time to give a short course on research methodology and techniques. There is no such short course.

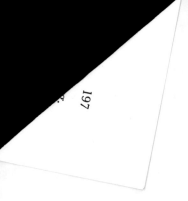

CHAPTER TEN

Notes on the Art of Research Management

Marie R. Haug

Some useful warnings on the problems of data collection and analysis, particularly in evaluative research, have been sounded in Professor Borgatta's paper. He is well advised to stress the issues of adequate design, relations with host agencies which retain authority for the researcher at critical check points, and the pitfalls of shot-gun or fad-bound research analysis.

My approach, however, will be somewhat different. It is the intention of this paper to review some of the peculiar organizational problems of contemporary social research in general, and to distill from experience some specific management strategies which may be more or less successful in overcoming the difficulties inherent in the system. These problems and strategies are largely ignored in traditional research methods courses, perhaps because such mundane matters are considered administrative details beneath the dignity of academic training. Yet management processes have a critical impact on the conduct and outcome of the research enterprise.

Only in the case of the rapidly disappearing lone researcher-professor and his faithful student assistant is management a less important issue. Unfortunately genius on a shoe-string is becoming quite rare, and is perforce limited to secondary analysis of others' data, or to using captive groups such as students, patients, prisoners or other subjects already in the researcher's charge. The much more common current format is the "project," involving one or more researchers, assistants and clerk-

198

technicians. Such a project may be located temporarily in an agency, as is frequently the case in evaluative research, or it may be housed in a university or research center, in which instance it will do evaluative, demonstration, exploratory or experimental research in one or more agencies on a visiting basis, or focus on some segment of the population without regard to agency affiliation. In brief, problems of researcher-agency relations represent only one area of research management; there are others of at least equal concern. It may help to understand these problems if they are put in the context of bureaucratic-professional tensions.

The Peculiar Institution

The relationship between professionals and bureaucratic administrators has been the subject of considerable study, speculation and theory. Professionals are purportedly masters of a unique scientific body of knowledge, their ethos is one of service to the public, and their pride is personal autonomy in work planning and performance. Professional patterns of interaction are collegial, as is found in a company of intellectual equals, where nobody is the boss (Sussman, 1966). In contrast, bureaucratic administrators cannot function without reference to a hierarchy of organizational authority. Their work may require a certain expertise, but the tasks are related to a particular location in the bureaucratic structure rather than to a body of knowledge, and actions are governed by a system of impartial rules and regulations without a direct humanitarian rationale. Persons in a bureaucratic system do not enjoy occupational autonomy but are subject to orders passed on by their superiors in the system (Blau, 1955).

The differences between the professional and the bureaucratic models of action are managed in any single organization by relative segregation, the familiar split between staff and line. This strategy is facilitated by the fact that the behaviors described are archetypical rather than typical — nobody is ever pure professional or pure bureaucrat. An entire literature has arisen on the conflicts and accommodations of bureaucracies and professions, including not only line-staff relations, but also the difficulties encountered when both roles must be played by one individual. Here the common solution has been segregation in time rather than space. Social workers, nurses, teachers, clergymen, professors and other practitioners move from more professional into more bureaucratic roles as they are advanced into administrative posts, and slough off the collegial robe as they don the authoritative hat.

Neither of these strategies of reconciliation quite fit the research project situation. In that context, the bureaucratic and professional models of action are combined in sequences depending on the stage of the total research process, and to the extent that these stages frequently overlap, the researcher may on occasion find himself trying to play both roles simultaneously.

There are three major phases in any research project with characteristic variations in work stance (See table 1). The initial stage includes the definition and formulation of the problem in researchable terms, a task which sets the degrees of freedom on design, data collection, analysis

TABLE 1 — *Variations in Work Styles by Research Stage*

Research Stage	Work Style
Problem Formulation and Design	Professional
Sampling, Data Collection, and Processing	Bureaucratic
Analysis and Report Writing	Professional

and other study activities. During the early problem formulation and subsequent design period, the model of action is professional, collegial. The researcher as "scientist" struggles with the conceptual and methodological issues attendant on putting his vague questions and interests into a precise statement specifying exactly what he wants to know, and how he plans to find it out. This is the period when interchange of ideas, consultation, argument and appeals for advice dominate — or should. Problem formulation as a prelude to design is a stage which is often overlooked or perhaps assumed to have occurred when it has not. Borgatta's emphasis on design without reference to this necessary prior step may be a case in point. In any event, failure in adequate problem specification is·a root source of many mishaps in later research stages. Since problem formulation is a process which calls upon the researcher's body of theoretical and methodological knowledge and requires autonomous decision-making on his part, it is the prototype of the professional portion of the research role.

But in order to get the project under way and then to carry out the various steps of sampling, data gathering and data processing, the researcher must switch to a bureaucratic style. He is now an administrator, with authority over a "crew," even if it is only a crew of one or two assistants or clerks. He is responsible for integrating and supervising the performance of tasks best described as nasty details — looking for holes in sampling frames, getting data collection forms prepared, or interviewing prospective interviewers, or arranging for videotapes of behaviors, and overseeing all the facets of accurate, expeditious data collection. Once the data are in hand a new set of administrative tasks confronts the researcher, as he must supervise coding the information, arranging for transmission to punch cards or magnetic tape, pursuing errors by way of card-cleaning, and giving instructions for "print-outs" of the findings. In all this complex of duties the researcher is now, like it or not, a straw-boss who commands and coordinates others' activities.

In the final stages, the autonomous, collegial style again pertains. Usually analysis and re-analysis of the findings as well as the writing of reports, papers, and books brings the researcher back into the professional role. Throughout the time sequence, however, administrative responsibilities will tend to overlap with the professional. At the final stages there will be mop-up supervisory tasks to perform, just as at the beginning there were some preparatory ones, even during the design phase. In short, role segregation, the classic solution to the tension between bureaucratic and professional styles, is not really available to the researcher. He fluctuates between these modes of action in sequential segments of time as the major research emphasis changes, and even within each segment is forced to juggle both administrative and contemplative duties at the same time.

Problems of research management thus boil down to the strategy of administrative behavior — tactics and techniques of governance and leadership which will get the multitude of detailed research tasks done, and done properly, without bogging down the investigator and detracting from the exercise of his professional expertise. Training in research *methods* is of limited use in preparing to meet problems of research *management*. Indeed a little experience in the business world is undoubtedly (*sic*) ! better preparation, in terms of both skills and attitudes, than the most sophisticated course work in methodology.

Assuming that most researchers have not had such a practical background, the remainder of this paper will address itself to a number of the tricks of the trade with relevance to administrative issues. These strategies[1] were deduced, developed by trial and error, and accumulated over a number of years of research experience in different types of situation. These experiences range from "in-agency" research where a study was housed in a residential treatment center, to "semi-detached" research in which the investigators came to the rehabilitation settings to collect data, to "external" research in which the researchers were located in an academic setting and acquired their data by long-distance from rehabilitation personnel. Although the proximity to the agency and the method of data gathering varied widely in each situation, management problems and solutions were remarkably similar.

Management Issues: "Hired Hands"

A good administrator is one who can delegate authority with the confidence that necessary work will be done fast and well. For the researcher not connected with an ongoing center or institute, this means rounding up an *ad hoc* staff which is committed to the work, capable, and willing to stay through to the end of a study.

Borrowing staff from a host agency is no solution. The capabilities and practices of such personnel will be geared to the style of the agency rather than the research, and although they may be faithful in appearing for work, their commitments are likely to lie elsewhere. Similar arguments obtain against using students as research workers. Useful as it is for the student to receive apprenticeship training in connection with an ongoing study, from the point of view of the researcher there are difficulties. Students come and go: they may receive fellowships, graduate, drop out of school, marry, be taken into the army. For some, the research will be only a routine chore, as their major interests lie in completing course work and passing examinations. Although their capabilities are likely to be high, they are better viewed as trainees and research interns than as part of a regular staff component.

Where then is a research crew to be found? The best source, and to judge by many existing staff rosters a fairly common one, is among older married women, housewives. *Cherchez la femme* has apparently been the solution for more than one harassed project director. Women with school age or older children are prime candidates for interviewers, coders, typists, and data processors. As far as interviewers go, this procedure has become so much a way of research life that most big centers hire no one else (Sudman, 1967, p. 105). Women, however, should also be considered as "deputy directors," to manage the crew and supervise the numerous housekeeping and organizational tasks involved in running a study operation. Because of their experience in handling the dual roles of home manager and gainfully employed worker, women have often learned to juggle sets of disparate activities, keeping them in harmony and in appropriate temporal sequences, in short have been forced to become good administrators in order to survive. Furthermore the fact that many women are geographically immobilized because of their husbands' jobs means that the market for their skills and abilities is limited, making them more available than men with equivalent capabilities. Finally, women often are seeking more than money alone: they will be attracted by the new ideas, challenges and intellectual excitement to be found in research work.[2]

Rehabilitation research should be particularly appealing, because of its humanitarian assumptions, to women interested in a job with a social service component. For this reason such research can also find potentially committed workers among the disabled themselves. It is apparent that those whose opportunities have been narrowed by irrelevant personal characteristics can be viewed as a pool for capable study personnel. This should not be interpreted as license to employ cheap labor, or exploit people trapped to a degree by their biological make-up. Rather, these suggestions are designed to alert scientific investigators to a relatively unused source of a staff which can readily develop commitment to research goals.

Commitment is the way out of one of the difficulties of a bureaucratic and hierarchical work situation. Normally in such an organization lower echelons have little interest in the seemingly distant overall goals of the enterprise, and yet have considerable negative power for affecting goal attainment. Hired hands can select the messages which reach the boss through screening of phone calls, arrangement of appointments and even control over flow of correspondence. By their tempo of work and selective attention to tasks they can "make decisions" about the nature and timing of production, whether the output be nuts and bolts or research questionnaires.

Roth (1966) has suggested that "hired hands" in research actually may falsify or fudge results because of their *lack* of understanding and commitment. This is certainly a danger where a project is run in military style, but should not occur where the investigator wins the working crew's support by sharing goals, methods, dilemmas, and problems. In short, the objective should be to professionalize the administrative phase of the research process to the maximum consistent with staff potential. Although it will usually not be possible or even advisable to involve the research crew in either the formulation of the problem or the analysis of findings, it is almost invariably feasible to engage them in joint discussion and solution of the critical problems of data collection methods, and to the degree this is done, commitment and support on a professional level are likely to follow.

This discussion argues that one can expect professional behaviors of subordinates in the bureaucratic phase of research activity, even though for them there is as a rule no professional pay-off in terms of high salaries, status, or academic advancement. Investigators can win lower echelons' identification with research goals by sharing over all humanitarian objectives and calling upon individual instincts of workmanship. To the extent that women, and especially women in their middle years, are bound by social norms, notions of service, and the Protestant Ethic, this outcome will be more likely with a feminine staff.

Management Issues: Errors and Hardware

Errors are the nightmare of the conscientious researcher, and they can be discovered at any stage of the research, worst of all after the findings are in print. Conceptual errors in design, including mistakes in sampling, measurement, controls, and analysis, are not usually a management concern, the most common exception being the organization of sample follow-up to minimize lost cases. Very much a function of management, on the other hand, is the control of processing errors, such as "goofs" in coding, punching, tabulating, and computing.

A high rate of lost cases will cast doubt on the validity and generalizability of research results. Yet covering all the members of a sample is a difficult and expensive proposition. NORC has found that it takes an average of 2.7 call-backs to complete interviews in a probability sample, and even more for males, young persons, and big city dwellers (Sudman, 1967, p. 12). First wave responses on mailed questionnaires rarely run as high as 50 per cent, even with a population which is deeply interested in the research issues. If case records or observations are used instead of interviews or mailed questionnaires the problem is not necessarily solved. As noted elsewhere in these papers, case records can be missing or incomplete, and observations are impossible when subjects drop out or disappear.

The methods used to reduce the lost case rate to a minimum while maintaining adequate sample size are essentially issues of design. Unfortunately the inexperienced researcher may believe that the way to secure a large number of usable responses is to oversample. Journals still proudly report studies in which a 40 or 50 per cent response rate produced several hundred cases for analysis. These investigators fail to realize the extent to which a self-selected sample can distort results. Individuals who choose to continue in a program or choose to be interviewed or choose to return a questionnaire are likely to differ in various ways from those who choose *not* to cooperate. The yea-sayers constitute, in effect, a self-selected sample, not a randomly selected one, no matter how carefully probability rules were followed in the original sampling. Any time a response rate below 90 per cent is accepted, even when key characteristics of non-participants are known, the findings can be considered suspect to some degree.[3] It is true that the results *may* not be off by very much or perhaps not at all, but the point is that the researcher can only guess: he does not really know.

A methodologically sounder strategy is to select a smaller group in the first place, and then marshall all possible managerial skills to include every case in the researcher's data net. A final "sample" of 360 cases produces more confidence in the generalizability of the findings if it represents 90 per cent of an original sample of 400 than if it covers 36 per cent of an original sample of 1,000. And the smaller the original randomly selected set, the fewer individuals it is necessary to pursue to achieve a respectable response rate.

The decision to select a smaller sample and follow its members to the ends of the earth in order to minimize unidentifiable error requires careful deployment of time and resources. Research staff must develop a "skip-tracer" approach. Repeated call-backs and follow-ups, the use of special appeals, telephone requests and the like will be necessary. Ingenuity and persistence are needed to discover where movers or drop outs have gone. At the same time, the methods used should not appear to pressure or intimidate potential subjects, since this also could distort results. Sufficient time needs to be built in to the research plan to accommodate these activities, and create the expectation that they will be carried out.

If self-selection error is too little attended to, the situation is no better with respect to processing error, a distinctly managerial issue. As has been pointed out elsewhere (Sussman and Haug, 1967), mistakes in coding, punching, tabulating, and computing are too much ignored; such errors are not necessarily random in any one study, and can be costly in terms of inaccurately evaluated outcomes. The most serious source of processing error is in the coding phase. Systematic coding bias can result from idiosyncratic interpretations of data; assignment of different meanings by two coders or by one coder whose interpretations modify over time will produce variations in any coding where some judgment is required. Where judgment is at a minimum, as in pre-coded instruments, coders can still err purely by accident.

One strategy used successfully to minimize this type of error is independent double coding, with the code sheets verified against each other and discrepancies corrected prior to punching or taping. Such a procedure is analogous to the use of independent judges in other stages of research. In making up IBM cards it is routine to verify the original punching by essentially a repetition of the punching procedure. Double coding is suggested here as an equally if not more important verification step.

Other small techniques for avoiding processing error are worth mentioning. For example, no research project should be without a "log book," in which all decisions concerning research steps, data interpretations, and coding category meanings, as well as all minutes and records should be kept as a running account of development. It is amazing how easy it is to forget, and *write it down* slogans are no joke.

A word of warning is in order, however, about *over*-correction of errors. Borgatta is undoubtedly more literary than clinical when he refers to "paranoia about truth in research." It is not well to see errors where there are none, because corrective efforts can compound mistakes: in the process of repunching a guilty IBM card, an operator eliminating one "goof" has been known to produce two new ones.

The process of error correction, once the coding phase is completed, is known as "card cleaning," and involves a search for discrepancies, inconsistencies, and anomalies in the data as clues to coding and punching errors, which are then eliminated by returning to the original raw data as a basis for revising the card. The danger here is that the raw data are reviewed out of context, and an apparent discrepancy may in fact be a deviant case correctly coded and punched; changing it will then mean that other coding decisions are made wrong by reference. And even where there is a real error, its correction can produce new mistakes purely by mechanical accident. Skilled research management, in short, requires the ability to say "enough is enough," and achieve closure at some point. Be a nit-picker when it comes to accuracy, but not a paranoid.

Another note of caution concerns excessive reliance on computers. Not every researcher has access to electronic hardware, and even those who have computer time available may find themselves low on the priority list and unable to get output as rapidly as is desirable. Unfortunately there is a certain snob status attached to computers, so that failure to use these mechanical aids is somehow considered lowbrow, ignorant, and not with it. The fact is that computers are convenient time-savers with large numbers of cases and complicated calculations, but are often inefficient with smaller samples or simple runs. Using an expensive piece of machinery to print out straightforward distributions is a poor allocation of resources, unless an N is unusually large.

In order to avoid becoming a slave to the computer and its canned programs, wise research managers will arrange to have a duplicate deck of IBM cards available, and access to a mechanical card sorter. In this way distributions can be checked and new ideas on cross tabulations explored without undue delay. Furthermore it is advisable to develop a "Bible," listing frequency distributions on every variable from such a separate deck. Computers are not infallible machines, and even perfectly de-bugged canned programs can be improperly processed. In brief, computer-based errors are possible, and having a set of marginals available for verification of results is comforting if not downright essential on occasion.

Management Issues: The Fight for Time

The institutionalization of research in agencies, universities, projects and centers has not been without some psychic cost. The mounting money needs of even modest studies have brought heavy dependence on granting agencies. Accordingly most contemporary research is timebound. Output pressures have taken away temporal autonomy, as reporting deadlines must be met to assure continuous financing or fulfill prior obligations.

Investigators are no longer in control of their own timetables. Research stages are less geared to the demands of the questions being studied or the data being gathered than to the demands of the funding organization for progress reports, budgets, and final summaries. There is a problem in choreography here, to fit the research sequences to the rhythms of the granting agencies. Reports, reviews and check points are a familiar bureaucratic need, and carrying out such regulations a standard administrative task. But the management of time requirements is no less distasteful for being common, and it is particularly unpleasant for professionals, one of whose chief perquisites is the right to control their own time.

One way to beat the system is to anticipate its demands. Researchers who manage to prepare partial reports, working papers and study memoranda as they go along have a body of material available to put together when a government or foundation deadline approaches. This is admittedly a case of freedom by advance recognition of necessity, but the procedure has the added side effect of enriching the details of findings and capturing fresh ideas and serendipitous notions as they arise instead of allowing them to be forgotten in the final formalities.

In the end, however, the only solution is a successful fight for time. The battle is originally joined when a research plan or study proposal is drawn up. A time budget prepared at that point needs to allow a sufficient period for each stage of the investigation to be carried out with reasonable deliberateness. NORC, which has had wide experience with research schedules, suggests that, after realistic estimates of a study's sub-parts have been summed, at least an additional 25 per cent be added as a "time for uncertainty." It is my impression that many researchers underestimate the time needed for final analysis and report preparation. NORC found that this terminal stage, *not* including publication time, has averaged nine months in their studies over the last several years, and has been known to last 21 months (Sudman, 1967, pp. 190–191).

The fight for time, moreover, does not end with approval of a liberal research schedule. Researchers must wrestle out special time for reflection *within* the context of the ongoing study. A time to think, to engage in mental factor analysis (the best kind), to speculate, dream, compare, notice oddities or similarities — all this is essential to the creative process. An investigator who is so bogged down with managerial details as to lose time for reflection is shutting the door on both theoretical insights and serendipitous ideas. Reflection is the prerequisite for meaningful research results which go beyond routine reports of findings. On the other hand, the researcher must try to keep his creativity within some constraints. For instance, going off on a new tack in midstream, revising a research design on the basis of a new hunch, is probably more likely to foul up the original study plan and timetable than it is to lead to a great discovery. Judgment argues that some products of reflection are best reserved for later research engagements. Any good administrator will make time for release from management duties to think about what he is doing and why. If he is also a successful researcher, he will know when to modify an existing design, and when to file away an idea for subsequent investigation.

The fight for time can be seen in a different context with respect to the design itself. Longitudinal studies are based on a future time perspective, and usually provide for data collection at the beginning, middle and end of a specific number of months or even years. This is in contrast to the more common social science research plan, in which information is gathered at one point in time, although subjects may be asked to give facts on their personal *past* histories.

Longitudinal research is frequently more expensive than a cross-sectional study, and presents some difficulties of its own. If it utilizes a panel scheme, in which the same subjects are questioned or observed over a future time span, there is the problem of keeping track of their movements. Unless the sample members are institutionalized, this can be quite a project, as modern man is exceedingly hard to pin down, and the poor and disadvantaged are the most mobile of all. Even if different subjects are to be under scrutiny in the different time segments, the follow-up savings may be compensated for by extra costs of analysis and statistical manipulation to account for sub-sample variations. Some funding agencies also seem to shy away from longitudinal studies, so that it may be somewhat more difficult to win approval for such a proposal. Whether this tendency is due to reluctance to commit financing into the future, or to some reason idiosyncratic to an agency, is an empirical question.

Despite these hangups, the fight for time to do a longitudinal study is well worth winning. This design can be structured to approximate the classical experimental before–after model, and to this extent is desirable for evaluative research and theory testing. Only in straight descriptive surveys or pilot studies can it be argued that longitudinal designs are usually inappropriate. In general, the quasi-experimental logic possible in research conducted over time is ample reason for designing and carrying out longitudinal studies.

One other time problem is emerging now that demonstration projects and accompanying evaluation research are becoming more wide-spread both in rehabilitation and other helping fields. The way most such demonstrations are now structured, there is no provision for continuation if the projects are found to be worthwhile. Usually there is at least a one year gap between a final report announcing that the experiment was a success and the completion of the red tape necessary to having it continued; by that time much of the momentum of accomplishment may be lost.[4] Time sequences need to be devised which will permit immediate continuation funding to be approved on the basis of preliminary or informal evaluations of project effectiveness. Whatever method may ultimately be developed, evaluation researchers need to be sensitive to the problems of time lapse, and their solution. Time is important to subjects as well as to investigators.

Summary: Pass it on

The most successful and productive researchers are those who are either good administrators themselves, or have learned to capture good administrators and put them in strategic positions in the management of the research enterprise. That is the message which this paper has tried to convey. Nor is it intended to downgrade the role of either the professional researcher or the bureaucratic manager. In today's condition of institutionalized social science research and welfare demonstration projects, involving large sums of money and commitment to publics that some social benefit will accrue, the obligation is to combine professional and managerial strategies for optimum results. Both skills and both roles are essential, and this is the art of research in a nutshell.

It is sad, then, that the secrets of this art are so hard to come by. Courses in methodology do not teach it, text books do not cover it, and even symposia like this one can only touch lightly on its many facets. Apprenticeship is really the only way to pass the art on to students and future investigators. Study directors, professors, and instructors of any variety should feel an obligation to take on one or more student apprentices, who can pick up the many techniques, strategies, and tactics which make up the nitty gritty of successful social research. Pass it on.

Notes to the Chapter

1. Strictly speaking à la von Clausewitz, strategy is a broad overall plan while tactics refer to the specific actions to carry out the strategy. In this sense, the discussion up to this point has concerned strategies, while that which follows will be somewhat more tactical. But in looser terminology, both strategy and tactics are considered in the balance of the paper.

2. While it is true that there is considerable drudgery and repetitiousness in many research tasks such as coding and punching, workers can be sustained through these stages if they are interested in the larger goals and the final outcomes.

3. Technically this statement applies only in instances where the purpose is to estimate the parameters of a population. However, even when estimation is not at issue, if random sampling is used at all, low response rates introduce an unknown and possibly distorting error into any findings.

4. I am indebted to Professor George Wolkon for drawing this problem to my attention.

References

BLAU, PETER M.
    1955   *The Dynamics of Bureaucracy.* Chicago: University of Chicago Press.
ROTH, JULIUS
    1966   "Hired Hand Research." *The American Sociologist,* 1 (August): 190–196.
SUDMAN, SEYMOUR
    1967   *Reducing the Cost of Surveys.* Chicago: Aldine Publishing Company.
SUSSMAN, MARVIN B. (ed.)
    1966   *Sociology and Rehabilitation.* Washington, D.C.: American Sociological Association.
SUSSMAN, MARVIN B., and MARIE R. HAUG
    1967   "Human and Mechanical Error — An Unknown Quantity in Research." *The American Behavioral Scientist,* 11 (November): 55–56.

THE IMPLEMENTATION
OF RESEARCH

CHAPTER ELEVEN

The Implementation of Research Investigations

HOWARD E. FREEMAN

The temptation is great to confine this paper to anecdotes. Anecdotal accounts may not only be instructive but also entertaining. Interviewers and field workers apparently have a strange proneness for sexually seductive engagements, for being privy to state secrets, for learning about the confidential and private activities of politicians, organized criminals and corrupt businessmen, and for obtaining tips on the stock market and real estate speculations. No matter how routine the investigation and no matter how dull the content of a study, somehow the data collection phase provides innumerable believable and unbelievable tales that perhaps should be assembled and not merely transmitted as part of cocktail party chatter.

The temptation is equally great to concentrate, in this document, on the grave deficiencies that exist in the methodology of social research. Even persons most sympathetic to social science and identified with the research endeavor realistically must be amazed at the haphazard and inconsistent ways in which projects are carried out; the cynic has a field day when he examines our so-called craft. How little we know about the interview is enough of a case in point. Although a number of systematic considerations of the research interview have been undertaken (Reisman and Benny, 1956, Richardson *et al.* 1965), it still is not possible to specify the range of contingencies in the interviewing process. Refusals are sometimes related to the lack of training and persistence of interviewers, at other times to their personalities, and at still other times to social and temperamental characteristics of informants (Dohrenwend and Dohrenwend, 1968). Likewise, biases in informant responses, on the one hand, may be related to too great a status discrepancy between the data collector and the respondent, and on the other hand to too close a social affinity between them (Dohrenwend *et al.*, 1968). One esteemed expert, on social research that is, has been said to remark: "Doing research is like making love in a Volkswagen. It seems impossible but if the need is great enough, and the parties involved resourceful and not easily discouraged, it's simply amazing what can be accomplished."

It is not my intention here to provide either a disparate series of anecdotes or a systematic examination of methodological defects. Anecdotes and criticism are unavoidable. But I will make use of anecdotes and criticism in examining elements of design, in pointing up directions for the general development of social research methodology and in describing some of the special issues in social policy and applied research investigations, rather than focusing on them for their own sake. My perspective perhaps is an over-simplistic one. Increased support of innovative work in method is required and many of us need intensive instruction in existent methodological procedures. But both the current political and social climate and the pressures of the academic enterprise reinforce the continuance and acceleration of research endeavors, however blundering, unrefined and disorderly be our present styles of work (Freeman, 1963, National Science Board 1969). Given the current and projected state of affairs, it does seem reasonable that the implementation of research studies can be enhanced if investigators are at least alert to the range of considerations that commonly render the findings of some investigations highly questionable. I also would like to examine the various objectives and purposes for which research is undertaken, since many of the *ad hoc* solutions that have to be accepted in the implementation of studies, however imperfect they be, are related to the objectives and purposes of the investigations. I also will try to offer, when I can, pragmatic advice on the conduct of research investigations (See Freeman and Simmons, 1960 for an earlier effort along these lines). Most of the advice that I can come up with is at the level of "folk wisdom" and, needless to say, may be regarded as debatable by other research investigators and proven wrong if followed either uncritically or blindly in future investigations.

Components in the Conduct of Studies

Those of us who have been in the research game any length of time are acutely aware of the ability and perhaps skill of some of our colleagues to conduct innumerable investigations with apparent "success," while other of our colleagues are confronted with all types of problems that somehow result in their studies never being reported or even completed. While few researchers can claim success in every one of their ventures, particularly if success is defined in terms of a product, i.e., a creditable monograph or journal publication, there is no doubt that a wide variation exists in production records of investigators. Undoubtedly a strange and complex mixture of intuition and temperament has much to do with the investigator's "batting average," at least in terms of the way I have defined success.

A key element undoubtedly is the ability of some persons to locate important and interesting research problems, while others somehow never quite come up with an exciting research question. Efforts to codify the sources and stimuli for research investigations (Merton, 1959) do not tell the entire story. A special type of intelligence, one's interpersonal network, and an individual's social values are probably key determinants of problem selection. There are undoubtedly a host of other determinants of problem formulation that remain to be identified.

There also is the matter of "packaging" research results so that they are attractive to the publisher and journal editor. Skill in writing, the availability of colleagues to critically react to preliminary drafts, and secretaries to type neat manuscripts conforming to style requirements, as well as a degree of egomania and of recklessness, probably are related to publication records.

In a sense, these last remarks are by way of a digression. I want to acknowledge that neither do I know, nor do I think anyone really knows, the extent to which variations in either problem selection or the communication of research account for the wide differences that exist in the production records of different researchers with similar academic training and experience. It would be foolish, of course, to deny the importance of problem selection or the communication process. But my guess is that the differences in research success are also related and perhaps primarily associated with a varying awareness and differential skill in coping with some five dimensions of the research activity. I doubt if many investigators maintain the equivalent of the airline pilot's flight check card and run down a list as part of the process of undertaking research. I do believe, however, that some investigators in their studies, implicitly, deal with various design elements while others ignore them or, perhaps even worse, are oblivious to their importance. Each of the five — cooperation of subjects and relevant organizations, reliability, validity, precision and accuracy, and efficiency — requires at least some discussion.

There is some logic in discussing these matters in the sequence presented, for I contend that they form a Guttman-type scale in the order noted: unless it is possible to carry out an investigation, there is no point in worrying about its reliability; unless one's data are reliable, there is little reason to worry about their validity; cooperation, reliability and validity are prerequisites for a concern with precision and all four of the components are antecedent to a worry about the efficiency of the investigation.

Some of the audience for these remarks, at this point, will be tortuously bored by the repetition in the previous paragraphs. Others will be angered because they will feel I am beating dead horses and that everyone accepts the important character of the five elements mentioned. But I do think it is justified to be repetitive, anecdotal and critical here in order to make the point. It is to my mind important enough to be worth belaboring.

I want to dwell for a minute on this matter of reliability for even further emphasis. At the present time, with the exception of methods for obtaining certain social characteristics such as age and sex, we have almost *no* measures with known reliability. Not only is there a tendency for investigators to create their own measures and blithely go ahead using them without ever thinking about the matter of reliability, but scales that have been used in literally thousands of investigations persist in the literature without any test of their reliability.

I would bet, for example, that in the past decade probably five thousand studies, and that may be an underestimate, have used as an important measure the anomia scale developed by Srole. At this point, I insert a table from a paper with my colleague Richardson. (Freeman and Richardson, 1969). The data shown in Table 1 are the anomia responses of a representative sample of retired UAW workers 75 years and over. The two sets of responses were obtained from the study group at points one year apart in time.

In the paper reporting these results, we consider a number of alternatives for the very low correlation, including the likelihood that the scale may be unreliable among the very old retired UAW workers, that anomia is a fleeting quality among the very aged, and other reasonable possibilities. Considering the consistency in other data collected as part of the same interviews by NORC at time-points a year apart, and even though it is possible to create other alternatives for the findings, I know "in my heart", or at least in my gut, that it is a matter of instrument unreliability. What I would like to see are some studies that either would contradict our findings, or that would tell me that the results are due to a reason other than reliability, or, if reliability is the explanation, that demonstrated that the unreliability is idiosyncratic to using this scale on this particular sample. In the meantime, however, I am not exactly comfortable reading the many papers in which the anomia scale has a central place.

TABLE 1 — *Association Between First and Second Anomia Scores of UAW Retirees*

		Anomia Score I*			
		(Low) 5–8	9–10	11–12	(High) 13–15
	5–8 (Low)	38	37	20	17	112
Anomia	9–10	35	70	60	40	205
Score II	11–12	40	48	64	65	217
	13–15 (High)	16	55	71	147	289
		129	210	215	269	823

$x = 114.30$ $df = 9$ $P = 0.01$ Tau-C = 0.25

---

* Anomia scores ranging from 5–15 were computed on the basis of 3 points for an Agree response, 2 points for a Don't Know, and 1 point for a Disagree response for each of the five individual anomia items.

I know about the old Jewish proverb that says "a 'for instance' is not proof" and I hope I may be forgiven for using as an illustration a finding from my own bizarre research on very old men. But I want to drive home the point that the elements of research strategy that are included in virtually every introductory text book on methods, even if they do not use the same terms I have, are pretty well passed over by most persons engaged in the craft of social research. If investigators were forced by the editors of our major journals to supply reliability coefficients for all scales used, it would undoubtedly cut down drastically the number of printed pages that all of us complain about not having had a chance to read quite yet. I have picked out the reliability issue perhaps only because we do know most about means for assessing it, but I daresay the same qualification to the conduct of studies would hold for any other of the five components noted above.

I would like to approach the five elements somewhat more systematically. I shall not attempt to provide formal and comprehensive definitions for each of them. Rather, I would like to indicate at least some of the means by which research can be improved with respect to these elements.

Cooperation

In the olden days, before social research became one of the United States' major industries, sociologists were pretty much restricted to studying the behavior and thoughts of persons they knew, namely their students. When I was a boy, which unfortunately was before the S.D.S., students were acquiescent, if not proud, of being the subjects of research investigations. Clever investigators always included a sufficient amount of material in surveys about sex, or, in the few cases in which experiments were undertaken, implied that there would be opportunities for interesting social contacts before, after, or during the research. They had no difficulty, or practically none, with either refusals or other uncooperativeness on the part of subjects, or with failure to be able to carry out the study because some group or organization would not allow it to take place.

Most social investigators have gotten over the idea that informants, or the groups to which they belong, are going to be as cooperative as students used to be. I think we must face up to the realization that it is going to be increasingly difficult to secure cooperation of subjects and the relevant groups whose cooperation is required. We know from as far back as almost twenty years ago that an unwise decision on what a population was like could arouse a community sufficiently so that a home town boy and his wife, he a psychiatrist no less, were almost tarred and feathered before being booted out of the town (Cumming and Cumming, 1957).

In trying to understand the problems of cooperation, it is important to try to separate out the issues related to the community and environment in which the research is undertaken, the ones associated with the need to have key influentials on your side, and the problems of securing the cooperation of the actual research subjects or informants. It seems reasonably clear now that communities or groups are unlikely to sit still and allow themselves to be investigated by persons they do not like or cooperate in studies that they feel have little relevance to them. Whitney Young has pointed out in speeches a number of times, and I wish I could capture his exact words, that black communities have been studied cross-sectionally, longitudinally, horizontally, vertically, superficially, and in depth, by interviews, questionnaires, field teams, projective techniques, and concealed cameras and recording devices. His remarks are pertinent to a Boston community I know, for I am one of the many who have researched it (Watts *et al.*, 1965).

Roxbury has not only been studied by Brandeis, Harvard, Boston University, Simmons, Northeastern, and the University of Massachusetts, but has been "loaned out" as a research site to our colleagues in universities in other parts of the country. It is an ideal research site, close to public transportation, relatively safe, and large enough to be truly called a black ghetto yet small enough so that sampling is relatively easy. But how many research invasions by whites is this community likely to tolerate? Many of the investigations conducted in it are irrelevant to the welfare of the population of Roxbury and virtually all of the investigations that potentially could have resulted in social action of benefit to Roxbury residents either were completed too late or ineptly handled from the standpoint of stimulating social change. I would contend that, in these times, we are likely to exhaust almost completely the feelings of good will and cooperation of the various "special populations" on which so much of our research effort is centered.

Certainly it is not always possible to develop research investigations so that they are relevant to populations studied. If social research is going to prosper, however, it is necessary to make certain that a significant proportion of our studies be directed at matters that are of concern to informants and that the potential of investigations be assessed in terms of their likelihood to result in progressive social change. A continuation of the attitude on the part of social investigators that it is their right to study whatever they please and whoever they please can shortly yield a situation so antagonistic that neither needful basic research studies nor important social-policy oriented ones are likely to be feasible. It is critical, I think, to recognize the disastrous consequences of a continued insensitivity to the needs and social action values of populations studied. The past presidential election, for example, was the first time, to my knowledge, that public opinion groups ran into significant numbers of the general population who simply did not give a damn about being included in the Gallup or Harris or some other poll. Among the poor black and the otherwise disadvantaged, it may not be a matter of individuals simply refusing to participate, but collectivities of individuals strenuously preventing research investigators from studying anyone in their locale. I know of no efforts on a national level, or indeed a local one, to promote the potential utility of research to the many special groups involved, and I believe such efforts are seriously required.

In the case of individual studies, in addition to the general problem of developing them in the ways most relevant to the study populations in order to enlist cooperation, there are a variety of means that the investigator can use to indicate his gratefulness for being permitted to undertake his work. In our study of middle-income negroes in Roxbury, for example, it was the funding agency who insisted that we have a staff member with the assigned responsibility to relate us and our study to the population (Watts *et al.*, 1965). Quite frankly, at that time we accepted this item in the budget only because it seemed easier than to argue against having this type of activity accompany our research. Since we did have the money, however, we went out and recruited a "community-relations type." By chance, our choice was a fortunate one. We hired an individual who had been a resident of the community for a large number of years, was a mediator between the various political factions in it, and knew almost everybody there because of the other job he had held. He was employed by one of the large liquor distributors as a public relations man, and spent a considerable proportion of the time sitting in local bars and buying drinks for customers. He did more, however, than obtain some free "positive-neutral" publicity for us in the neighborhood newspaper and sway some families who refused to be interviewed to cooperate with the study. He was a visible indication to all of the community that we were sufficiently aware of exploiting them to have at least employed someone they knew, and generally trusted, as part of the research team. As I noted, I take no credit for having such a person on the research staff, but it was a useful lesson. Social investigators need to consider, much more than they have, the requirement to include during field work a "community-relations component." Further, there needs to be some explication of the various tasks which a community-relations person may engage in and the qualities he should have for the job.

A word also should be said about the need to recognize the many dimensions of power and influence that exist today within the communities and study groups that we seek to investigate. While it has been a traditional approach on the part of social investigators to request the cooperation of persons with either legal responsibility or sufficient formal power to prevent the conduct of a study, typically we have not gone beyond such efforts. In these times, for example, it is probably not only essential to obtain the permission of the high school principal and parents in order to conduct a study of students, but of the various organized student groups as well. It is not only necessary to secure the cooperation of the commissioner of welfare in order to investigate families receiving public assistance, but also to obtain the support of the welfare mothers' group. For the most part, research investigators simply have not thought in these terms. In these times, it is probably essential that we imitate our colleagues in anthropology who, at least in their work in foreign communities, have tried very hard to be sensitive to local social structures and value systems. Sociologists have been so fortunate in meeting minimal community resistance in their efforts that they have tended to overlook this matter. It is foolish to continue ignoring the problem of community cooperation.

Along the same lines, it is necessary to re-evaluate, or at least shift our concerns, with respect to the individual study-group member. Because of the impact of a psychotherapeutic orientation during the period in which survey research and other types of field interviewing studies were gaining in popularity, most of the concern with the researcher–study group member relationship was framed in terms of rapport. By now, it seems clear that there has been an overconcern with rapport and a lack of attention to other matters that are more important, or at least as important, in order to obtain a continued cooperation in social research endeavors. In the first place, we should accept the proposition by now that once people agree to cooperate in studies, there is virtual certainty that they will discuss almost any topic as genuinely as they know how, without the need to build up an intensive interpersonal relationship. The numerous studies of sexual conduct should convince us that little is to be gained by creating therapeutic situations out of data-collection ones. In the second place, all of the evidence suggests that biases stemming from over-rapport are at least as extensive, if not more so, than biases accruing from under-rapport (Weiss, 1968).

But I think two issues have been insufficiently taken into account. Although there have been a number of reviews of the matter of privacy, including a socio-legal consideration for example by Ruebhausen and Brim (1965), a statement on privacy in storage of data (Sawyer and Schechter, 1968), and an instructive paper on the problems of confidentiality among a sensitive population (Rainwater and Pittman, 1967), there remains an unusual apathy about the matter of privacy amongst social investigators. I would argue that, in these times, unless deception of any sort is critical to the conduct of an investigation, there is no excuse for it. Moreover, in those cases in which deception is undertaken, as in the case of the Rosenthal study (1968), it is essential that the investigator be aware of what he is doing and be able to defend the harmlessness of his deception. Even in such cases, however, I believe that deception is defensible only when the potential social benefits of the study are extremely great and there is no other way to approach the investigation.

In all instances in which it is possible, study groups are entitled to know the purposes of the investigation, the limits of confidentiality, and the safeguards that are being taken in order to protect them and the data. Most important, as Ruebhausen and Brim (1965) point out, social scientists have a unique stake in the maintenance of privacy and the responsibility to serve as their own watchdogs so that academic colleagues, commercial researchers, and various community groups do not interfere with the privacy of community members. Rather than connive with various groups of responsible officials and gatekeepers who have access to study group populations in order to obtain samples and quasi-official status that legitimizes the investigators' seeking out of informants, the investigator should accept the responsibility to develop appropriate mechanisms to ensure the privacy of potential study group members. I literally cringe when I realize that in my research experience ministers and rabbis have given me access to their teenage parishioners without even inquiring about what I was going to study, or how I was going to study it. Mental hospital superintendents have allowed me to review the records of patients about to be discharged, and to talk to them and their relatives with but a superficial review of either my credentials or the protocols, and school authorities have provided names of boys thought to be delinquents and potential delinquents, merely because the study has a quasi-official relationship with another city agency. I would suggest that in these times cooperation for any particular study, and also for the long-range continuance of the research enterprise, requires that we pay much more attention to the matter of privacy.

Second, it is important that we become more concerned with the dignity of the individuals involved in research investigations. I recall some years back while training interviewers to undertake the field aspects of a study of relatives of former mental patients, one of the social workers, during a training session, asked whether they should call the interviewees by their first or last names. My response was probably inexcusable. I told her that it did not make any difference and that she should do whatever would make her feel comfortable. Certainly it would seem to me, at least now, that participants in studies are entitled to as much dignity and respect as can be provided to them. The successful conduct of studies, and again the course of the research endeavor, require that attention be paid to the seemingly trifling elements in the encounter between data collector and data provider. Courtesy, appropriate forms of address, interviews at the convenience of the informant, and overt acknowledgement of appreciation should be built into data collection efforts.

Currently there is considerable debate about the appropriateness of paying informants, particularly when studies are undertaken of disadvantages groups. I know of no research investigation that indicates that it makes much difference in terms of biases, but it is interesting that anthropologists often have provided gifts for community members, sociologists have bought lunches for groups such as Wall Street lawyers (Smigel, 1964) and psychologists often have paid students who participate in experiments. I think I would argue that it is perfectly proper to remunerate participants in studies, particularly when their involvement results in a monetary loss or a re-arrangement of any consequence in their life patterns.

I have known studies in which investigators were quite aware that blue-collar workers were being docked from their jobs for the time they spent as informants and that housewives used taxis and paid for babysitters, and yet these investigators have been entirely comfortable about ignoring such matters. Naturally the use of monetary rewards can be undignified if they take on the semblance of a bribe or serve to make the informant uncomfortable because of the ways they are presented. As a generalization, I would contend that the matter of whether you pay a person or do not pay them depends upon the particular circumstances of the investigation. But there is no reason to argue from any principle that the researcher has the right to expect cooperation from persons merely because of the psychological gratification that is obtained from participation in an investigation.

In summary, with respect to the matter of cooperation, I would like to indicate that investigators today must recognize that the very climate of the times requires a much more extensive effort, or perhaps program is a better term, a program that recognizes that there is no normative responsibility on the part of anyone to serve as a subject, informant or data source and that no researcher has the right to invade the personal and social lives of community members. Regardless of the cost and time involved, it is critical that we think of these programs as part of investigations in order to ensure both the success of the individual study and, as I have noted, the viability of the research enterprise.

Reliability

I have already indicated the critical need to be concerned about reliability in some of my earlier remarks. At the present time, we do not even have an adequate codification of sources of unreliability. As I pointed out, the field of sociology is conspicuously absent in estimating the reliability of measures and undoubtedly the inadequacy of instruments is a major source of unreliability. In addition, however, we have paid scant attention to the environments in which we collect our data. Although psychologists have become aware of the influence of the environment on responses since the discovery that marked differences among IQs between criminals and non-criminals was a myth accounted for, at least to a certain extent, by differences in testing situations, for the most part social researchers, particularly survey investigators, go blithely along presuming that the locus of data collection makes little difference. I would like to see the differences in test-retest scores of mothers when the first data collection occurs on a sunny day while the children are out playing, and the second occurs on a rainy day when the children are confined to the house. I also would maintain that, in addition to environmental circumstances, such as the presence of other individuals, resulting in differences in response, the sheer mechanics of data collection are strongly influenced by environmental considerations. What data-collectors write down, how many items are improperly administered, and so on, are, or may be, related to the setting in which one works, although I know of no studies along these lines.

Moreover, we often presume that personal and social characteristics of informants make little difference and rarely, I would say practically never, worry about differences in reliability of sub-aggregates within a study population. If one includes, within the phenomenon of unreliability, consistency in response of individuals when the direction of items is reversed, then certainly the problem of sub-group differences in reliability needs to be reckoned with in most studies. I described before the test-retest results on the anomia scale of retired UAW workers who are 75 years of age and over. One explanation is that the scale may be reliable, as I noted, with younger population, but not with groups this old. Perhaps concern with consistency in response when the direction of items is reversed and the possibility of sub-group differences in reliability to scales represents an overextension of the concept of reliability. I am willing to stand corrected on whether it fits in this section on reliability, but I do contend that it represents an important and uninvestigated problem of method.

Finally, there is the problem quite well studied, or at least some aspects of it have been, namely the reliability of data collectors. While it is generally presumed that the results of structured interviews are recorded with acceptable reliability, certainly we know that most interviewer-completed rating forms employed as part of field studies suffer seriously with respect to reliability. The utility of using most interviewer ratings obtained in research investigations of individuals' personality attributes, levels of living and social sensitivities is highly questionable.

I recognize that these comments are quite damning. Let me again emphasize, however, the foolishness of continuing a sociological tradition of unreliable research. It renders a concern with the other problems—validity, precision and efficiency—meaningless.

Do I have any practical hints to offer? There are no real solutions except for investigators actually to undertake reliability analyses as part of the pre-testing phases of their studies. Unlike psychologists, sociologists' studies rarely include tests with a sufficient number of items to permit a split-half measurement of reliability. The only solution, unless we wish to change considerably our styles of investigation, is to invest heavily in test-retest procedures during pre-testing.

As far as the discipline goes, there is a definite need for the development of measures with known reliabilities for different populations. In particular, investigators who have undertaken panel studies have probably shirked their responsibility in this respect. Such studies provide an unusual opportunity to undertake test-retest studies of frequently-used scales, even if they are not totally relevant to the objects of the study. While subsequently I will comment on the need for economy in measurement in order to handle some of the problems that face the field, I think here is one case where the need is so urgent that a cooperative enterprise is required with various investigators in panel studies making use of scales frequently employed by themselves and their colleagues.

In the absence of scales with known reliability, my feeling somehow is that one is always better off making use of scales that others have employed in investigations. Even if reliability is unknown, there may be some basis for presuming reasonable reliability if scales have been identified as predictors of a wide range of phenomena. Indeed, the consistent correlations between anomia and "F" scores may be regarded as an indication that I have treated Srole's scale too harshly. It is hard to imagine that many investigators would be fortunate enough to have unreliable scales repeatedly predict other measures. Also, sociologists probably should seek, whenever possible, to use rankings rather than ratings. In general, rankings will turn out to be more reliable in comparison with ratings (Borgatta, 1960). Particularly in the case of judgmental measures, the investigator is well advised to rely on rankings rather than ratings.

I also would like to suggest that the era is over in which just about anyone can collect data. I understand fully the entrepreneurial motivation of both profit and non-profit organizations to provide interviewing and data collection services. Despite the self-interests involved in the promotion of these groups, I think it only fair to acknowledge that there is some hope of an increase in reliability by the utilization of well-trained field workers who have considerable experience in the collection of data. I have in the past made use of both graduate students and otherwise personally selected interviewing staffs. The fact of the matter is, however, that regardless of how well intentioned the investigator is, he is unlikely to attend to the time-consuming tasks of training and supervision that are essential to the development and maintenance of a sophisticated field staff. Organized groups that make data-collection "their business," at the very least, provide the resources likely to minimize some of the problems of unreliability connected with the collection of data.

Some individuals may regard my discussion of unreliability as much too broad, encompassing the concept of bias often discussed in research methodology. I recognize this fault, but I think I can defend the position that the concern with bias is a relatively academic matter. Most of the faults with field work, including the impact of the data collection staff, are actually matters of reliability and not of bias. Indeed, though perhaps an extreme statement, I would argue that we really have no decent tools for assessing biases in data collection because we employ so few instruments and so few procedures that maximize reliability.

Validity

At a discursive level, there is no lack of consideration of the problem of validity. Indeed, if sociologists are preoccupied with one issue, it is whether or not empirical investigations are at all tied in to the conceptual ideas that exist in the discipline. It is simply remarkable how many of our important theoretical and conceptual notions have failed to be operationalized well. In virtually all cases, although the various levels of estimating validity have been documented (Elinson, 1963), our field relies on "face validity" — agreement among colleagues that what we are measuring actually reflects the underlying phenomena. On the one hand, our failure to deal with the validity problem in other ways can be related to the way concepts are manufactured and employed in social research. It could well be argued that essentially most of them are interesting journalistic verbiage, words that portray an image which is impossible to grasp solidly in order to develop sound operational measures of them. On the other hand, it can be argued that empirical researchers are so intellectually uncreative and overly concerned with mundane matters that they fail to develop adequate measures of critical conceptual ideas.

Although it may be somewhat of an exaggeration, the problem of valid measures is a major reason that there is minimum exchange and interaction between empirical investigators and so-called conceptualizers and theorists. The blame, of course, lies in both sides. Many "theoretical scholars," on the one hand, when confronted with the requirement to develop their variables in measurable terms, simply retreat into a discursive monologue and completely ignore the requirement of operationalism. "Hard nosed empiricists," on the other hand, frequently fail to relate sympathetically to those persons who are active in the development of concepts and theoretical notions. At the present time, I think it is fair to say that there exist two sociologies, a sociology of interesting but untested ideas and a sociology of uninspired but empirically supported research findings. Not only is this trend likely to continue but it limits extraordinarily the prospects for a sociology directed at social change and amelioration of the social problems that face contemporary society.

There are two key issues in this respect. First, I would like to indicate that there has been failure on the part of sociologists to develop what might be called, as Curtis and Jackson (1962) describe it, "multiple indicators." Second, there has been the most naïve and irresponsible acceptance of verbal reports and attitudinal statements in lieu of the measurement of interpersonal behavior (Tausky and Piedmont, 1968).

It is apparent that, in most cases, it is simply not possible to derive one single operational measure that is going to be regarded as an entirely adequate reflector of an important sociological concept. As a consequence, one strategy for the investigator is to make use of a variety of operational measures of a particular concept in an investigation. Given multiple measures, it is more possible to examine the issue of whether a relationship exists. What happens in many empirical investigations now is that the failure of empirical findings to support conceptual ideas can be dismissed on the grounds of "invalidity," and oftentimes the critics are absolutely right. The investigator is accused of setting up a "straw man" by the way he measured a phenomenon. Many times he does just that, for the game of social research often is to find a body of data lying around and then to suggest that by coincidence there exists within it some good measure of a particular concept, allowing empirical assessment of a conceptual idea. In more careful investigations, perhaps, the operational measure is derived from the conceptual idea and the analysis is not entirely an *ex post-facto* one. Regardless of whether it is *ex post-facto* or not, however, the "straw man" criticism of the empirical study frequently is legitimate.

Thus, one of the possible means of decreasing an investigation's dismissal on the grounds of lack of validity is the use of multiple indicators; for example, the employment of several different scales to measure authoritarianism rather than complete reliance on a single five-item measure. If one wants an illustration of a field in which the advice to use a multitude of indicators could be most well-taken, it is in the measurement of community power. As Walton (1966) has shown, given the various ideological bents of investigators and the conflicting results of studies in which the money has been bet on a particular measure of power, the idea of using multiple indicators is recommended.

But I think I would argue that if there is any single validity problem that is primary, it is the naïve idea on the part of social researchers that what people say is congruent to what they do. There exists a virtually incontestable body of literature to substantiate the point that it is simply impossible to rely on verbal reports and so-called attitudes if one is interested primarily in behavior. (Bullock 1951, Freeman and Sherwood 1965). Perhaps it seems silly to indicate to established research investigators that there is a great difference between prejudice and discrimination, between sexual immorality and promiscuous conduct, and between a future time orientation and impulsive behavior, but we continue to be comfortable about making such assumptions.

It is time that we stopped using attitude indicators as supposedly valid measures of social behavior. In part, our survey research methodology and other means by which we question people need to be revised, so that we ask what people do or did, not what they think they would like to do or might do. We also must improve both opportunities and means for observing behavior directly.

There are innumerable problems, particularly of reliability, with so-called called field observation. But while I am not overly sympathetic or enthusiastic about field observation as the panacea for the problems in method of contemporary sociology, there is a point to the fanaticism of individuals identified with this method. It is simply that the possibility of always obtaining valid verbal responses from individuals about their social and interpersonal behavior is, to say the least, highly questionable. Consequently, if there is any single bit of advice about the matter of validity that can be offered, it is simply that we should not presume that, because survey research and the interviewing method allows for large samples and in most cases quantification, it should be adopted without due consideration to the purposes of the investigation. Increased validity may require emphasis upon direct observation or at least a re-casting of the research approach.

Precision

Precision or accuracy of research findings depends, of course, to a large extent upon reliability. Without a reasonably high degree of reliability it is impossible to expect a high degree of accuracy, and there is no reason to be interested in the precision of invalid measures. In addition, both the size of the sample and the method of sample selection are related to precision. The concept of precision can be defined in several different ways. It is frequently used to refer to the extent to which estimates obtained from samples reflect accurately the population for which one wishes to generalize, and this is a sufficient definition for my purposes here.

In general, sociologists have not concerned themselves much with the matter of precision otherwise, at least in large-sample, quantitative studies, there would be more frequent employment of confidence limit statements. I think it is fair to say that while the body of knowledge which sociologists have accumulated allows a large number of statements of relationships between variables, we are not in a position to state with much accuracy the magnitudes of association between even the most common phenomena subjected to investigation. Take the matter of social participation: in an article a few years back, Teele (1965) reviews a large number of the contemporary studies of the social participation of community members and demographic correlates of participation. Even if one overlooks the diffuseness of results stemming in part from the wide variety of ways that social participation is operationalized, one cannot but be struck by the inability to make any estimates of the magnitudes of association between social and demographic characteristics of persons in the various study groups and their social participation. Is it only the different samples employed in four studies that Teele cites by name that result in percentage figures of 30, 40, 50, and 75 with respect to working-class membership in voluntary associations?

It is probably a fair question to inquire as to whether or not at this level of development in sociology it is important to be precise or whether we should be content with merely identifying stable relationships and not concern ourselves with their magnitude? Certainly this is an improper stand if we are going to continue to undertake multiple variable analyses and to do more than constantly discuss one zero-order relationship and then another. Moreover, a good many of the practical uses to which social research is put require a modicum of precision, including of course the important one of identifying the size of various "social problem" groups. Again, in evaluation studies, particularly if there is going to be any interest in the development of "cost-benefit" comparisons, a rather high degree of precision is important. There is simply no way that either the body of knowledge of sociology or the application of sociological research to community problems can advance without drastic improvements in our ability to be precise.

Are there any immediate means to improve the precision of the current type of work in social research? I think so. One way is to pay more attention to the matter of reliability. A second is to reduce the refusal rate, particularly in large, sample-survey investigations. I have previously discussed at some length the issues involved in achieving cooperation from study groups in community populations. I would argue that the standard must be extremely high with respect to refusals before one begins to regard sociological research ventures as successful and worthwhile.

The several reputable survey research services in general community studies are able to achieve at least a 90 per cent completion rate. Investigations of "captive" and "quasi-captive" populations are often able to include 95 per cent or more of their drawing group in their studies. Moreover, some panel-type investigations can retain 80 per cent or more of the drawing group, even when interviews are conducted a number of months apart, yet even today one can still pick up any of our refereed journals and find either papers that do not even mention the attrition rate from the drawing group during the conduct of study or else report losses of anywhere from one-quarter to one-third of the sample originally selected.

Much earlier, I made the proposal that our journal and monograph editors might adopt a policy of rejecting all work that failed to include statements about reliability. I wonder what might happen if, in the notice to contributors that appears in our major journals, a statement like the following was included: "Except in very unusual cases, no cross-sectional study will be considered except if a systematic sampling procedure has been employed and the rate of refusal is below 10 per cent." I simply do not believe that high refusal rates usually are unavoidable. Rather they occur because of an inattention to the matter of securing needed cooperation, and simply because our discipline fails to exercise sufficient social control so that persons make enough of an investment in their field work.

Precision also is related to the response rate to individual measures within studies. It is one matter for a large number of people to be observed, interviewed and questioned, and another to have the appropriate information from them and about them. In many investigations with high completion rates, there frequently are low response rates to particular measures. Except when investigators star the "total" column on their tables and indicate the number that did not respond, the non-completion rate to measures is not even made explicit. I confess that after having refereed papers for four different journals, I cannot recall one time when I ever took such information into account in reaching a judgment on the worth of the findings. Perhaps I am more negligent in evaluating others' work, but I think there is a generalized apathy on this account and one likely to continue unless there is rather vigorous effort to change our norms. Again it would be useful if contributors to journals were required, in addition to a statement about the sample and the sample-completion rate, to discuss in a sentence or two something about the average response rate to the measures in the study.

I am not sure I know how to improve the response rates to measures. But I believe that pre-testing in many investigations is carried out ritualistically and insufficient attention paid to this phase of study development. How many of us really consider seriously the issue of item ordering and whether or not this may have something to do with the completion rate to different measures? My guess is that you could count the number of studies on your fingers, and certainly on your fingers and toes, in which pretesting has been carried out in a sequential manner with experimentation in question ordering and interview schedule design. Yet it seems reasonable that these matters are associated with the response rates to measures.

Finally, I wonder how much precision is lost because of inadequate editing of interview schedules and field notes, and sloppy code instructions. Having suffered perhaps as much as anyone, I am most sympathetic to the problem of going back to a deck of IBM cards or a coded data file because, during the analysis phase, it becomes apparent that overlapping categories were employed (so you combine them), inconsistencies between responses were not properly adjudicated (which you ignore) or the data coded in ways that prevent its dis-aggregation (which speeds up the analysis). Like the pre-testing of interview schedules, I would contend that "dry runs" of codes are undertaken ritualistically. What has ever happened to the idea of coding up a small proportion of the data and doing a prototype of the analysis? I fully understand that in these days of high costs, desire for speed in the analysis phase and the information overload we face because of the ability for computers to spill out tables, there are great pressures to slip over as fast as possible the editing and coding processes. I suspect, however, that considerable improvement in the precision of studies would result from more attention to these matters.

Efficiency

By efficiency, I am referring to the minimal expenditure of resources, money, manpower, and the like, required to conduct a research project. Naturally there is a relationship between expenditures for research and the conduct of successful investigations in terms of the elements I have discussed previously. I would say, however, that most academic research centers are notoriously poor in the management of their resources and investigators who work out of their own academic cubicles are probably even more wasteful. Along with most of my colleagues, I, of course, would hate to see the complete adoption of a "money-orientation" and a sacrifice of intellectual contributions that may stem from leisurely explorations of data and "side ventures." Nevertheless, it is necessary to be concerned with the matter of efficiency. Not only are we facing an increasingly difficult period for securing resources, but at the same time the cost of research activities is rising drastically. Most to the point, there is simply too much for all of us to do to be complacent about engaging in wasteful endeavors.

There are a number of issues regarding the efficiency of studies that are obvious and can be touched on very briefly. A constant dilemma for the research investigator, and particularly for the organized research institute, is the extent that waste is permissible because of a responsibility to function as a training institute. Medical centers have an impossible job trying to cost out their training function in comparison with patient care. I am not proposing that it is possible for us to make good estimates either. There is reason to question, however, many instances of the employment of graduate students when more efficient operations could be developed by using regular staff persons and where the training received by the students is minute. I would argue that it is hard to defend the utility of using graduate students on long term projects as coders and clerks. There are simply more stimulating and provocative things that they can do and besides, the cost considerations argue against their working at such tasks.

Other ways of doing things, that stem from our using the scholar in the humanities as a reference person, also need to be reconsidered. Four or five telephone calls to individuals who have been working in a particular content area may provide many more leads than hours of library work. An airplane trip half-way across the country may be more economical in the long run so that someone's program can be used on the computer it was written for, rather than spending hours, perhaps days, and many minutes of computer time gimmicking it up for one's own machine. We also are going to reach the point, I believe, where trained professional editors are going to have an important place in the research enterprise, rather than rely on our secretaries to fix the split infinitives and to get rid of the "data is" phrases.

But the real key, it seems to me, of efficient research comes about through the appropriate selection of research approaches and research designs. Most of us are socialized to be relatively inflexible in the ways we go about developing investigations. Persons enamored with the survey research method are loath to opt for a field observation approach even when this method may be as reliable, valid and precise and more efficient. Informants and catalogs of secondary data may be adequate to answer research questions and yet there is sometimes an insistence by investigators of undertaking their own field investigations. Abstruse and indirect approaches may be used when very direct and economical means can produce the same results.

Finally, I would like to point out that there is a tendency for almost all of us to collect too much data. A large number of studies, and I will confess I am as guilty as the next one, include numerous background measures without any real idea of why they are needed and frequently the distributions on them are never even really scrutinized. I would also love to have back all the secretarial time I and my colleagues have wasted having tape-recordings typed and distributed, of research-planning meetings, exploratory interviews, and the like.

Undoubtedly each of the five elements I have discussed could be considered in much further detail. I have not even exhausted my own personal homilies on how to deal with the problems that are around the matters of cooperation, reliability, validity, precision and efficiency. Moreover, virtually every social researcher has his own personal notions of how to overcome defects and his own views on which deficiencies in method are likely to result in disasters, or at least in limited successful productivity of research results.

There is, of course, an advantage to continually trading ideas on how one pragmatically overcomes some of the problems that I have discussed. One reason, I believe, that certain institutions develop a greater proportion than their share of successful researchers and become recognized as the important centers of activity is that there is both a critical mass of persons and a climate for the exchange of ideas at a very pragmatic level. It is probably not only intellectual isolation that makes it so difficult for individuals in less active settings to be productive, but the inability to keep abreast of practical innovations, the tricks if you will, of undertaking research.

I do believe, however, that what is urgently needed, as well as an exchange of pragmatic hints, are strenuous efforts to explicate general schemes that can be used by the investigator when he is designing a study. Outside of the introductory text-books on method, our literature on research is primarily devoted to the explication of special techniques and there is an extremely limited reference shelf that the investigator can fall back on in order to avoid major pitfalls. Instead of continuing the discussion in terms of tricks of the trade, therefore, I would like to at least briefly look at the possibilities of developing useful general schema.

Development of Design Selection Procedures

At the outset, I would like to offer the proposition that there is no single best research method. It is simply impossible for the field to move ahead if participants in it continue to maintain their doctrinaire orientations and constantly promote a particular approach regardless of the nature of the research problem. Zelditch (1962) put the matter well and I quote him: "There is, in fact, a tendency to be either *for* or *against* quantification as if it were an either/or issue. To some extent the battle lines correlate with a relative concern for 'hardness' versus 'depth and reality' of data. Quantitative data are often thought of as 'hard,' and qualitative as 'real and deep'; thus, if you prefer 'hard' data you are for quantification and if you prefer 'real, deep' data you are for qualitative participant observation. What to do if you prefer data that are real, deep, *and* hard is not immediately apparent (p. 567)."

Zelditch goes on to point out that the only fruitful way of looking at the matter is to ask the question "what kinds of methods and what kinds of information are relevant?" In the paper I have quoted, he discusses with clarity some of the concerns. He notes, first of all, that the problems of validity and reliability are found regardless of the method used and chooses not to consider them when looking at the virtues of particular approaches. He argues that the social researcher has available to him three fundamental strategies. First, he may undertake enumerations or surveys. In enumerations and surveys, he points out, data may be obtained by either direct observation or by interviews and questionnaires. A second strategy is that of participant observation. I think we now prefer the term field observation to describe his second strategy, for it better encompasses studies in which field workers do not fully integrate themselves and identify with the group. The third strategy, he notes, is that of interviewing informants. Informants may be persons who either have formally or informally undertaken enumerations and surveys themselves or have been "participant observers" by virtue of their interpersonal and social involvements.

Each of these strategies has its obvious advantages and disadvantages. Enumerations and surveys most often allow opportunities for obtaining quantitative data and for systematic sampling. In addition to being expensive and thus often inefficient, there are other limitations as well. Many types of information are simply not known or not salient to large numbers of persons and so the investigator may face the problem of having to try to unravel the "meaningful" from the non-meaningful responses.

Field observation allows the investigator an opportunity to observe interpersonal relationships and processes and thus to study "behavior" directly rather than relying on verbal reports of it. But as we know, quantification of field methods is limited, systematic sampling difficult, and complete and accurate recording a serious problem. Informants may be the most economical way of obtaining data and for many purposes more data can be obtained through the reports of a few informants from large samples. There is often considerable difficulty, however, in estimating the accuracy of informant reports and, because one uses but a few of them, great risks of bias. Moreover, poor selection of informants clearly has serious consequences because of bias and inaccuracy. As Zelditch lays out in more detail than I have here, each strategy has its advantages and its limitations.

It becomes important then to look at the various strategies in terms of the types of information that one wishes to know. Zelditch discusses three information types, (1) frequency distributions; (2) incidents and histories; and (3) institutional norms and statuses. The cross-classification of methods and informational types is shown in Figure 1, which I have reproduced from Zelditch's paper. It is instructive in that it provides considerable guidance in the selection of appropriate methods in relationship to the type of information that is sought.

FIGURE 1 — *Methods of Obtaining Information*

Information types	Enumerations and Samples	Participant Observation	Interviewing Informants
Frequency distributions	Prototype and best form	Usually inadequate and inefficient	Often, but not always, inadequate; if adequate it is efficient
Incidents, histories	Not adequate by itself; not efficient	Prototype and best form	Adequate with precautions, and efficient
Institutionalized norms and statuses	Adequate but inefficient	Adequate, but inefficient except for unverbalized norms	Most efficient and hence best form

Zelditch's paradigm, of course, requires considerable extension and elaboration. It is possible, first of all, to extend the number of information types so as to include, for example, such additional ones as personal values, internalized beliefs and attitudes, and learned behavior. Likewise his categories of methods can be extended to include documentary analysis, field experiments and laboratory experiments, as well as possibly other means of obtaining information. Moreover, it would indeed be useful to specify subsets within each of the information types so that, for example, various kinds of frequency distributions could be looked at separately. The development of a broader and more detailed paradigm is far beyond the scope of this paper and would necessarily require a cooperative enterprise of considerable magnitude and an opportunity to test out the resulting paradigm by reviewing a large number of studies as well as obtaining the reactions of a wide assortment of investigators. Ideally, of course, such a paradigm should not merely concern itself with the issues of precision and efficiency but with the other elements mentioned before, namely cooperation, reliability, and validity.

In lieu of a general paradigm, I would argue that it is incumbent upon each investigator, in thinking through the design for a study, to have evaluated explicitly the various methods in relationship to the type of information that the investigation is supposed to provide. Presumably we do so implicitly in the developmental stage of a research project, but I have never seen the process explicated. It would mean essentially filling in the appropriateness of each method for each design element before one moved ahead very far in the development of the investigation (Figure 2). I would like to suggest that if such an evaluation of our studies were undertaken, we might be able to figure out better how appropriate our efforts have been. I would go further to suggest that probably many studies would be done quite differently, either a different method would be selected or a combination of methods rather than a single one would be employed. I must confess I tried out the idea with several rather large studies I have undertaken in the past few years. It would be too lengthy a digression to report the results of this effort and also, I am afraid, it would be rather embarrassing personally. If I am a representative sample of one, however, let me assure you that there is a need for this kind of exercise to be undertaken in the development of every investigation.

FIGURE 2 — *Evaluation of Research Approach*

METHOD

DESIGN ELEMENTS

Cooperation Reliability Validity Precision Efficiency

	Cooperation	Reliability	Validity	Precision	Efficiency
Enumeration Sample Survey					
Participant observation					
Interviewing informants					
Documentary analysis					
Field experiment					
Laboratory experiment					

I do not want to underestimate the extent of the effort required in order either for an individual investigation to be examined as I have proposed, or for the social research community to develop a comprehensive general paradigm. The idea of moving in the direction of developing means for measuring methodology is not a new one. Several years ago, Dodd (1966) published an interesting paper describing a preliminary effort to create a series of scales on which research studies could be rated. Up to now, at least to the best of my knowledge, only exploratory and fragmented efforts to examine the appropriateness of the procedures in investigations or, more important, the appropriateness of procedures planned for investigations, have taken place.

I believe it is critical, as Dodd points out in reporting his exploratory effort, for the fields of social science to develop formal mechanisms that permit us to revise our ideas on the best techniques and tactics for undertaking social investigations, and to be able to assess the degree of effectiveness in the behavior of social researchers. The analysis of the measurement of community power by Walton (1966) points up how far we have to go. In his study he classified some thirty-three investigations that dealt with fifty-five communities by the method used, i.e., reputational, decision-making, case study, or some combination of the three of them. What he found is that sociologists have more frequently employed the reputational method, while political scientists tend to prefer the decision-making and closely related methods. Further, political scientists, compared with sociologists, tend to find less monolithic power structures. Finally, the use of the reputational method tends to be associated with the identification of a monolithic power structure. He is able to show quite convincingly, unfortunately, that discipline leads to method, and that method leads to the description of the power structure in a particular study. It is simply dismaying how far we are from the development of what, for want of a better term, one may think of as a "definitive" body of knowledge about social behavior and social process.

In planning this paper, I considered rather carefully the desirability of putting this section ahead of the consideration of the separate elements discussed. The reversing of the order of the two sections could easily be defended. I was afraid to do so however, for I do not want to identify myself with the small but vocal group of "research cynics" among our colleagues, who give the impression that all substantive research should cease until we are more systematic in our research strategy. Rather, I believe that social research needs the simultaneous accumulation and availability of "helpful hints" and the cumulative development of a general scheme for the selection of appropriate research strategies in order to maximize cooperation, reliability, validity, precision and efficiency. At the present time I would argue that there is a lack of considered effort in either direction. If there is insufficient reason to work on both tasks from the standpoint of building up knowledge in the social sciences, the utilization of social research for applied policy purposes commands attention to these tasks. Indeed, many of the current limitations of the application of social science, to my mind, stem from an inability to maximize the various elements noted. I will try to develop this concern in the next section.

Social Policy and Social Research

Many of us who are engaged in research careers feel a strong responsibility to use our craft to effect social policy development and orderly social change (Freeman and Sherwood, 1970). In these times, the development of social policy is dependent to some degree on the utilization of social research methods. In the planning of action programs, in the development and implementation of social rehabilitation efforts, and in the evaluation and assessment of existing and innovative programs, there is recognition of the potential of social research instead of complete reliance on impressionistic ideas and ideological commitments. While social policy development is not an orderly process, there are more or less stages to it; at each stage there are important opportunities for the social researcher to contribute to policy development.

Planning

Planning is the process by which policy makers develop communal goals and assess the extent to which current community conditions or behavior depart from these goals. The statement of goals, of course, may be based solely upon philosophical or political views and may not be amenable to research. More often than not, however, concrete goals are formulated on the basis of a consideration of expert opinions and an understanding of the values of either community members or at least selected aggregates among them. Whether it be expert opinion, the views of the community as a whole, or selected segments within it that are the underpinnings of the policy goals, in all cases systematic research is valuable and called for.

In addition to goals, however, as I have noted, it is critical that the policy maker have knowledge of the extent to which existing conditions or behavior depart from the objective or goal. The assessment of the deviations between what exists and what should exist, is a task certainly amenable to social investigation.

The planning process, or at least the two aspects of it noted, require descriptive data, and there is literally an entire industry that is now devoted to providing information of this type. Yet, if we look at the descriptive data available in any of the fields within the purview of the sponsors of this conference, one realizes the gap between research needed and findings available. The lack of "successful research" on the incidence and prevalence of social deviations and social disorganization limits considerably the opportunities for social planners to undertake their work competently. I do not need, for example, to indicate to you the difficulties in coming to any conclusion about the rates of crime and delinquency, drug addiction and child-abuse in the United States, yet, particularly in these times, there is a strong mandate for the development of better mechanisms for their control. How far we have to go is perhaps indicated by the invaluable planning data that have been developed in a few fields, such as in the area of health, because of a commitment to a continuing national health survey. But even in the field of health we lack adequate knowledge when it comes to the deficiencies of sub-population groups such as the very aged (Freeman and Richardson, 1967). In these times, when planning is generally accepted as a necessity in order for marked modifications to take place in the social lives of many of our community members and the social conditions under which they live, much of the activity necessarily takes place in the absence of adequate information.

The key notions of incidence and prevalence need to be developed much more than they have been. Even in medical epidemiology, except perhaps in the study of acute illness, the concepts need to be sharpened. Incidence refers to the number of new cases per some unit of the population, prevalence to the number of existing cases per some unit of the population. Two problems arise and are most troublesome when one is concerned with social disorganization, although they exist in medical studies as well.

One of the problems is the selection of an appropriate denominator. Incidence and prevalence rates require for denominators what are known as the "population at risk." For example, a comparison of incidence rates for syphilis of two communities would be misleading if one community had an extremely high proportion of young children and a second community had an extremely low proportion of young children, and yet the general population was used as the denominator. Ideally it would be better not only to eliminate children from the denominator but nonsexually active persons as well, regardless of their age. In developing incidence and prevalence rates for social deviations and conditions of social disorganization, the population at risk becomes exceedingly difficult to define. With the possible exception of delinquency and biologically related types of deviance and disorganization, the populations at risk that we are interested in are bounded by complex matrices of social and psychological factors. For example, in establishing a denominator for the prevalence of families on welfare, the families in the community who are eligible for benefits from other types of programs, such as veterans pensions, annuities, and the like, need to be taken into account. The ability of descriptive social investigations to contribute to the planning process requires considerably more conceptualization and empirical data on populations at risk.

The second problem is related to a lack of definitiveness in our ideas about what constitutes a social rehabilitation or "cure." Medicine has this problem too, except in the case of nonrestorative types of disorders such as cancer. Psychiatrists, for example, have varying views as to what constitutes a "cured schizophrenic." Thus any notion of the prevalence of schizophrenia in a community is dependent upon whether one holds the view that once a schizophrenic always a schizophrenic, or that schizophrenia is defined by a series of active symptoms, or that schizophrenia is regarded as no longer present if hospitalization has been avoided for a given number of years. The development of prevalence rates on matters such as crime, delinquency and so on, is at least as difficult as the one faced in defining schizophrenia. It is critical, however, for planning purposes, to have rates of various social disorders and problems. One of the requirements, therefore, for successful research in our field is much more consideration of a series of uniform operational definitions of various types of social problems. It is simply not possible for our research areas to develop well unless attention is paid to this matter. In order to make any sociological sense out of the problem of mental illness, for example, obviously we need some consistency in what we regard as a mental patient (Mechanic, 1969).

In lieu of uniformly consistent definitions throughout a field, the individual researcher must explicate carefully the particular behavior or condition that he is studying. Further, it is incumbent upon him, in offering comparisons between his result and others', to be fully aware of and communicate differences and similarities in the criteria employed. Part of the lack of communicativeness in work in fields such as mental health, crime, delinquency, child abuse, and the like, comes about because of the diversity and inconsistency in how study groups are defined. Moreover, from the standpoint of the planner, there needs to be congruence between his perspective on the constitution of the problem group and the one employed by the researcher. As in the case of comparisons between research studies, there often are considerable differences in the way action-oriented persons and social science trained investigators conceive of social problems. This lack of congruence represents an important barrier to the utilization of social research.

Program Development and Implementation

Program development and implementation usually requires research data for two purposes. In order for the process of program development implementation to be a rational one, the policy maker must have information that allows him to define the target population for the program and also to specify an impact model on which to base the substance of the program (Freeman and Sherwood, 1965). The identification of the target population for a program is primarily a predictive research task. The allocation of scarce resources requires a commitment on the part of policy makers for the selective provision of various services and rehabilitation efforts. Means are needed in virtually every area of social rehabilitation to identify economically and effectively the population to be served.

The problem of the specification of the impact model is a complex one. An impact model is an explicit statement of a series of relationships between program elements and hypothesized outcomes, and between hypothesized outcomes and changes within a group in the direction of a desired objective (Freeman and Sherwood, 1970). The relationship between, for example, improving education and reducing delinquency, usually rests upon an impact model that hypothesizes that a particular educational program will improve educational attainment; that improved educational attainment will result in youths who are delinquency prone becoming more similar to those who ordinarily are not delinquency prone; and that becoming more like boys who are not delinquency prone will reduce the delinquency of the boys prone to this type of behavior.

Ideally, specification of impact models should be based on experimental studies. Since experiments are not usually available and indeed are often impossible, impact models must rely on correlational analysis. Since these correlational analyses are only useful if the independent–dependent relationships can be demonstrated to hold when "contaminating variables" are taken into account statistically, there is a strong need for studies that allow the use of multi-correlational statistics.

In selecting the target population, the objective is to develop an efficient and effective means of directing to a particular program those persons or other units who are in need of and amenable to it. With the exception of criteria derived from either legal or similar types of commitments, the object is to identify the characteristics of the sub-aggregate within the larger population in such a way that a maximum proportion of those who should receive the services, and a minimal number of those for whom the services are extraneous or perhaps even harmful, are included. Let me provide an illustration. If a public health department wishes to serve medically indigent families by providing dental care for them and their children, they wish to have a means of identifying as many of the medically indigent families as possible, so as to promote their use of the dental clinic. But, at the same time, it is not desirable to provide services to those persons who are able to make use of private dentists.

The statistical techniques for undertaking such selection procedures are well known. The critical consideration, however, is to devise a selection procedure that can be implemented effectively. Family income may be the best single predictor of medical indigency, or at least family income when family size is taken into account. But this variable may be exceedingly difficult to measure reliably, validly, and precisely. This may be the case not only because of seasonal variations in income, second jobs, multiple earners, and the like, but because it may be difficult for school authorities or public health officials to have either the means or the degree of cooperation with families to obtain this type of information. Therefore, less efficient predictors may have to be used and a more complex predictive procedure developed. If social researchers are going to provide an input into the program development and implementation process, they have to be aware of the implementation aspects of procedures for the selection of target populations as well as the technical procedures employed in developing them.

Correlational studies also form the basis for virtually all impact model development. As noted, ideally, impact model development should stem from experimental research. But controlled studies are rarely available or even feasible to initiate. As a consequence, there has been a major effort on the part of social investigators to develop quasi-casual approaches to understanding social phenomena. Duncan's (1966) path analysis approach is only one illustration, and there are other approaches as well (Schuessler, 1969). But, from the standpoint of program development and implementation, the investigator must also take into account the manipulative ability of variables included in his analysis. In order to do so, he must know something about the limits of social action programs and the potentialities for social change in particular areas. Otherwise, after having completed analyses designed to make causal inferences, he or the policy makers are placed in the position of "deriving" manipulable program elements. In the process of doing so, they may wander quite far from the measures included in the quasi-causal study, with resulting lack of change when action programs are introduced. If there is one single example to cite about this point, it is the large number of investigations that apparently document the importance of social economic factors in the educational and emotional experiences of a person.

Even if one can demonstrate with considerable confidence the importance of social economic factors, how does one go about developing impact models once one is aware of the determinants? Usually one begins by raising questions about the differences between individuals of different socio-economic statuses, and then tries to develop ways to make up for, or remedy, the discrepancies. From the standpoint of impact model development, however, it would be much better to have included in the actual prediction study direct measures of the kinds of things that ordinarily one includes as program elements, rather than socio-economic status. Underlying many of our remedial programs to improve educational performance of children is a view that middle-class children have much broader and intensive types of social stimulation. Consequently, there are considerable federal and local funds and tremendous amount of manpower going into the development of programs to increase the social stimulation of lower socio-economic children. It seems to me eminently reasonable to argue that we would be much better off, however, if instead of looking at correlations between the socio-economic status of parents and educational performance, a study was developed that measured directly the social stimulation variable and put this in the predictive analysis.

If successful research from the standpoint of program development and implementation is going to be undertaken, it is necessary that we not only take into account the potential manipulability of our variables, but also somehow, to forsake some of the habitual "stock" variables included in research and substitute ones more directly relevant to programs.

Evaluation

The evaluation procedure consists of two important tasks (Suchman, 1967). First of all, it is critical that we have some knowledge of whether or not programs are carried out in the ways that they were planned and developed. In order to have knowledge of the extent to which programs are carried out in conformity with the principles under which they were developed, some combination of quantitative data on the populations served, and who could be served, and field studies of the ways that the programs are conducted, are required.

In order to accomplish the second task, namely to evaluate whether or not the program had an impact, some type of experimental evaluation is required, and there are many complex technical problems involved (see, for example, Bohrnstedt, 1969). Experimental evaluations in these times, furthermore, often need to be undertaken in ways that provide information on their "cost benefit" as well as on their efficacy.

There is no reason in this paper to stress the importance of evaluation research from the standpoint of social policy development and the social rehabilitation fields. This matter has been considered elsewhere in detail (Freeman and Sherwood, 1965) and, indeed, one of the papers presented here is emphatic on this point. I would like, however, to point up the important benefits from extensive evaluation studies to the academic disciplines of the social sciences themselves. It is simply unreasonable to believe that either laboratory studies or nonexperimental field research in themselves are going to be sufficient for the development of a science of social behavior. It is also difficult to imagine widespread community support, either in terms of cooperation or the provision of financial resources, for broad experimental studies in the community if the purpose is primarily the accumulation of "basic knowledge." Rather, it seems to me, experimental evaluation studies are the major opportunity that we have to undertake causal investigations.

Because of the current commitments, the programs of treatment and rehabilitation, and because of the "need to know," experimental evaluation studies represent an activity with benefits to the suppliers of resources, the community itself, and the social sciences. Investigations that can contribute to the subject matter of the social sciences and, at the same time, provide useful and meaningful results from the standpoint of the development of a more rational series of social policies and action programs, may indeed be the most challenging arena of work for social researchers during the remainder of this century (National Science Board, 1969).

Concluding Comment

Let me try to summarize briefly the points I have raised in this paper. Initially, I proposed that there are five essential design elements, cooperation, reliability, validity, precision and efficiency. My position is that they need to be considered in the order just noted. There is simply no way of developing a successful investigation unless one has confidence that it is possible to secure the cooperation of the various parties who can stymie a study. These include of course the subjects or informants, but there are other individuals involved whose cooperation is necessary in order to sample, or who have legal and quasi-legal means to prevent an investigation. If cooperation is assured, reliability becomes the next concern. There is no point in considering other design elements unless one has been able to develop reliable measures and means of recording data. Next, one needs to worry about the validity problem, and in worrying about the validity problem I have particularly emphasized the limitations of accepting verbal responses as indicators or reflections of interpersonal and social behavior.

Then, there is the problem of precision or accuracy, and the importance of having some confidence in the data presented or some range at least of the degree of precision of data. Finally, I have indicated that there is a need to worry about the efficiency of research given limits of financial and human resources.

With these design elements in mind, the subsequent sections of the paper have tried to consider some practical ways of developing studies that are consistent with the design elements, to point up the direction for general development of a methodology of social research and to describe some of the special issues in applied, or what I have termed social policy, investigations. These three sections admittedly are incomplete. I do not pretend to know all of the "tricks," and certainly there are differences of opinion about how one pragmatically maximizes the design elements. Also, I have stressed that there is much less than a desirable effort being made on a general level to improve our methods. This section of my paper reflects the limited consideration that has gone into the relationship between type of information and appropriate method. The varied ways in which social research is used in the development of social policy and action programs has made it impossible for me to do more than alert the reader to what I consider to be some of the key issues. If nothing more, however, perhaps I have been able to impress the reader with the limited state of our craft, and, by disparaging comments, perhaps will have stimulated activities in the necessary direction. Certainly I hope my view is clear. The conduct of studies is both a critical art and an orderly technical process, and both are underdeveloped.

Finally, let me go back to the starting point where I suggested five design elements. Really a sixth should be added, and it is antecedent to any of those I have noted. This is the matter of "relevance." Studies cannot be successful unless there is relevance either to the substantive matter of the social sciences or to the many persons who are engaged in programs of social action and social change. Ideally perhaps, studies should be relevant to the worlds of both scholarship and social development. While this may not always be feasible or desirable, I would be remiss in my assignment if I did not at least point out the importance of the *relevance* of research as well as the other design elements.

REFERENCES

BOHRNSTEDT, GEORGE W.
1969   "Observations on the measurement of change." In Edgar F. Borgatta (ed.), *Sociological Methodology*, pp. 113–136. San Francisco: Jossey-Bass, Inc.

BORGATTA, EDGAR
1960   "Ranking and self-assessments." *Journal of Social Psychology*, **52** (November): 279–307.

BULLOCK, HENRY A.
1951   "Racial attitudes and the employment of Negroes." *American Journal of Sociology*, **56** (March): 448–457.

CUMMING, ELAINE and JOHN
1957   *Closed Ranks*. Cambridge: Harvard University Press.

CURTIS, RICHARD F., and ELTON F. JACKSON
1962   "Multiple indicators in social research." *American Journal of Sociology*, **68** (September): 195–204.

DODD, STUART C.
1966   "Scient-scales for measuring methodology." *American Behavioral Scientist*, **9** (June): 3–19.

DOHRENWEND, BARBARA SNELL, JOHN COLOMBATOS, and BRUCE P. DOHRENWEND
1968   "Social distance and interviewer effects." *Public Opinion Quarterly*, **32** (Fall): 410–422.

DOHRENWEND, BARBARA S., and BRUCE P. DOHRENWEND
1968   "Sources of refusals in surveys." *Public Opinion Quarterly*, **32** (Spring): 74–83.

DUNCAN, OTIS D.
1966   "Path analysis: sociological examples." *American Journal of Sociology*, **72** (July): 1–16.

ELLINSON, JACK
1963   "Methods of sociomedical research," Chapter 18. In Howard E. Freeman, Sol Levine, and Leo G. Reeder (eds.), *Handbook of Medical Sociology*. Englewood Cliffs: Prentice-Hall.

FREEMAN, HOWARD E.
1963   "The strategy of social policy research." In *The Social Welfare Forum*, pp. 142–156. New York: Columbia University Press.

FREEMAN, HOWARD E., and OZZIE G. SIMMONS
1960   "The use of the survey in mental illness research." *Mental Hygiene*, **44** (July): 400–410.

FREEMAN, HOWARD E., and ARTHUR H. RICHARDSON
1969   "Anomia and social behavior among the very old." (Mimeo.)

FREEMAN, HOWARD E., ARTHUR H. RICHARDSON, JAMES F. CUMMINS and HAROLD W. SCHNAPER

1967   "Use of medical resources by Spancos: II. Social factors and medical care experience." *Milbank Memorial Fund Quarterly,* **45** (January): 61–75.

FREEMAN, HOWARD E., and CLARENCE C. SHERWOOD
1970   *Social Policy and Social Research.* Englewood Cliffs: Prentice-Hall.

FREEMAN, HOWARD E., and CLARENCE C. SHERWOOD
1965   "Research in large-scale intervention programs." *Journal of Social Issues,* **21** (January): 11–28.

MECHANIC, DAVID
1969   *Mental Health and Social Policy.* Englewood Cliffs: Prentice-Hall.

MERTON, ROBERT K., L. BROOM, and L. S. COTTRELL (eds.)
1959   *Sociology Today,* Chapter 1. New York: Basic Books.

NATIONAL SCIENCE BOARD
1969   *Increasing the Nation's Use of the Social Sciences.* Special Commission on the Social Sciences. Washington, D.C.

RAINWATER, LEE, and DAVID J. PITTMAN
1967   "Ethical problems in studying a politically sensitive deviant community." *Social Problems,* **14** (Spring): 357–366.

REISMAN, DAVID, and MARK BENNY (eds.)
1956   "The interview in social research." *American Journal of Sociology,* **62** (September): entire issue.

RUEBHAUSEN, OSCAR M., and ORVILLE G. BRIM
1965   "Privacy and behavioral research." *Columbia Law Review,* **65** (November): 1184–1211.

RICHARDSON, STEPHEN A., BARBARA S. DOHRENWEND, and DAVID KLEIN
1965   *Interviewing.* New York: Basic Books.

ROSENTHAL, ROBERT
1968   *Pygmalion in the Classroom.* New York: Holt, Rinehart and Winston, Inc.

SAWYER, JACK, and HOWARD SCHECHTER
1968   "Computers, privacy, and national data centers: the responsibility of social scientists." *American Sociologist,* **23** (November): 810–818.

SCHUESSLER, KARL
1969   "Covariance analysis in sociological research." In Edgar F. Borgatta (ed.), *Sociological Methodology,* **1**: 219–244. San Francisco: Jossey-Bass, Inc.

SMIGEL, ERWIN O.
1964   *The Wall Street Lawyer,* Chapter 2. New York: Free Press.

SUCHMAN, EDWARD A.
1968   "The sampling of behavior." *American Sociologist,* **3** (February): 49–51.

TEELE, JAMES E.
1965   "An appraisal of research on social participation." *Sociological Quarterly,* **6** (Summer): 257–267.

WALTON, JOHN
  1966   "Discipline, method, and community power: A note on the sociology
          of knowledge." *American Sociological Review,* **31** (October): 684–689.
WATTS, LEWIS G., HOWARD E. FREEMAN, HELEN M. HUGHES, ROBERT MORRIS, and
  THOMAS PETTIGREW
  1965   *Middle-Income Negro Family Faces Urban Renewal.* Waltham, Mass:
          Brandeis University.
WEISS, CAROL H.
  1968   *Validity of Interview Responses of Welfare Mothers.* Columbia University:
          Bureau of Applied Social Research.
ZELDITCH, MORRIS, JR.
  1962   "Some methodological problems of field studies." *American Journal of
          Sociology,* **67** (March): 566–576.

CHAPTER TWELVE

Consent, Cooperation, and Control in Rehabilitation Research

GEORGE H. WOLKON

The five design elements of cooperation, reliability, validity, precision, and efficiency proposed by Professor Freeman as essential to developing a successful investigation seems a useful way to organize the issues involved in "The Implementation of Research Investigations." I not only agree that cooperation with and among all persons in the broad research settings might be seen as the first item in a Guttman type scale with the underlying dimension being carrying out a successful research project, but also suggest that cooperation is a necessary but not sufficient condition to perform useful, valid and relevant research. The nature of the cooperation is a major determinant of the quality of the reliability, validity, precision, and efficiency obtained in the actual research. The goal of this paper is to discuss the issue of cooperation in more detail and to examine its ramifications in terms of the total research design and research outcomes.

Consent To Do Research

It is obvious that except for certain kinds of participant observation, spying, works of hate and other kinds of unobtrusive data collection methods (Webb, Campbell, Schwartz, and Sechrest, 1966), official permission from persons in power positions is needed to carry out research. Freeman's point that there are developing multiple loci of power in many settings is well taken. Argyris (1968, p. 189) reports the embryonic development of student (subject) organizations (unions) to offset directly the power and control of academic instructor researchers.

As social scientists, our diagnostic skills in locating the formal and real power centers and developing tactics of entry into those centers should be well developed. In practice, this expectation is not borne out. The basic reason for what are in essence our misjudgments is a naïve optimism and trust in the Weberian organization chart. We think that when the legitimate leader or leaders give consent that there will be cooperation from and among the leaders, other persons filling squares in the organizational chart, including the clients, staff, and the researchers. Further, we think that consent of the leaders or agency directors implies control over the treatment program and the participants, staff, and clients, in that program.

Consent to Cooperate: The Director

Perhaps the first step in developing the tactics of obtaining the kind of consent that will lead to the quality of cooperation desired is to ascertain the motivation of the agency director and other leaders for giving consent. The point is that the giving of consent does not insure cooperation and that the director's motivation for giving consent or for even apparently stimulating research in his own agency, may lead to different levels of cooperation which will affect the reliability, validity, precision efficiency, and relevance of the research project.

Under ideal circumstances, the motivations of the director and the researcher mesh perfectly: to add to the knowledge of social science, to contribute to the understanding of the substantive problem area, and to improve the service program. When this does occur, many of the potential problems discussed by Freeman, and others in this conference, cease to be of meaningful concern. An example would be if the question of evaluating a service program can be changed with mutual agreement from, "Is it good or bad?" to, "What kinds of clients benefit in what way from what type of services?". The change in question implicitly if not explicitly, assumes that the new or experimental program represents the best thinking of the practitioners at that time. If not, there is no point in carrying out or evaluating the service program.

In order to suggest improvements in the service program, we must make reasonable inferences from our data. If our data are well integrated with our own discipline's conceptual and theoretical approaches, our inferences will be sounder than if our data are theoretical. This means that in terms of research design and in terms of the data that are collected, the differences between basic and applied research dissipate. The major difference will be in the kinds of reports that are written; e.g., reports dealing with the evaluation of the treatment program, systematic descriptions, or attempts at theory building and verification (Wolkon, 1963).

The ideal viable cooperative situation will also allow for side studies — answering questions not directly relevant to the original goals of the research project by (a) collecting a small amount of specific data along with the data of major relevance, (b) using already collected data to answer questions developed in the research process, and (c) collecting new specific data to answer questions developed in the process of research. This kind of cooperation clearly affects what Freeman has called "efficiency"; i.e., "the minimal expenditure of resources, money, manpower, and the like to conduct the research project." In a narrow sense, side studies lower the efficiency for the individual research project in that resources are used for other than the project's major reason for existence. On the other hand, given the financial expense and other resources needed for data collection and, even more important, for the formulation of good questions, side studies seem most efficient for the field as a whole. Like any war, the war on ignorance must take advantage of targets of opportunity.

Why spend time discussing an ideal state when the realities of research implementation and its consequent compromises are the realistic foci of the day? I guess all I am saying is: don't compromise too quickly in the attempt to obtain consent for this kind of cooperation, or the word "compromise" will truly deserve its pejorative connotation. More important, the word "research" may in time suffer from the same connotation.

Am I over-optimistic, even euphoric? Maybe. The experiences I am going to report are not randomly selected from a defined population and thus are not offered as compelling evidence for optimism.

While engaged in research at Hill House (Mental Health Rehabilitation and Research, Inc.) in Cleveland, the issue of side studies came up a number of times. The director of the agency and I decided to attempt to specify the need for post-hospital services for psychiatric patients returning to the community. The purpose was to help the agency and the community in planning services. Our major source of data was a number of interviews with mental health professionals. Within the limitations of the research design, the purpose was accomplished (Wolkon & Tanaka, 1965). As with most interviews, there was a great deal of information that was not used for the major purpose of the research effort. The agency director and I discussed whether we should spend our resources in examining the interviews in a way which would help us understand the continuum of care — a related but not directly relevant question. Not only was it decided that internal personnel should be used, but money was allocated to hire someone from outside to work on the project. This side effort resulted in a paper, which at the least is interesting, entitled, "Disease or Deviance: Effects on the Treatment Continuum" (Wolkon & Melzer, 1968).

A more dramatic side study, although it required no extra expenditure of funds, was done at the same agency and was totally unrelated to the major project. A section of the literature was reporting conflicting explanations concerned with the firm finding that first-borns achieve more than later-borns. One possible explanation postulated a differential need for achievement for different ordinal positions. We had collected need achievement data from psychiatric patients in order to predict vocational functioning and also had birth order data. A colleague, George Levinger, had been investigating marital functioning and had obtained birth order and need achievement data for his own purposes. With agency support, we tested the relationship between birth order and need for achievement for three independent samples at extremely little extra cost to the field (Wolkon and Levinger, 1965).

Despite our thinking that side studies are efficient for the field in general, you may have become convinced by these experiences that exploiting targets of opportunities do not win wars. We would probably agree; but not exploiting them will postpone if not eliminate the possibility of winning. The director's consent to cooperate must be genuine if the described overall efficiency is to be one of the outcomes of the research project.

The tone of the above implies that once consent is obtained, the threat of lack of cooperation emanates solely from the agency director and not from the researcher. Obviously, this is not so. The general research design in the agency described above was that of evaluation of the impact of a social rehabilitation program for recently released psychiatric patients. The method of intake allowed for the randomly selected patients to refuse to participate in the treatment program (more will be said of this below). This situation was indeed a research problem; methods were explored to purify the control group. But it was a service problem, too. The director and staff wanted to know how they could deliver service to the patients who needed it but who were refusing the opportunity to participate. They asked the researcher to explore this problem, to redirect his current efforts and resources (not to give them up). The resulting investigation of the intake process was the most important contribution of the entire research program, both theoretically and in terms of immediate application and technique (Wolkon, 1968, a, b). Recently, an opportunity to test the theory and techniques in other settings was made available. The researcher asked the cooperation of the agency director for some of the agency's resources — personnel — to work and collect data in other settings. The request was granted and the results are being prepared for communication. Cooperation is indeed a reciprocal process.

Let us return to other motivations agency directors may have in giving consent and their potential consequences for the quality of subsequent cooperation.

Despite the criticisms we ourselves have about research and the complaints that administrators and practitioners level at research, research is perceived by many agency directors and others as bringing status and prestige as well as future funding to the agency. If status is the prime motivator for the giving of consent, cooperation will occur only when glory to the agency is a real possibility. Travel funds to present papers at conferences will easily be forthcoming, if the papers say the agency is good or if they are not directly relevant to the agency. This is probably not so for a paper with constructive criticism. Obtaining specific consent to have service personnel shift a portion of their time from serving clients to the completion of research forms will probably not be given. What will be important are the status symbols of research — an organizational slot for a researcher that is filled, a research plan that can be talked about, publications and conference papers, students and hopefully some sort of university affiliation. The content, quality and relevance of the research will be much less important. The task of the administrator will be to create the symbols of research at the least possible cost to the organization. A brief true story may dramatize the point. We are attempting to develop a vocational rehabilitation program for chronic unmotivated released psychiatric patients. We proposed to the director of a vocational agency that in order to increase and sustain motivation of the clients, the following program be implemented. During the first couple of weeks in the program the clients should be paid daily in cash, and then weekly in cash and finally weekly by check. The director rejected the motivating technique not on the basis of probable therapeutic success but because of administrative feasibility. Indeed, the director maintained before and after this event that he wanted to and was cooperating with us. This kind of cooperation not only threatens useful research, it threatens the development of innovative service programs. After a year of negotiations, the techniques were agreed to.

Many agency directors, with or without a demonstration grant, want to demonstrate with objective, rigorous, and systematic evidence that they, their program, and staff are doing a good job. A basic issue here is whether the findings are private or public. Clearly if we are interested in the field of rehabilitation, they must be public, even though it may hurt the agency's short run interest. A more subtle and at the same time more extreme implication for cooperation has to do with potential sources of data. If the treatment program is thought to be good, any interference with it, such as talking to clients about their problems — a research interview or a questionnaire or personality measure — will be seen as disrupting the treatment process. The type of institution, somewhat confounded with their own self-evaluation, will also affect the sources of data. For example, a psychoanalytically oriented institution is much more likely to refuse consent for a researcher to talk with their patients than is the administrator of a state psychiatric hospital with many marginal chronic schizophrenics. The availability of sources of data will clearly affect the design, the variables investigated, including whether or not they are manipulable, and the relevance of the design to the practitioner. This "ideal" type of director will also not be swayed by the logic of a research design that eliminates alternative explanations but more concerned with whether the data will demonstrate that a good job is being done. Implicit in these points is the fact that the evaluation question cannot be transformed as it was under the condition of true cooperation because the program is already good and therefore cannot be improved. Thus, a research project that tries to combine basic and applied research is unlikely.

No agency director can admit to these self-serving motivations because of public pressure. Research, especially evaluation research, is good, pure, and needed according to the public which supports many agencies through taxes and Red Feather contributions and by boards of trustees of the agencies. For the directors committed to their program Elison's (1967) tongue-in-cheek suggestions might be considered:

1. A control group should not be used.
2. If a control group is used, it should be selected purposively, rather than by random methods, and matched on "relevant variables."
3. If a prospective design cannot be used, the matching for the control groups should be done retrospectively.
4. Effort variables should be used as criteria of success rather than effect variables.
5. The evaluation should be done preferably by those in charge of the program.
6. The results should not be published in scientific literature, but should be issued as a report to one's self or the program director.

In this day and age of satisfying the consumers of service I would add to Elison's list, the evaluation of the service by those clients who voluntarily have chosen to remain in the program for a long period of time. The fact that dissonance theory offers a reasonable alternative explanation will not bother the director nor his board of trustees because musicology is not relevant to rehabilitation.

Perhaps persons engaged in research should form another power bloc and refuse to work and consult in agencies of this type. We should withhold our services until they are forced to see the error of their ways. This is unlikely; for some of us sincerely desire to be where the action is; can certainly use, if not need, the money; and may sincerely believe that some data, no matter what their limitations, are better than none. Where are the problems with solutions?

Consent to Control: Staff and Program Operation

When the agency director consents to cooperate, he often states that his staff is most interested in and willing to cooperate with the research. Further, he may state that he has sent his staff an inter-office memo informing them of their expected interest and cooperation. In essence, the director implies control over his staff. When research, especially evaluative research, is imminent, even the best practitioners who are most interested and want to be sincerely cooperative become somewhat anxious (which may or may not deter from their helpfulness). The first week I became associated with the agency in which I was going to do evaluation research, there was a welcoming party. When I was introduced to the husband of one of the social workers in the agency, he jokingly said, "So you are the one who is going to decide if my wife keeps her job!"

The magic of research is certainly overpowering and frightening. How can this fear and anxiety among the staff be overcome? No matter what the research problem, cooperation from the staff is necessary at some level in order to understand the service program, the nature of clients, etc. Are there differences between the formal program and what is actually occurring? Why? What are the crucial criterion variables as the staff sees them? What kind of language system does the staff use? Can it be meaningfully related to that of the researcher? Perhaps the research design requires that the staff keep systematic records, complete new forms and use rating scales. Perhaps, as in demonstration projects, the staff, i.e. the staff's intervention, is in fact the independent variable. Sometimes, the staff is asked to intervene in ways that are different from what they had been doing. Finally, any of us engaged in research want, at least should want, some of our work to be relevant and useful to the practitioners. As a minimum, we would hope that the agency in which the research was done would adopt our suggestions. This requires that there be an ongoing involvement of and cooperation with the practitioners.

One brief example where consent of the directors, although implying control and cooperation of the staff, did not result in the desired state follows. Krause (1966) reported a research project "aimed at reducing the sizable number of failures of applicants to keep a first appointment in a family service agency. He devised four specific and different procedures for intake workers and used a Latin Square design to take into account the effects of differences of worker performance and intake composition. This research plan is useful, technically competent and innovative.

Let us examine its implementation. The design required that each worker use each of the four procedures on randomly selected clients, even if in the worker's professional judgment it is not the best procedure. It should be kept in mind that the stimulus for the research was that what the practitioners were doing in intake was not leading to satisfactory results as seen by the practitioners. It is clear that the director and staff consented to this design. Nevertheless, there was no control over the implementation, neither internal nor external. In a revealing footnote, Krause reports that 60 per cent of the original sample was not exposed to the treatment procedures, because in the workers professional judgment the clients were in some way ill-suited to the experiment or because the workers did not apply the procedures for personal reasons. Krause's study was somewhat valuable but could have been more so if there were control over the cooperation of staff.

Consent of the director also implies he has control over the treatment program and its clients. The Krause study clearly shows the lack of control over the treatment program. We have all heard reports of school superintendents discussing the educational program and the reports of teachers telling of the management programs, of directors of psychiatric hospitals discussing their therapeutic programs and the reports of observers concerned with management and custodial programs, of directors of rehabilitation agencies telling of their rehabilitative programs and observing layoffs and hirings of clients based on the materialization of contracts in their shop and not on the therapeutic needs of the client. We have heard presidents of companies and their boards of trustees issue policies of fair employment practices and observed personnel directors and immediate supervisors sidestep them. In an earlier paper, Freeman and Sherwood (1965) included this as one aspect of accountability. Indeed, this is the responsibility of the director of the agency. The research person does, however, have a stake in it. His own interests in the social problem and the theoretical relationship between the intervention, the intermediate variable and outcome variables will be overshadowed. He may, however, still be able to evaluate the program by writing an expose.

One ideal plan for establishing control over the program and personnel, is for the researcher to be the director, i.e. the administrative director, not the director of the operations of the service program. This, as indicated above, does not solve all the problems but does help. The classic example is the Harwood Manufacturing Company. A psychologist owns and runs the company. Much testing of social science theory to applied problems has been accomplished. One need not be in industry to have this type of control. A former student of mine, Bill Shalinsky, was interested in applying Schutz's (1958) theory of interpersonal relations and group composition to children in a camp setting. His applied problem, was how to put the children together in cabins so that a camping experience would be more pleasurable and beneficial. He was also the program director of the camp. He had control over the kids, i.e. he decided what kids go in what cabins. He supervised and trained counselors and defined as part of their job the completion of rating forms for each child, etc. It should be pointed out that Shalinsky's work was both basic and applied and is reflected in the formal reports he has written (Shalinsky, 1968, 1969, a and b).

Even with the researcher having apparent control over the treatment program and subjects, many of the programs we are interested in understanding and evaluating are voluntary for the clients. In most psychotherapies and rehabilitation programs, motivation of the client is not only conceived of as a major determinant of continuing in the program but also of the progress he makes within it. Elsewhere we have argued that practitioners should not accept low motivation for needed services (Wolkon, 1968, a,b). Although entry into and continuance in a program is of legitimate and major concern to both practitioners and researchers, it makes evaluating the intervention program extremely complex.

Consent to Control: Clients as Recipients of Service.

When clients are voluntary, the actual implementation of the classical control group design, no matter how attractive and desirable, cannot be guaranteed and, in fact, is quite unlikely. Clients are able to choose to begin to participate in a rehabilitation program; if they begin, are able to choose to drop out of the program prior to obtaining maximum benefit from the program. Assuming that voluntary programs will remain voluntary based on civil liberties and assuming that motivation is essential for success in resocialization, are not volunteers the population of crucial concern? The answer is obviously, "Yes." But what does this do to our evaluation of the treatment procedure that is, can we establish the effects of the independent variable?

Perhaps the refusal rate and the drop-out rate are not large enough to be concerned about. That is, do all persons who need service choose to begin and continue in the programs? The answer is clearly "No." In our own work at Hill House, two-thirds of the psychiatric patients clinically evaluated as needing post-hospital rehabilitative services refused an opportunity to participate in them (Wolkon, 1968, a). The implication seems clear. When one is primarily interested in evaluating a treatment program, do not randomly assign from the population which manifests the greatest need, but randomly assign from the population that has applied for the program. This plan takes into account the issues of voluntarism, eliminates the possibility of refusals, but raises even more sharply the ethics involved in refusing treatment, and sharpens the issue of the potential difference between those who need service and those who demand it. Freeman and Sherwood (1965) discuss this issue under the concept of accountability. Does the program serve the persons it was designed to serve?

The question of whether starting with the population of applicants allows for statements concerning the effects of the treatment program is still unresolved. What are the drop-out rates of persons who begin a voluntary program? In out-patient psychiatry, a high drop-out rate (30–65 per cent) has been reported consistently for ten years (Eiduson, 1968). At the Hill House rehabilitation center one-half of the persons attended less than 10 times where at least 50 sessions are expected (Wolkon, in press). Another rehabilitation center for ex-psychiatric patients reported that they had carried out a randomly assigned control group evaluation (Beard, Pitt, Fisher, & Goertzel, 1963). They accepted applicants for their program on a random basis. They then compared the outcomes of those accepted with those not accepted. Yet they reported that 50 per cent of those accepted for the program failed to make more than one visit to the agency.

What was the treatment program that was evaluated? The application for help with the subsequent decision to continue or not, the program itself, the interaction between self selection and the program, or the self selection itself? At the very least, attendance (amount of exposure to the independent variable) should be related to the criterion variables and client characteristics should be related to attendance and to outcomes. In some of our work we have found that the greater the attendance, the better the outcome; and the high attenders do not have the best prognoses. Alternative explanations concerned with self-selection are nevertheless still present (Wolkon & Tanaka, 1966; Wolkon, in press).

Despite the control over the service program which we might naïvely and optimistically infer from the consent and cooperation of the director and staff, the lack of control over client participation will severely impede a straightforward evaluation of the effects of the service program. It seems necessary that in evaluation research with voluntary clients systematic data directly relevant to the probability of each person's continuation in the program and their prognoses be obtained from the treatment and control groups. These data should then be used to divide the control group into sub-groups corresponding to the different levels of exposure of individuals in the treatment group to the independent variable.

The description of the clients successfully and unsuccessfully served by the program is also an integral part of the evaluation as is a recommendation of programs for those who need something but refuse available programs.

Consent to Control: Clients as Respondents

The director's consent to cooperate also implies control over the clients as respondents for the research. In mental hospitals the implied control is well-founded. The patients know that in order to get released they must conform to the authority structure of the institution. In our study, one patient was somewhat reluctant to be interviewed. As the interviewer was attempting to convince the patient to participate in the research, the patient's psychiatrist overheard the discussion and intervened. He said, in almost these words, "In order for you to go home, I have to consider you well. Taking part in this interview will be a sign that you are well. If you do not cooperate, it means you are still sick." The patient then "chose" to cooperate.

The type and level of control will obviously affect the refusal rate of the respondents. In addition to lessening the precision of the study, the type of control may also affect the reliability and validity. If we include within the concept of control the auspices under which the research is being undertaken, including the set given to the respondent, problems of reliability and validity become even more obvious.

In the Hill House project, the patients were told that the hospital staff would not see the individual responses and the interview would in no way affect any treatment decisions. They were told the purpose of the interview was to help others, people who might find themselves in similar situations in the future. We had hoped to eliminate major attempts of the respondent to fulfill his goal of either being released from the hospital or remaining there. We thought this approach would lead to more valid responses. On the other hand, we thought that the lack of direct and immediate relevance to the respondent might have lessened the reliability of the responses which of course limits validity. We made the decision without compelling data.

The problem of control over people not in total institutions is even more vexing. We all believe that the refusal rate can be substantially reduced if we use the right letterhead, if the auspices of the research are perceived as legitimate and powerful. This probably is true. Let us briefly examine three studies dealing with recently released psychiatric patients.

Angrist, Lefton, Dinitz, and Pasamanick (1968) sent letters to the former patients saying that, "As part of our program, the staff of Columbus Psychiatric Institute and Hospital is seeing former patients in order to find out how they are doing." Angrist, *et al.* (1968, p. 62) reported that, "Only a few families resented being contacted." They further reported a total respondent loss, including no contacts, of only 8 per cent. Freeman and Simmons (1963) in their interviews with relatives of former psychiatric patients used a letterhead of an organization called "Community Health Project." The first sentence in the letter further specified the auspices, "At the request of the Public Health Service, the Community Health Project, in collaboration with (name of hospital) is making a survey . . ." Later in the letter confidentiality was mentioned. These authors report (p. 29) that 49 interviews of 698 (7 per cent) attempted were not included in the report. In the majority of these the designated relative refused to be interviewed or terminated the interview prior to its completion. However, they further point out that 50 of the interviews attempted required either a reassignment of interviewers and/or a letter over the signature of the patient's psychiatrist suggesting that the interview may be beneficial in helping the patient remain out of the hospital. Freeman and Simmons explicitly acknowledge that the latter two methods of increasing response rate may affect the obtained responses and they stated their preference for the potential bias as opposed to a higher rate of uncompleted interviews.

The real problem is that we do not know the nature nor the extent of the potential bias in response due to the auspices and perceived power of the interviewer. As a gross statement of the comparative findings between these studies, it may be said that the Freeman and Simmons study found no relationship between role expectations and performance with re-hospitalization while the Angrist *et al.* study did find such a relationship. The studies differed in a number of ways; eg., the sex, chronicity and social class of the patients, the instruments, etc., were somewhat different. As described above the studies also differed in the stated auspices of the research. Angrist *et al.* said they were from the hospital and made no mention of confidentiality as compared to Freeman and Simmons who, for the most part, were identified as separate from the hospital and mentioned confidentiality.

One could raise the issue that the respondents in the Angrist *et al.* study were influenced to justify their decision to have the ex-patient re-hospitalized or not. That is, those relatives who re-hospitalized the patient justified their decision by reporting low performance on the part of the patient or vice versa; if the patient were not re-hospitalized, the relatives state he is performing well.

In the Hill House follow-up study in the community we used the letter-head of a research organization and said the interviews were confidential. Of those asked for an interview, 27 per cent refused. The refusal rate may have been higher because the interviews took place about 18 months after hospital release as compared to 6 months for the other two studies. If the refusal rate could have been lowered by using the implied power of the psychiatric hospital as the "inducement" to cooperate, to what degree would the increased rate of responses have reflected the inducement in terms of unreliability and lack of validity?

The situation, set, and relationship between the interviewer and the interviewee are reflected in the verbal responses obtained. The problem that we face is not to eliminate these "demand characteristics" (Orne, 1962) because they cannot be eliminated; others may be substituted but demand characteristics will always exist. Our task, then, is to understand them in order to take them into account in our interpretations and designs.

If our interpretation of verbal responses and attitudes indicate a one to one relationship with behavior as Freeman and others (e.g. Deutscher, 1966, in press) have suggested, indeed we are committing a grievous error. On the other hand, if we are interested in predicting future behavior and we decide that the best predictor we have available, given our resources and ingenuity, is the person's attitude, then we must use it.

The value of an attitude measure as a predictor of behavior depends on the accuracy of the prediction in relation to the purpose at hand in comparison to the availability and accuracy of other predictor variables. The arguments against using attitudes as predictors of future behavior generally imply that better predictors exist and that the only reason we use attitudes is ease and feasibility. Often behavior samples are suggested as a better predictor of behavior, if not a panacea for all research problems. As in any prediction problem, we must decide on the nature of the criterion variable prior to deciding on the best predictor. Does future behavior mean a specific act such as voting for a presidential candidate or does it refer to a currently unspecified set of future behaviors such as how a congressman will influence and be influenced by his colleagues and constituency and how he will vote during his term in office; or such as typing skills as compared to being a "Gal Friday" including the administration of chicken soup when necessary.

When specific behaviors are the criterion, then behavior samples taken in situations with similar demand characteristics as the actual behavior may be the best predictor; for example, a typing test or a confidential survey (see Deutscher, in press). When the criterion variable is an unspecified set of future actions, an attitude measure may be the best predictor.

There is no question that our measurement of attitudes must be improved. Rokeach (1966–67) has suggested that in addition to obtaining measures of the attitudes towards the subject we also obtain measures of the attitude toward the situation in which the attitude will be transmogrified into behavior. He is suggesting that we attend to the demand characteristics of the criterion situation. The moral is that the demand characteristics of the research interview situation should parallel as closely as possible the demand characteristics of the situation to which we are predicting. The fact of multiple actions and situations of the criterion situation presents a stimulating challenge. But let us not dismiss attitudes as predictors of future behavior. Let us try to understand their relationship. (For an excellent discussion, see Ehrlich, 1969.)

Summary

This paper discussed the multi-faceted aspects of cooperation in relation to research design and research outcomes. It was indicated that consent to do research from people in power positions does not guarantee either cooperation with potential participants or control over them. The motivation of the agency director was proposed as a major determinant of the quality of cooperation. Control over the implementation of the service program — the independent variable — was discussed. The lack of control over the client's amount of exposure to the service program implies extreme difficulty, if not impossibility, in applying a classic control group design with voluntary clients. It was suggested that in many situations, the demand characteristics of the interview situation has opposite effects on response rates as compared to reliability and validity. The complexity of the relationship between attitudes and behavior was interpreted in terms of the demand characteristics of the predictor and criterion situations. It was stated that the demand characteristics cannot be eliminated but must be understood in order to create more appropriate research designs and interpretations.

REFERENCES

ANGRIST, S., LEFTON, M., S. DINITZ, and B. PASAMANICK
1968   *Women After Treatment.* New York: Appleton-Century-Crofts.
ARGYRIS, C.
1968   "Some unintended consequences of rigorous research." *Psychological Bulletin* **70**, 3: 185–197.
BEARD, J. H., R. B. PITT, S. H. FISHER, and V. GOERTZEL
1963   "Evaluating the effectiveness of a psychiatric rehabilitation program." *American Journal of Orthopsychiatry*, **33**, 4: 701–712.
DEUTSCHER, I.
1969   "Evil companions and naughty behavior: Some thoughts and evidence bearing on a folk hypothesis." In J. Douglas and R. A. Scott (eds.), *Deviance.* New York: Basic Books (in press).
DEUTSCHER, I.
1966   "Words and deeds: Social science and social policy." *Social Problems*, **13**: 235–254.
EHRLICH, H. J.
1969   "Attitudes, behavior, and the intervening variables." *The American Sociologist*, **4**, 1: 29–34.
EIDUSON, B. T.
1968   "Retreat from help." *American Journal of Orthopsychiatry*, **38**, 5: 910–925.
ELINSON, J.
1967   "Effectiveness of social action programs in health and welfare." In *Assessing the Effectiveness of Health Services Ross Conference on Pediatric Research*, pp. 77–81. Ross Laboratories: Columbus, Ohio.
FREEMAN, H., and C. SHERWOOD
1965   "Research in large scale intervention programs." *Journal of Social Issues*, **21**, 1: 11–28.
FREEMAN, H. E., and O. G. SIMMONS
1963   *The Mental Patient Comes Home.* New York: John Wiley and Sons.

KRAUSE, M. S.
1966 "Comparative effects on continuance of four experimental intake procedures." *Social Casework*, 6: 519–525.

ORNE, M. T.
1962 "On the social psychology of the psychological experiment: With particular reference to demand characteristics and their implications." *American Psychologist*, 17: 776–783.

ROKEACH, M.
1966–67 "Attitude change and behavioral change." *Public Opinion Quarterly*, 30: 529–550.

SCHUTZ, W. C.
1958 *FIRO*. New York: Rinehart and Company.

SHALINSKY, W.
1968 "Criteria used in cabin composition." *Camping Magazine* (May).

SHALINSKY, W.
1969 "Group composition as an element of social group work practice." *Social Service Review*, 43, 1: 42–49(a).

SHALINSKY, W.
1969 "Group composition as a factor in assembly effects." *Human Relations*, 22: 457–464(b).

WEBB, E. J., D. T. CAMPBELL, R. D. SCHWARTZ, and L. SECHREST.
1966 *Unobtrusive Measures*. Chicago, Illinois: Rand McNally and Company.

WOLKON, G. H.
1963 "Perspectives and procedures of the Hill House research program." Paper presented at the National Institute of Halfway Houses.

WOLKON, G. H.
1968 "Effecting a continuum of care: An exploitation of the crisis of psychiatric hospital release." *Community Mental Health Journal*, 4, 1: 63–73 (a).

WOLKON, G. H.
1968 "Structural interventions and the use of rehabilitation facilities by psychiatric patients." *Rehabilitation Literature*, 29: 40–42 (b).

WOLKON, G. H.
in press "Characteristics of clients and continuity of care into the community." *Community Mental Health Journal*.

WOLKON, G. H., and G. LEVINGER
1965 "Birth order and need for achievement." *Psychological Reports*, 16, 1: 72–73.

WOLKON, G. H., and A. E. MELZER
1968 "Disease or deviance: Effects on the treatment continuum." In M. Lefton, J. K. Skipper, and C. H. McCaghy (eds.), *Approaches to Deviance*. New York: Appleton-Century-Crofts. 339–348.

WOLKON, G. H., and H. T. TANAKA
  1965   "Professionals' views on the need for psychiatric aftercare services."
          Community Mental Health Journal, 1, 3: 262–270.
WOLKON, G. H., and H. T. TANAKA
  1966   "Outcome of a social rehabilitation service for recently released
          psychiatric patients." *Social Work*, 11, 2: 53–61.

CHAPTER THIRTEEN

Integrating Theory and Practice*

ROBERT C. LEONARD AND JAMES K. SKIPPER, JR.

We conceive of the problem of integrating social theory and social practice as one of social organization, with both cultural and structural components. Society constructs specialized roles and organizations for doing research and for carrying out social action programs. Each of these kinds of organizations develops a culture for rationalizing and sustaining its own activities. The problem, then, is to integrate this division of labor so as to achieve the common goals of the overall system. This problem is familiar to both academics and practitioners. Likewise the solution we discuss — development of practice-oriented basic research programs within universities is not without precedent. We take the problem of putting knowledge to work to be the shared responsibility of both academic organizations and work organizations. So although our conception of the problem and the steps we propose focus on the university as a center for research, firm links between work organizations and the university are necessary.

Our proposal may appear radical or impractical for many kinds of social practice. Likewise, it may appear to place an unreasonable burden upon the university. We are convinced it is neither. Rather, it is the most efficient and effective way to build upon our existing organizations. The best research has been, is being, and will continue to be done within universities. The practical professions can do no better than to call upon universities — as specialists in the development, preservation and dissemination of knowledge — for assistance in the development of knowledge that will help improve professional practice. At the same time, this collaborative effort can contribute to the university. Practical wisdom gained through repeated experience is an important source of knowledge and practical usefulness can be a severe test of scholarly theories.

Action-oriented research within the university, may be familiar to all who are acquainted with university-affiliated professional schools. On the other hand, not all professional schools accept empirical research, and of those that do, not all accept social research. Among those that do try, not all succeed in developing sustained efforts in practice-oriented social research. The reasons for lack of such research are seen in the dual requirements placed upon it. The kind of research program we speak of has the following characteristics: (a) It is academically respectable, i.e., *basic* research meeting all our best scholarly standards; (b) it is done by fully qualified academics who meet regular university criteria for appointment. At the same time: (a′) It is practical, i.e., usable and acceptable by the practitioner in his natural habitat; (b′) it is done by fully qualified practitioners who meet all legal, professional and/or bureaucratic criteria for appointment within the work organization. Trying to do rigorous research that has direct and yet important applications to the ongoing flow of client service may well be the most difficult task a scientist could ever choose. This would be reason enough for its relatively slow development in contrast to purely academic research on the one hand and, on the other hand, to empirically loose speculation from "clinical experience" or unthinking organizational bookkeeping.

The university's task is to create a structure — e.g., within the professional school — that will minimize strains on the practitioner-researcher while at the same time maintaining the two standards of scholarly competence and practical relevance. At first glance this may seem an unrealizable goal. On the other hand, our personal experience with, and observation of, the nursing and medical professions suggests it is possible, under the right conditions. Study of the same problem in the many other professions and tinkering trades which occupy space in the modern American university might add evidence of the feasibility of this type of research program. The first factor we discuss is conflict between the practitioner and academic cultures, which produces strain for the practitioner-researcher role.

The Two Cultures of Thought and Action[1]

RATIONALITY VS. RATIONALIZATION

At the outset, we should remember that thinking and doing reside on a two-way street. Certainly within the history of social science theory,

the cause-effect relation between thought and action has a
problematic. Since "theory" after all is nothing but another
the process of thinking, a theory can just as well be determined by
action as it can be a guide to future action. These two processes might
labeled "rationalization" and "rationality." We have the insight from
Freud that thoughts are often rationalizations for actions of the past;
that is, action determines thought. In contrast, the proposal here to
integrate theory and practice through practice-oriented research presumes
using the theory to guide the practitioner in his work. This is simply an
extension to a new area of a general historical process toward increasing
rationality of action through application of science.[2] Academic research
is used to link thought and action through the development of scientific
theories of practice.[3] This "rational" use of (scientific) thought for
guiding social action is the reverse of the process of "rationalization"
identified by Freud. In the first case, thought guides action. In the
second, thoughts are rationalizations for actions of the past — that is,
action determines thought.

The relationship between thought and action is further complicated
when a practitioner's performance is "evaluated" by conformity to
accepted procedures (i.e., a theory of practice). Obviously, one way to
improve the integration of theory and practice is to pick the theory that
fits closest to already established procedures. The practitioner is expected
to justify — i.e., "rationalize" — his actions. Thus it is quite understandable that the fit with commitments already made in action would
often be a primary criterion for accepting or rejecting a theory of practice.
Is is easy for practitioners to believe that what is accepted procedure is
automatically good (i.e., "therapeutic") for the client and to reject
previously unaccepted procedures as bad. Any questioning of accepted
practices, or proposal for new ones, may involve an admission that
established practice has not been helpful to the client, or perhaps even
harmful. In the medical and nursing professions we have noted this
even when there is no empirical evidence to support accepted procedures. Even more startling: when an accepted procedure is shown to
be harmful, some practitioners will continue its use. Rodman and
Kolodny discuss this as "denial and displacement" (1965: 104–105). It
is harder to accept the new evidence than it is to continue to accept the
old theory. From the point of view of the customer receiving services,
this is at least unfortunate and perhaps most often simply unethical and
immoral behavior by the practitioner.

But, whatever the moral status of such rationalization by practitioners

...ut their effectiveness, such a process should
...cientists who have been sensitized by Freud's
...cted in the more recent research on cognitive
..., practitioners must understand that scientific
...must be accepted, if not understood, before
...rationality to social action rather than just
...ion. Furthermore, this problem may be more
...but personal over-commitment to a theory is
far from ....; ivory tower scientists. Some famous controversies in the history of science have been generated by individuals who seemed to have their mind made up, and did not want to be confused by any more facts. Placing the additional burden of practical usefulness upon a theory exacerbates the problem. A good deal of misunderstanding between practitioner and scientist might be avoided if the complexity of the practical uses of theory were recognized by both.

At the social system level, much talk about action can be identified as what Marx called ideology. Ideologies are, again, rationalizations for occupants of positions — e.g., occupations — in the system. This view of professional ideologies is in contrast to the hope that professional theory — e.g., principles of practice — can be used to (rationally) guide professional action. But it is this latter conception which we propose for linking action to thought through scientifically based theories of professional practice.

IVORY TOWER AND PRACTICAL WORLD OF WORK

There is a problematic relationship between thought and action: does present thought guide future action or is it rationalization for actions of the past? For the individual practitioner this problem is institutionalized in a conflict between cultures within a division of labor — between the "thinkers" of the ivory tower and the "doers" of the practicing professions. There is indeed a conflict between these two cultures. We have seen it clearly in our work with the development of university-based patient care research programs. But we have also observed it elsewhere, directly and through the reports of those doing research in practice settings. It is also a matter of personal experience for most academics who experience strain between their research and teaching. How often do academicians study their own teaching? How often do they apply their own research methods to improvement of their own professional practice? The answer is: almost never. As an administrative assistant in the president's office of one of our top state university systems put it, privately: "The universities are the 'dark continent' of administration. The government and business have been investigated to death by academicians but they won't touch their own organization."

In some sense, the basic strain between scholar and practitioner may never be eliminated, but only controlled. The members of each culture may have a "trained incapacity" of seeing the same things as significant, worthwhile, or real. We may expect varying degrees of success in joining the two, depending on the area of scholarly endeavor we are trying to integrate with action. Civil engineering, with at least a two thousand year history behind it, must face different problems in the use of pure mathematics than does vocational rehabilitation which barely has any history at all and yet tries to integrate the scholarly developments of sociology, which itself has barely been born. From a moderately developed profession, such as medicine, we could perhaps draw examples of successful, and unsuccessful, approaches to integration of scholarly knowledge with practical action most useful for our purpose here. It is clear from the twenty-year history of medical sociology, that we have much to learn about the application of social science research to the improvement of the performance of social practitioners. A recognition of the two cultures is a prelude to the action-oriented research solution of the problem. We next briefly delimit these conflicts between the two cultures to highlight this barrier to integrating theory with practice through action-oriented basic research.

WHAT IS "WORK"?

The academician has as his acknowledged goal the development of knowledge for knowledge's sake: "Here's to pure science, may it never be of use!" The academic culture places highest value and pays the greatest rewards for "pure" research. Practical implications matter little. The primary consideration is simply whether there will be an increase in the knowledge of the science. Immediate benefits for the general society are given low priority. Indeed, the scholar can *lose* the respect of his academic colleagues by showing too much concern with practical affairs of the general society. In contrast, the priority of values within the practitioner culture is reversed. The professional is inclined to value action over contemplation, to value "practical" research over "theoretical" research. The practitioner is inclined to be impatient with heavily qualified scholarly discourse that provides no clear implication for practice. The action-oriented professional practitioner is likely to regard the knowledge-oriented scholar as someone who "does not care for people." On the other hand, the researcher is inclined to be impatient with mundane things like organizational meetings which last too long and are too frequent.

Within the work organization run by practitioners, the scientist goes home from a day of meetings, and conferences, feeling exhausted as though the day had been wasted and futile, while the action-oriented professional is satisfied with a day's work well done. The solution of a stream of immediate particular action problems provides little satisfaction to the scholar who is concerned with discovering eternal truth, while it is the very essence of work life for the practitioner. In contrast, the practitioner who finds himself within the academic setting will be startled by the lack of communication with his colleagues. He will very likely feel isolated. The norm of locking oneself behind closed doors and communicating only with the typewriter or computer for hours or even days on end can seem unnatural for those socialized into the action-oriented culture of the practitioner. The practitioner can go home from a day of reading and writing feeling exhausted and discouraged by a day futilely wasted, while the scholar would be pleased by the same day's progress.

The Organizational Problem

"Basic" vs. "Applied"

Beginning with the practitioner's problem is often regarded as degrading by the ivory tower scientist. This is often cast, with derogatory connotations, as an issue of "basic" versus "applied" research. However, it is difficult to see why a problem chosen by one's dissertation chairman, or from a perusal of old and musty books is necessarily more "basic" than one dictated by practical societal needs. Letting one's research focus be directed by the availability of funds is, likewise, hardly more "basic." We should hasten to make it clear that we do not insist that science must "save us," any more than it is necessary to ask "knowledge for what?" (Lundberg, 1947; Lynd, 1939). Sheer armchair speculation, as well as laboratory and other kinds of research with no known practical application are completely legitimate exercises in the ivory tower. All that is necessary for our argument is to accept that these are not the only legitimate kinds of research. Furthermore, if it is possible to do superior social research and at the same time contribute to the solution of practical problems, then the university would be foolish to not seize the opportunity to do so.

CULTURE CONFLICT INEVITABLE?

The sociologist can see these problems as arising out of a division of labor which produces role conflict from the diverging values of two cultures. One might be tempted to regard as a solution elimination of these divergent cultures. But as sociologists, we are also inclined to suspect that this could only be accomplished by eliminating the division of labor, which would consequently lose the benefits to be derived from specialization. Perhaps the two cultures are essential. Perhaps the basic academic scientist *must* value knowledge for its own sake, while the professional practitioner, in turn, must replace doubt with action — when the demand arises and not "when all the facts are in." Indeed, a faith in the principles of one's profession may be necessary for effective practice — while skepticism about these very same principles may be essential, on the scholar's part, for effective research. Granted that these cultural differences increase the effectiveness of both practitioner and research, our problem is now clear: how can the performances of these two be integrated in spite of the differences?

Professional Schools as Sally Ports

What is needed is a buffer organization, a point of transition from the ivory tower to the day-to-day demands of professional practice. Within this transitional culture, a balance may be struck — a balance between the university's prime commitment to knowledge and the larger society's practical demands for action. We have such organizations now: the professional schools within the universities. Ideally, in the professional school, practitioner-researchers can learn how to get the results society demands of their profession while they do not themselves carry their theories into practice. Instead they teach others how to do so, through their publication and through education of practitioners. These profession-oriented academicians have plenty to do while limiting themselves to developing knowledge and transmitting it: in that sense, their role calls for pure research. Their job is to find out how to do it, but not to do it. But the only way to find out how to solve a particular practical problem may be to actually work on it — e.g., "try out" a surgical procedure — in other words, engage in professional practice. Within these professional schools, the twin values of commitment to professional service and to basic knowledge could be equally developed. Then there could be a meeting ground for the basic scientist and the skilled practitioner, within a single role, the practitioner-researcher role.

Within this transitional organization, there remains a problem if we are to avoid simply perpetuating the conflicts between the two cultures. However, there would seem to be no inherent reason why research could not contribute to *both* basic scientific theory and also to the improvement of professional practice. How this is to be done and how much is actually achieved cannot be left to chance. It depends upon the appropriate organization and the development of the appropriate research strategies. Our contention is that a careful examination of the appropriate uses of research in a profession can reveal ways to direct our efforts toward kinds of research that can integrate basic science and everyday social practice. Before elaborating on this conception of the professional school as a sally port between the ivory tower and the man in the street, we will briefly consider as a contrast some other approaches to "integrating" knowledge and action.

Contrasting Approaches

BASIC SCIENCE IN PRACTITIONER EDUCATION

Discussions of the integration of social research into the various professions often concentrate on education of the practitioner. This overlooks the important potential contribution the social sciences can make to practice-oriented *research*. We would do well to ask, "Can the abstract conceptual scheme of the behavioral sciences be utilized in such individualistic ways?" (Sheldon, 1963). Our answer, in general, is no. It is unreasonable to expect the individual practitioner to bridge the gap between abstract theory and particular action situations by simply picking principles to "apply." We should remember that the basic principles of the academic disciplines are very seldom based on research which was designed to develop principles of professional practice. These principles are not specifically addressed to the situations confronted by each particular practicing profession in its daily work with clients. Blind application of any "principles" that are based on research done in situations other than those confronted by the practitioner is at best haphazard and quite possibly filled with danger. Even if the so-called "basic" principles are well tested and widely accepted by the particular academic discipline, there still may remain a large gap between the general principle and its application to specific practical situations. It is ineffective and inefficient to teach these abstract general principles to novice practitioners and then expect them to discover the particular applications in practice.

The impulse to teach basic social science in the education of the practitioner is, of course, progress to the extent that it is a recognition that common sense and good intentions are not sufficient — they are no substitute for scientifically tested principles. But such an approach is far from sufficient. We cannot take the findings of social science research and immediately apply them to the practitioner's situation. However, this is often expected from the student practitioner while, very significantly, these same students are not expected to have the ability for critical appraisal of the "findings" that are taught in social science courses for practitioners. To close the gap between the basic ivory tower disciplines and the everyday situations faced by practitioners, practice-oriented research is needed. This research can be "basic" to the academic disciplines; at the very least, it is testing the generality of those basic propositions which have been established for other areas of human behavior. Quite possibly, basic new discoveries about human behavior will be made. This practice-oriented research is "basic" research, in the strictly academic sense.

ACADEMIC CONSULTANTS

Practice-oriented research needs justification both to the practitioner culture and to the academic culture. As academic sociologists, it is significant to us that the original aim of sociology was to provide a scientific basis for the construction of utopias. As Zetterberg puts it:

> One of the most appealing ideas of our century is the notion that science can be put to work to provide solutions to social problems. If 18th century physics gave us the modern engineer, and . . . 19th century biology gave us the modern physician to deal with health problems, so 20th century social science dreams that it shall give mankind the social practitioner to deal scientifically with social problems. (1962, p. 16.)

Zetterberg goes on to propose the role of consultant for sociologists. This consultant would translate "established knowledge" into prescriptions for practice. This, he suggests, can be done without further research. We might agree with him that often the social scientist's response to requests for help are proposals to "do some research" that is beside the point as far as the practitioner's problem is concerned. And we agree completely with Zetterberg that:

> Applied sociology should proceed from the client's problem to something very abstract — theoretical problems and theoretical solutions — and back to the client's problem with a practical solution. (1962)

What we insist is that any "practical solution" that is derived from abstract sociological theory, or even from a combination of professional experience and sociological theory, is nothing more than an hypothesis to be tested. Again, we could agree with Zetterberg that: "Nothing improves theory more than its confrontation with practice." (p. 189.) But, we insist, such confrontation must be made under conditions yielding data that conform to our most rigorous principles of research methods. Such confrontations of academic scholarship and social action must conform to university standards of scholarship. Prescriptions for professional practice should be put to rigorous tests before being incorporated into the practitioner's theory of practice (cf. Leonard *et al.*, 1967). Only if this step is taken can we regard the practice as "scientifically based." As field testing of prescriptions for practice contributes to the development of the profession, at the same time it contributes to basic social theory through rigorous testing in realistic situations. But how much is actually achieved in action-oriented research depends on how it is organized.

OTHER FORMS OF ACTION-ORIENTED RESEARCH IN THE UNIVERSITY

Developing a practicing profession as an academic discipline is the best way of developing a research bridge between the world of the everyday problems of the practitioner and the world of the ivory tower scholar. Other ways are often discussed. We will briefly consider two of the most popular of these before going on to elaborate the research-practitioner role: (a) the interdisciplinary team, (b) hired-hand research.

Division of labor between the practicing professions does not correspond to the division of labor within the basic academic disciplines. Consequently, development of a body of principles for guiding the professional practitioner requires cutting across the academic boundaries of knowledge. Consequently, one frequent impulse is to try to incorporate the knowledge of the various academic disciplines that might be applicable by the development of "team" research. Rodman and Kolodny (1965) provide a good framework for discussing this approach, based on their own experience and an extensive bibliography on researcher-practitioner relations. The theory developed and tested by such a team is integrated with professional practice through social integration of practitioners into the "team." Inclusion of experienced practitioners, who are actively engaged in professional practice, as full-fledged members of the team, may increase the likelihood that whatever theory does emerge from this approach will be integrated with actual practice. But simply including practitioners is not sufficient; they must have a high position of prestige and power. Yet to hold a high position within the academic culture the practitioner must excel by academic standards, i.e., by being a good scholar. In other words, to be successful the "team" approach still requires the development of the practitioner-researcher role.

Related to high rank for the practitioner-research on the inter-disciplinary team is high evaluation of practical relevance and practitioner skills. Both practical and academic values must be adopted. A qualified practitioner can gain academic prestige by doing strictly academic research — this is all too frequent. The laboratory or the computer room becomes a way of escaping direct service to clients. Or, more subtle yet, the same person may apply two sets of standards. In the laboratory, rigorously conducted research will help develop a potential treatment which is then carelessly "tried" on the next series of customers who happen to come in for treatment. In the "pure" research, scholarly standards are followed, but when the very same person then does "clinical" research, the same standards are not applied. True integration of theory and practice cannot permit this double standard. An interdisciplinary approach that does not enforce standards of the academic culture upon all members of the team in all phases of the research will fail in its task.

A final comment might be made about the role of nonpractitioner members of the interdisciplinary team. With the practitioner-researcher ranking the importance of various hypotheses according to their practical usefulness, the other academic members are to some extent cast in a consultant role. This differs from the consultation discussed by Zetterberg (1962), in that it is research consultation. But, at the same time, many of the points Zetterberg makes about successful consultation and the use of general social theory seem equally applicable for this role.

Another popular way to try to put the basic sciences to use in professional practice is to hire scientists from those various disciplines to do research presumed to be relevant to problems of the profession. The "hired hand" approach may succeed in taking the publication pressure off the nonresearchers in the professional school, but is not likely to do much to produce useful theory for the workers out in the field. For other reasons, already well stated by Roth (1966), this approach may not do much to produce research good for *any* purpose, practical or academic.

The dilemma facing the practical professions is that those who are in a position to know what the basic problems are, i.e., the practitioners, do not have the training necessary to do research on those problems.

When practitioners do attempt research, the results are usually disappointingly inconclusive because of faulty procedures. On the other hand, those who have the necessary research skills are identified with academic disciplines where the research tends to be only peripheral to professional practice. Many studies done by academicians will be, from the point of view of practitioners, only exploratory. The psychologist or sociologist has a good time finding out all kinds of facts about the practitioner's world which are new to him but just common knowledge to the practitioner. Such research runs the risk of at best producing hypotheses that any experienced practitioner already knows. At worst, this research produces nothing at all because the researchers try to impose their own theories. In other cases, the researchers may not know how to behave in the practice setting, or else they design their study to test hypotheses that are irrelevant to begin with as far as actual practice is concerned. Combining the necessary ingredients of clinical experience with clients as well as training in basic scholarship in a "team" is a temporary expedient. It is a temporary expedient that is inferior to combining the necessary ingredients for successful practice-oriented research within the skill complex of each individual researcher.[4]

The Practitioner-Researcher in Academe

The third approach, which we propose here, is training practitioner-researchers. In this approach, in contrast to the others, all of the necessary skills and knowledge are incorporated within the repertoire of each individual researcher. This means combining the knowledge and skills that are typically found in both the ivory tower and in everyday work organizations.

In turning practitioners into practitioner-researchers, we are converting the culture conflict into a role conflict. Developing such a training program is not always easy; there are a number of barriers to its success. A first problem which one confronts in the meeting between academicians and experienced practitioners is the fundamental one of simply *why* research? This is a question that is seldom asked within the core of the ivory tower, but it is one that practitioners are likely to raise immediately. Sometimes when the question is asked, it is simply in a rhetorical way with the clear implication that practitioners really should not be doing research at all. Rather, they should be out there on the job taking care of the clients. Yet, it seems clear that if the practice of a profession is to rest on a scientific body of knowledge, then it must rely on practice-oriented research. Many of our more highly regarded professions — e.g., agronomy, engineering, medicine — have surely been aided in gaining their prestige by the scientific soundness of their practices.

Practitioner acceptance of scientific evidence rules is more of a problem than one might initially suppose.[5] Often the practitioner and the scholar have different standards for judging fact. Although academicians are likely to presume that we live in a scientific world, in actual practice, common sense is likely to be more often highly regarded. This rejection of science in favor of "common sense," or "practical experience," is even more of a problem for the social sciences than it might be for sciences that have already gained widespread acceptance. Our proposal presumes that common sense and good intentions are no substitute for scientifically tested principles. Social scientists are very familiar with this barrier to the application of academic knowledge through their teaching of introductory courses to undergraduates.

The possibility and utility of social science was an issue that was settled to the satisfaction of social scientists in the first quarter of the twentieth century. But it is still a current issue in fields populated by persons who have not had an introduction to modern social science. There is a question in their minds whether the "behavioral sciences" are really sciences at all in the same way as the biological and physical sciences. Are "interpersonal relation" or "administration" not simply matters that neither can be studied scientifically nor taught to practitioners? Is there not an *art* of working with clients? It would seem possible to recognize that there is an ingredient in professional practice that might reasonably be called an "art" of the profession. But we must warn against throwing out the baby with the bath. We should not confuse basic social scientific principles with the way they are used in a particular case. Individualized, sensitive, care of a client calls for the application of sound principles of practice if that practice is to be integrated with science. The "art" lies in adapting the general principles to each specific situation. Much of what mistakenly is considered to be part of the art of a profession is transmitted to young practitioners through the folklore of the profession. This folklore is a poor substitute for coherently stated and rigorously tested scientific principles. By properly conceived, practice-oriented research, the art of practice can be elevated to a new plane of excellence. This is not to deny the relevance of aesthetics for professional practice, but rather to insist that aesthetics and science are not mutually exclusive. The existence of an art of social practice does not preclude development of a science of social practice.

THEORY BRIDGES PRACTICE AND RESEARCH

In the strictly academic disciplines, the aim of research is to test theory, while the aim of theory is to guide research. This sort of circularity may seem pointless to the non-scientist. But it is — in a nutshell — the academic game. For academics it is an enjoyable game. More important: often enough skeptics of ivory tower science have been found to be in error down through history even by "practical" standards. There is good practical reason to support purely academic scholarship.

Theory in a practice-oriented discipline also has this function of guiding research but, in addition, it has another aim: to guide professional practice. A "practice theory" guides professional practice. It is a set of prescriptions for the practitioner. It contains a set of diagnostic categories and specifies appropriate treatment for each of these categories. The similar functions of theory in guiding practice and in guiding research highlights the "basic" nature of practice-oriented research.

Why theory?[6] For an academic discipline, theory is judged by its usefulness in research. Theory can be conceived of as a research tool (Glaser and Strauss, 1967). No further justification is required since research, i.e., scholarship, is what academics do. Improvement in our theories advances the science in improving our explanations for phenomena, or, if you prefer, our ability to predict and/or control.[7] To the extent that one theory does better at achieving any of these aims in our research, then to that extent, it is more useful theory. Theory can also be used to guide practical social action, which is outside the realm of the academic sociologist's role, but this "practical" use is not so far from its use in guiding pure research.

FIGURE 1

	RESEARCH	PRACTICE
1.	CLASSIFICATION	DIAGNOSIS
2.	HYPOTHESIS	PRESCRIPTION
3.	DATA COLLECTION	ACTION
4.	DATA ANALYSIS	EVALUATION

The use of theory for guiding social action is very parallel to its use in guiding social research. This parallel may be seen in Figure 1, where the steps in a social action program are designated as: (a) diagnosis, (b) prescription, (c) treatment, and (d) evaluation of the outcome of the treatment.

Diagnosis consists of applying a taxonomy and on the basis of the classification that is made of the "problem," a prescription can be made. This prescription is based upon some theory which specifies certain manipulations which are presumed to affect the diagnosed condition. On the basis of the prescription, the treatment is carried out, and in the complete professional cycle, the effects of this treatment are then assessed through a re-diagnosis.

Although carrying out a social action program in these steps may be seen as the application of already established scientific "knowledge," explicit inclusion of the evaluation step suggests opportunity for testing of these theories in actual ongoing social practice. If the prescribed treatment does not produce the expected results, then one interpretation is that there is something wrong with the theory. That is, the theory has been tested, found wrong, and must now be revised. Because of this parallel between social action and social research basic, practice-oriented research can simultaneously contribute to both. (Wooldridge *et al.*, 1968.)

The practical usefulness of social theory, at any given stage of development, must remain an open question. Zetterberg (1962) takes an optimistic position, believing that much useful application of present sociological theory is possible without any "further research." Many other sociologists might not be so optimistic as Zetterberg. Neither may they be so optimistic with respect to the possible contributions of social practice to sociological theory (cf. Wooldridge *et al.*, 1968). But in any case, characteristics of theory that make it useful for guiding research also make it useful for guiding social action.[8] Questions of the use of theory in research, or the nature of theory or problems of theory building are peripheral to our immediate discussions here.[9] More germane is the content of practice-oriented theory — the variables that are included.

Developing Practice-Oriented Theory

CHOICE OF VARIABLES

The choice of variables to include in practice-oriented research involves decisions about the practitioner's role. The content of practice-oriented theory varies with the ends set by the role of the practitioner and by the means that are prescribed as well as proscribed for achievement of those ends. From our experience, it seems clear that an essential precondition for establishing practice-oriented research is a clear conception of the practitioner's role. In this view the question "what is the role of . . . ?" is not a scientific question. Rather, it is a policy issue to be settled by the means that are typically used in establishing a division of labor. Jurisdictional disputes over the work and conflicts with rival professions provide topics for social science research, but settling those disputes must eventually hinge on political and value decisions, beyond the scope of science. That is to say: the choice of content of a practice-oriented theory must be made before the theory can be constructed and tested.

To professionalize social practice requires developing scientifically tested theories of practice. And, since the professional helping process involves working with people, this practice is a social process. Therefore, theories of professional practice that we are discussing are likely to include social variables. Likewise, of course, testing these theories will benefit from the research technology and general methodology developed by the social sciences.

The successful integration of behavioral science concepts into professional practice must somehow involve both general knowledge of the practicing profession and general social science. The applicability of social science principles will no doubt vary from one situation to another so there is a selective process necessary here depending on the role of the particular practitioner.

An understanding of selected basic concepts and the related social research literature might promote the next necessary step, which is more highly detailed identification of specific practice situation in which those variables are operating. Then systematic rigorous testing of these principles in practice can establish which are valid for those situations and which are not. In other words, we are suggesting that improvement of professional practice can come through the integration of social theory into professional practice theory. This will progress as more and more practitioners learn the general orientation of the social sciences and can in their practice identify the operation of social processes.

THE PRACTITIONER INFALLIBILITY SYNDROME[10]

A practitioner's performance is often "evaluated" by his conformity to professional ethics. There is an inclination to state practice principles in a didactic way. In sharp contrast, the practitioner-researcher must live in eternal uncertainty about those same absolutes by which the practitioner justifies his action. Practitioner training, which stresses that one must *not* make a mistake encourages a feeling of personal infallibility and a cultivated blindness to one's mistakes. Yet by analyzing mistakes one learns how to improve practice. The desire for certainty and the related reluctance to avoid examining one's own practice produces basic barriers to learning the research attitude by practitioners. It is a fundamental barrier to this method of developing practice-oriented research.

But, as one experienced person commenting on this manuscript suggested, it is equally a barrier to the "team" and "hired hand" approaches.[11] His comment is worth quoting at length:

> As you appropriately indicated, the practitioner is very sensitive to making mistakes. His ego suffers in direct proportion to the mistakes he makes *which others recognize as such*. On the other hand, during his graduate educational process, he has not had inculcated a value system which accepts evaluation as a legitimate ongoing process. ... (furthermore). ... The majority of service oriented folk are so "uptight" about this matter of self-evaluation that a researcher working with them tends to over-compromise his research design to develop the necessary rapport to be accepted by the practitioner. I would thus agree with your first training priority that the academics must strive for a practitioner/researcher graduate product who would be acceptable to the ethics of both worlds, research and practice.

A practitioner who is trying to learn to become a researcher may have difficulty accepting the ideas of an hypothesis. He may have an even harder time accepting scientific tests of these hypothetical principles of practice. The researcher may be elated and enthusiastic by the same study that disappoints, depresses, or even angers the committed practitioner. A *successful* experiment may be a program (action) failure. (E. G. Meyer *et al.*, 1965.)

Science vs. Ethics in "Evaluation"

We should emphasize that practice-oriented theory is scientific theory. This is the only way that research can be a link between thought and action. Yet most practitioner thought about practice centers on "aims, objectives, and professional ethics." This may be legitimate, and essential, yet the scientist is likely to suspect that intentions are best for paving that proverbial road to unintended consequences. This seems to be a difficult point. Although science "does not make value judgment," from the point of view of the practitioner this statement can appear hypocritical since in fact scientific research is proposed to "evaluate" their practice. If science does not make value judgments, then what does "evaluation" mean in the term of evaluation research? The answer is, of course, that the scientist substitutes consequences for intentions in the meaning of the word "evaluation." This is a necessary distinction which cannot be avoided in the case of practice theory which contains both ethical and scientific statements (cf. Dickoff *et al.*, 1968). Science meets ethics in developing practice-oriented theory, often to the great annoyance of the academic scientist and confusion of the practitioner.

MEASURING EFFECTS

The pivot point for integrating theory and practice is operationalization of the dependent variable, i.e., measuring the "effect." The problem is translating "aims and objectives" into observables. We can accept that intentions do make a difference: commitment to "aims and objectives" can facilitate producing the intended effects on the client. Yet we may still doubt that good intentions are either necessary or sufficient for effective professional practice. Both conscious fraud and unintended "psychological defenses" can produce avoidance of the central issue: actual effectiveness of the practitioner's actions. This is closely related to an often observed phenomenon of practitioner-centered rather than client-centered research in the practicing professions. (Henderson, 1956; Roth, 1962.) One reason for this is possible change in cherished practices which may be implied by rigorous research testing their effectiveness. The practitioner, quite understandably, reacts to the possibility of change by asking, "How much trouble will it be for me?" or, "What will this do to my career?"

We should not be surprised if the practitioner asks himself, "What will *I* get out of this change?" This is, of course, in contrast to asking what it will do for the customer, the organization, or society in general. But it must be recognized as a special problem in a research program such as the one we propose where practitioners must evaluate the effect on the client of their own, or their colleagues', performance. In our experience, once the practitioner, and his profession, recognize that knowing actual effects, in the scientific sense, can increase attainment of the goals they are committed to as practitioners, then this problem is eased.[12]

Conclusion

Development of the practitioner-researcher role, and its necessary supporting administrative structure, on university campuses probably most often involves the existing "professional" schools. Such development presumes that the primary purpose of a university is scholarship — not teaching people how to make a living — and the proposal is to make such professional schools equal to any other academic department on campus. But from the university's point of view, there is no sense in other departments which will simply duplicate already existing ones.

What distinctive contribution do practice-oriented departments have to offer to the research goal of the university? This question reverses the tone of much discussion using the "basic-applied" framework, where the presumption tends to be that the "applied" field is doing all the receiving. It is of course true that much pure academic research finds practical application — sometimes centuries later. But the opposite can be just as true: practice-oriented research in ongoing client-service situations can make fundamental contributions to general knowledge. In our opinion, the really excellent research coming out of professional schools uses the professional's practical experience and access to practice settings — it is "clinical" research but it is also basic research. It makes an addition to our fundamental knowledge which probably could only be made by experienced social practitioners. It is this basic clinical research that identifies a unique place for the various professions in the ivory tower.

The most successful way, we suspect, to integrate basic science and professional practice is through practice-oriented, basic, clinical research. Such research is, in the widest meanings of the words, *both* "basic" and "applied," with no compromise made in either academic standards or in practical import. It can answer both "How do you know?" and "So what?" It is the practitioner-researcher who possesses the necessary combination of skills and legal status for such research. We might hope that the universities could cooperate with the bureaucracies and professions to find ways so that individuals could fill this dual role of practitioner and researcher for the development of a distinctive kind of research that is both practical and theoretical, both basic and applied.

NOTES TO THE CHAPTER

1. Our distinction is different from C. P. Snow's (1959) who saw disaster in national policy decisions because communication problems between the two cultures of "literary intellectuals" and "scientists." He was dealing with the same phenomena, but sliced it differently, perhaps because his experience was with practitioners trained in the British university tradition. The most comparable group in this country would be those educated in academically conservative humanities-oriented colleges, perhaps followed by law school. The result is near total scientific illiteracy. Snow's view of the problem converges toward ours in his revised essay, written after a year's visit to this country, where he became aware of the social sciences as a "third culture" possibly bridging the other two (1963: 58,

66–67). As we elaborate later, sociology can also bring the academic and practical worlds together because professional practice is, essentially, a social process.

2. This historical process was a central object of Max Weber's sociological studies — to compound the confusion, often called a process of "rationalization" of the world. He identified bureaucratization as one such process toward increasing rationality. The use of scientific knowledge for guiding action is another, which may be identified as part of the process of professionalization.

3. In using the word "theory" here we are referring to essentially the same thing that is often called "concepts," "principles of practice" or simply "knowledge." This idea of practice theory has been developed in both social work and nursing as well as being recognized more generally in applied sociology (Chin 1962; Greenwood 1955; Gouldner 1956; Wald and Leonard 1964; Zetterberg 1964; Wooldridge, *et al.*, 1968; Dickoff *et al.*, 1968a, b).

4. Vocational rehabilitation is a new and interesting emerging profession which has been establishing positions on University campuses. The Vocational Rehabilitation Administration supports over a dozen centers for clinical research (Usdane in Sussman (ed.), n.d., p. XVIII). We expect that a comparison would reveal the most useful results to have come from those centers with high academic standards which have also developed best the researcher-practitioner role. If the training in these centers includes training for research as well as practice, then we would expect them to be the nucleus for the future of vocational rehabilitation research. An ingredient in this development is the training of rehabilitation practitioners who can develop research methods and theory appropriate to vocational rehabilitation problems, and to carry out studies of those problems.

5. Of course, the ivory tower scientist has his own faith in the rules that guide his conduct. But these are different rules about different conduct. The practitioner who becomes a researcher may find these two sets of rules in conflict, especially if he forgets which role he is performing. This conflict over which rules apply is especially problematic in clinical research, in the ongoing settings where one cares for clients. The problem we have pointed out is revealed in medicine, for example, in the gross neglect of "control groups." The very same man who will engage in rigorous research in the laboratory will simply assume the research results can be generalized to his practice and forget completely the scientific principles that he was using in the laboratory.

6. This is intended as neither rhetorical nor whimsical, Wrigley (1960) argues that there is no need for theory.

7. Rather than "understanding," etc., we might simply assert that sociological scholars do what they do because it is fun. This autotelic conception of the sociologist's activity contains important heuristic implications and may also have some implications for our criterion in choosing theory. One might suspect that choices of scientific theory are often based on aesthetic criteria or on what seems most pleasurable. There is a warning in this for the practitioner interested in applying "basic" science: academic disputes over choice of theory may sometimes have nothing to do with the facts.

8. This is in no way intended to contradict the distinction that Glaser and Strauss make between "substantive" and "formal" theories (1967, page 81), although we would not use those labels for the distinctions they have in mind.

9. See Robert Dubin's chapter in this book, and the Wooldridge commentary.

10. On the concept of practitioner infallibility, see Sharif and Levinson (1964).

11. Guy D. Spiesman, personal communication.

12. Thus, this approach achieves the same solution Pollock had in mind for the "team" approach (1956).

* We wish to acknowledge useful comments by Joseph Andriola, Reta Artz, and Guy Spiesman.

REFERENCES

CHIN, ROBERT
  1962   "Problems and Prospects of Applied Research," in W. G. Bennis, K. D. Benne, and R. Chin (Eds.) *The Planning of Change.* New York: Holt, Rinehart & Winston, p. 672.

DICKOFF, JAMES, PATRICIA JAMES, and ERNESTINE WIEDENBACH
  1968a   "Theory in a Practice Discipline: Part I. Practice Oriented Theory." *Nursing Research,* **17:**5 (September–October) 415–436.
  1968b   "Theory in a Practice Discipline: Part II. Practice Oriented Research." *Nursing Research,* **17:**6 (November–December): 545–555.

FREEMAN, HOWARD E.
  1963   "The Strategy of Social Policy Research," *The Social Welfare Forum,* 153–154.

GLASER, BARNEY G. and ANSELM L. STRAUSS
  1967   *The Discovery of Grounded Theory: Strategies for Qualitative Research.* Chicago: Aldine.

GOULDNER, ALVIN W.
  1956   "Explorations in Applied Social Science," *Social Problems,* **3** (January): 169–181.

GOULDNER, ALVIN W. and S. M. MILLER (editors)
  1965   *Applied Sociology.* New York: The Free Press.

GREENWOOD, ERNEST
  1955   "Social Science and Social Work: A Theory of Their Relationship," *Social Science Review,* **29,** 20–33.
  1961   "The Practice of Science and the Science of Practice," in Warren G. Bennis, *et al.* (eds.) *The Planning of Change.* New York: Holt, pp. 73–83.

HENDERSON, VIRGINIA A.
  1956   "Research in Nursing Practice — When?" *Nursing Research,* **4** (February): 99.

LUNDBERG, GEORGE A.
  1947   *Can Science Save Us?* New York, London, Toronto: Longsmans, Green and Company.
LEONARD, ROBERT C., P. J. Wooldridge, and I. K. Skipper, Jr.
  1967   "Small Sample Field Experiments for Evaluating Patient Care," *Health Services Research,* 2 (Spring): 46–59.
LYND, ROBERT S.
  1939   *Knowledge for What?* Princeton University Press.
MEYER, HENRY J., E. F. BORGATTA, and W. C. JONES
  1965   *Girls at Vocational High: An Experiment in Social Work Intervention.* New York: Russell Sage Foundation.
POLLOCK, OTTO
  1956   "Comments," *Social Service Review,* **30** (September) 298. Cited by Rodman and Kolodny (1965), p. 96.
RODMAN, HYMAN and R. L. KOLODNY
  1965   "Organizational Strains in the Researcher-Practitioner Role," in A. W. Gouldner and S. M. Miller (eds.) *Applied Sociology,* London: Collier-Macmillar Ltd, pp. 93–113.
ROTH, JULIUS A.
  1962   "Management Bias in the Study of Medical Treatment." *Human Organization,* 21 (Spring): 47–61.
  1966   "Hired Hand Research." *American Sociologist,* **1:4** (August): 190–196.
SHARAF, MYRON R. and DANIEL J. LEVINSON
  1964   "The Quest for Omnipotence in Professional Training: The Case of the Psychiatric Resident." *Psychiatry,* **27:2** (May): 135–149.
SHELDON, ELEANOR B.
  1963   "The Use of Behavioral Science in Nursing: An Opinion." *Nursing Research,* **12** (Summer): 150–152.
SKIPPER, JAMES K., JR., STEPHEN L. FINK, and PHYLLIS N. HALLENBECK
  1968   "Physical Disability Among Married Women: Problems in the Husband–Wife Relationship." *Journal of Rehabilitation,* **1:1** (September–October) 16–19.
SNOW, C. P.
  1959   *The Two Cultures and the Scientific Revolution.* New York and London: Cambridge University Press.
  1963   *The Two Cultures: And A Second Look.* New York and London: Cambridge University Press.
SUSSMAN, MARVIN B. (Ed.)
  no date *Sociology and Rehabilitation.* Washington D.C.: American Sociological Association.
WALD, FLORENCE S., and ROBERT C. LEONARD
  1964   "Toward Development of Nursing Practice Theory." *Nursing Research,* **13:4** (Fall): 309–313.

WEBER, MAX (Translated and Edited by E. A. Shils and H. A. Finch)
  1949   *The Methodology of the Social Sciences*, Glencoe: The Free Press. Originally written as a series of articles published between 1903 and 1917.
WOOLDRIDGE, POWHATAN J., J. K. SKIPPER, JR., and ROBERT C. LEONARD
  1968   *Behavioral Science, Social Practice, and the Nursing Profession*. Cleveland: The Press of Case Western Reserve University.
WRIGLEY, C.
  1960   "Theory Construction or Fact-finding in a Computer Age?" *Behavioral Science*, p. 184.
ZETTERBERG, HANS
  1962   *Social Theory and Social Practice*. New York: Bedminster Press.

CHAPTER FOURTEEN

Technology Transfer

WILLIAM M. USDANE

The utilization of significant research and demonstration findings is an integral part of the organization, management and tactics of social research. But the future facing technology transfer from outcomes to use by practitioners would be grim if the researchers were to be left in charge of their own research utilization. Researchers are mainly concerned with research. Their research outcomes continue to add to the information explosion. What can be done to transfer to the rehabilitation and welfare fields the accumulated technology that arises from the significant findings of ongoing and completed applied research?

This symposium has examined in depth some of the research methodological topics which only broadly concerned the group of sociologists who met at Carmel, California in 1965 (Sussman (ed.), 1965). There was need to press beyond the focus of the earlier gathering which was essentially involved in an introduction to the field of vocational rehabilitation for sociologists. This meeting has been held in a comprehensive rehabilitation center. Even so, despite the environment, the group has undoubtedly been aware of the unsolved daily problems facing the interdisciplinary team of professionals and sub-professionals. These workers have been engaged in the rehabilitation problem solving process with both the disabled as well as with the socially and culturally disadvantaged while symposium members discussed problems of social research. Where can help be obtained in resolving some of these daily problems except through the utilization of research outcomes in practice? Both the clients and the team members are consumers who need to be alerted to the store bins of accumulated knowledge resulting from research findings in the field of rehabilitation and social welfare.

There still remains the need of equal time for research utilization in yet another symposium since this one has not recognized its importance in the organization, management and tactics of social research. The request of the symposium coordinator[1] to ". . write your own original ideas . . . what do you think is neglected or needs further elaboration" has prompted an emphasis upon technology transfer. The overwhelming problems in a technocratic society can only begin to be met by what has already been tested and learned.

Few sociologists have indicated interest in the problems of research dissemination, innovation or utilization. Researchers themselves are caught in the publication hurdle of the professional journals which are from eighteen to twenty-four months behind in their backlog of accepted articles. Research outcomes are shared with findings by other researchers at professional conferences geared to the needs of the professionals rather than to those of the consumer, either practitioner or client.

In the Division of Research and Demonstration Grants of the Social and Rehabilitation Service (Department of Health, Education, and Welfare), specialized technology from over 1300 final reports needs to be translated from "established knowledge" into practice. The findings of these projects are strongly related to the Department's (HEW) priorities of 1969 which are focused upon model cities, neighborhood service centers, family planning, coordinated services for the aged, central city minority problems, motivating people to work, rural poverty, hunger and malnutrition, and violence, juvenile delinquency, law and order. Sociologists are needed to examine these problems, clarify their scope and meaning, help in carrying out these priority assignments in an orderly way, and, in the course of all this, assist in the dissemination, innovation, and utilization of the significant findings.

In view of the urgent social nature of the problems facing the country, there is good reason to turn to the sociologist for help. His role on the rehabilitation team until the sixties, has been almost nonexistent. Except for sociological research primarily in the area of mental illness, the rehabilitation research program since its inception in 1954 has essentially been unaware of the important role the sociologist can undertake in the organization, management and tactics of social research.

The Research Utilization Sciences

Richard Titmuss calls the society of today and tomorrow essentially technocratic. He states, "We are thus faced with more uncertainty and, at the same time, we want things to change more rapidly." But where can be found the instrument of change that is needed (Titmuss, 1968)? Perhaps what we need is essentially that composite discipline which is described by Leonard and Skipper, an interdisciplinary outcome between researcher and practitioner. Just as Bruner and his compatriots at Harvard have recently introduced a new composite discipline which is called "the growth sciences" (Pines, 1969:12), perhaps what is desparately needed today to promote technology transfer might be designated as the "utilization sciences." Since the researcher cannot be held responsible for the technology transfer of his significant outcomes to the field of practice, there is more than ever a need to develop "the utilization sciences." In the past few years, both basic and applied research programs have come into high visibility as the Congress has asked more and more strenuously for research results and the application. Any increasing budgetary requests for expanding Government programs in medical, social and rehabilitation research have brought demanding questions concerning the impact of research on existing problems of the disadvantaged; in fact, specific questions have been asked regarding methods whereby the outcomes can be absorbed into ongoing state welfare and rehabilitation programs.

The information explosion in the Division of Research and Demonstration Grants in the Social and Rehabilitation Service shows the immediate need to integrate theory and practice as pointed out by Leonard and Skipper. In 1968, 256 research final reports, including several types of information and publications, were received. Among them were 32 special reports and seven films. The 1968 yield compromised 20 per cent of all reports received since projects began submitting them in 1956. By the end of 1968, a total of 1,085 reports had been accounted for, not including 67 films. The rising influx of reports can be seen in the 192 received in 1967 as compared with 109 in 1966 and 84 in 1965. Journal articles from final reports increased from 630 in the 1959 Bibliography of Reports and Articles to 800 in 1962, and 2,404 in the 1968 edition (Regional Rehabilitation Research Institute, 1968).

The "utilization sciences" might comprise both those individuals who would serve as "change agents" in the technology transfer from final report to the practitioners on the rehabilitation team and those individuals involved in the varied steps needed within automated data processing.

Two recent publications from Springfield College (Cooper *et al.*, (eds.), 1968) and Northeastern University (Goldin *et al.*, 1969) address themselves to concepts, principles and research in the utilization of significant research outcomes. Appropriate personnel at universities, voluntary agencies and State health and welfare organizations could be organized around the concept of utilization and innovation just as medical research was organized around concepts of pathology.

The professional school can be utilized, according to Leonard and Skipper, as a balance between the university's prime commitment to knowledge and the larger society's practical demands for action. But the authors contend that these professional schools should not be utilized for research itself, but as a buffer organization between the 'Ivory Tower' and daily professional practice. The authors are not clear, however, since they mention twin values of commitment to service and to knowledge and claim that there can be a meeting ground for the basic scientists and the skilled practitioners *within a single role*. The research, as I read the authors, will still be done by the scientist and not within the professional school — but appropriate organization and development of research strategies can direct efforts towards kinds of research that can integrate basic science and the everyday social practice.

Field Testing Laboratories and Regional Research Institutes

The dilemma of the proper setting immediately occurs. The authors grant that the findings of social science research cannot always be immediately applied to the practitioner's situation. The solution, it is emphasized, is the need to engage in "practice-oriented research." By this, it is assumed the authors are considering demonstration or applied research. This type of research, however, is action-oriented with a necessary conceptual basis.

But no matter how applied the research, there is still the need for an additional step within the framework of the "utilization sciences." This step has recently been initiated in the first of several projects to be supported by the Division of Research and Demonstration Grants. Such a step can be realized within a "Technology Transfer Laboratory." This field testing laboratory has been in existence at the Jewish Vocational Service in Chicago only a few months. Here, within an ongoing rehabilitation facility, new patterns of service or newly devised techniques in working with the disadvantaged or the disabled individual can be innovated. The process of final report dissemination will already have been accomplished prior to the application of the significant results of demonstration outcomes in the Field Testing Laboratory. Adding only a minimum of staff and equipment, new patterns of services and innovative techniques can be coupled with or used in place of ongoing procedures. Administrators of other rehabilitation facilities will have an opportunity to observe the nature of the innovative pattern through its observable impact on staff, client and institution.

New Regional Research Institutes in Social Welfare will be started in each of the ten regions of the Department of Health, Education, and Welfare, supported by grants from the Social and Rehabilitation Service. Concentrating on a programmatic core area of social welfare research, each Institute will serve as a dissemination point for outcomes of significant research findings in its chosen core area both for the States in that region and for the other regions as well. The Institutes will serve as an informational back-up for the State Division of Vocational Rehabilitation "change agents" in the region. Already existing are nine rehabilitation Research Institutes conducting research in programmatic core areas of vocational rehabilitation. Each Institute is publishing its own series of monographs concerned with its selected core area. Northeastern University's Monograph No. 6 is concerned with the impact its publications have had on the practitioner-consumer who have received previous monographs (Goldin *et. al.*, 1969).

The Practitioner-Researcher

Leonard and Skipper acknowledge the fact that turning practitioners into practitioner-researchers will simply convert a culture conflict into a role conflict. I would agree with them that "there are a number of barriers to its success." There is considerable merit, however, in the authors' idea that properly conceived, practice-oriented research can elevate the art of practice to a new plane of excellence. No one can deny that theory can improve our understanding of prediction as well as guide practical social action. The diagram, Figure 1,[1] differentiates process from outcome, with "evaluation" listed under practice; unfortunately, nowhere does the schema provide for innovative utilization of new research results.

The age-old problem of the split of the cultures is emphasized by the authors, and there are several shades of the C.P. Snow Leavis cleavage coloring some of their initial remarks on thought and action. It is true that there is considerable difficulty in attempting to do rigorous research that has clear-cut and direct application to the ongoing flow of client service. This is a difficult request to make of a scientist concerned with basic research. Obviously this problem of application is not a part of the research involved with a "demonstration," or other applied research efforts.

The authors focus on the university as a center of research, outlining the need for firm links with the professions and bureaucracies involved in and responsible for social action. No mention is made in the paper of the universe of rehabilitation facilities composed of comprehensive and other rehabilitation centers, sheltered workshops, and the hundreds of District Offices of State Divisions of Vocational Rehabilitation. These settings are the major targets in need of immediate analysis based upon the principles derived from the organization, management and tactics of social research.

The authors state that before academic research can add rationality to social action, the practitioner must learn to use scientific criteria in accepting and rejecting theories relevant to this practice. These criteria can be learned, although this would take considerable time and training. For the validity of the idea that the practitioner should avoid more rationalization — deriving theory to suit accustomed action — can be assured if the "complexity of the practical uses of theory is recognized."

It occurred to me that the authors might be using the doctorate research model of themselves as obtainable at the practitioner's level. The practitioner is either trained at the Master's level (rehabilitation counseling, social work) or secures his position with a B.A. and some advanced university work. This is also the age, unfortunately, of the indigenous worker's involvement with the rehabilitation and welfare process.

There are approximately 70 graduate Masters' curricula in Rehabilitation Counseling emerging from problems of professionalism and working toward two other streams: doctoral programs and programs of support personnel at the bachelors' level. I would agree that there is grave need to prepare the practitioner-researcher at the same time.

In Duff and Hollingshead's *Sickness and Society*, one senior faculty member of the medical school sees only the difference between researchers and practitioners:

> "I like things the way they are. We are training researchers first, practitioners second. Those who enter practice are usually the second-rate students and some say we should teach them how to practice. But I feel we shouldn't waste our time on them. They can learn how to practice in a short time, later on. They won't do much harm in the meantime because given the nature of people and chronic disease they really can't do much good" (Duff and Hollingshead, 1968: 379).

These statements are made by someone not only unaware of the close relationship that must exist between researcher and practitioner, but also oblivious to some of the basic concepts of research utilization.

The authors then describe the professional schools within the university as "sally ports." Within them, they note, a balance between the two cultures can be struck. In the universities, the authors state the confrontation must be made under conditions which yield data that conform to our most rigorous principles of research methods. No one could disagree. But the setting of the university is that of training and research rather than practice. Again, as previously indicated, there needs to be a closely allied step for the training of the researcher-practitioner — that of the rehabilitation facility setting. Practice-oriented research, and its success when properly conceptualized, cannot be contained within the campus. Again, the argument given and concepts set forth by the authors are more acceptable in academic settings than in field service agencies.

Discussion of the interdisciplinary team and hired-hand research only increases the problems of technology transfer. Currently the Social and Rehabilitation Service (HEW) supports 19 Research and Training Centers, each containing a number of team members engaged in both basic and applied research. Twelve are in medical schools, three focus on mental retardation, three have a vocational emphasis, and one is concerned with the communicative disorders. Within them there are the beginning signs of the individual within those teams who may approach the definition and description of the practitioner-researcher of whom the authors speak. His role is sometimes to coordinate practice or service within administrative and managerial relationships. Usually he holds the doctoral degree, understands principles of basic and applied research, but recognizes the need to involve actively the practitioner on the team in the research process. His role as researcher-practitioner, however, is limited by the demands of administration and management.

In regard to the authors' consideration of consultants, difficulties arise in their non-involvement in the research process itself. Consultants seem to have dual problems: (a) over-commitment in a number of areas so that their input as a consultant is limited by heavy schedules of writing, teaching, and lecturing, and (b) their itinerant occupational disease — allowing them little time for follow through supervision of suggestions and recommendation whose implementation should have continued supervision.

The practitioner-researcher, however, is essentially an excellent idea, and in some ways is already in progress. The past few months have seen the approval of demonstration projects within the Social and Rehabilitation Service concerned with an individual called the "Research Utilization Specialist." These individuals began their first training course in June 1969 at the University of Florida.

The Research Utilization Specialist

With the establishment of a Research Utilization Branch within the Division of Research and Demonstration Grants (SRS/HEW) two years ago, and with the assistance of Drs. Everett Rogers and Edward M. Glaser, the next step was to develop someone who could act as a catalyst in the translation of research findings into programs serving larger numbers of disabled and disadvantaged more effectively.

The major step that started both the Branch and the consideration of additional action was a Task Force on Research Utilization appointed by Miss Mary E. Switzer, Administrator, Social and Rehabilitation Service in November of 1965. The Task Force presented its Final Report to the Administrator in January 1967, and she asked for immediate implementation. In addition, at its December 1966 conference on research dissemination and utilization, the Joint Liaison Committee of the Council of State Administrators of Vocational Rehabilitation and the Rehabilitation Counselor Educators heard of the need for a "change agent." Based upon the county agent's role as developed by the Department of Agriculture, Kurt Lewin's model identified in 1947 (Lewin, 1952), and Ronald Lippitt's material (Lippitt *et al.*, 1958), the Research Utilization Specialist was born at a planning session in Washington, D.C. in July 1968 (Hooker *et al.*, 1968).

The implementation of one of the Task Force on Research Utilization recommendations resulted in ten approved "Research Utilization Specialist" demonstrations. These five year demonstration grants are located in each of the ten regions of the Department of H.E.W. In addition, four other States appointed a Research Utilization Specialist without the support of a demonstration grant, and those individuals will attend all training sessions for the RUS during the coming year, to be provided by the Division of Training, Rehabilitation Services Administration, Social and Rehabilitation Service, DHEW.

As the change agent between research and service, the RUS (Rehabilitation Utilization Specialist) must be in the field where the innovation is to be introduced, utilized, and made effective as part of an ongoing program. Their training will include the process of role identification and relationship to their co-workers, the development of skills in problem identification and solutions involving significant research results, and appropriate systems enabling significant research outcomes to become a part of services for the disabled and the disadvantaged. The RUS will work closely with the Rehabilitation Research Institute in his region as well as with the Regional Research Institute in Social Welfare. Both Regional Institutes are involved in programmatic core research chosen conjointly by the University in which the Institute is located and the Regional Social and Rehabilitation Service office.

The objectives of the training program during its first phase were to introduce to the RUS some elementary change agent theory and skills, to sanction utilization activities within the State and region, and to form a work group for purposes of future training and support. The new staff member of the State Division of Vocational Rehabilitation will be placed on a level with State Supervisors of Staff Development and State Facilities Specialists. The term "research" carries with it a mystique generated mainly by those who fear statistical strategems, and by those whose doctoral degree was not attained due to lack of completion of the dissertation. More than these reasons, however, is a fear of "research" due to its impractical activity. This latter concern is held mainly by those individuals who cannot distinguish basic research from applied and who consider a demonstration involving service to people as nonresearch despite the evaluative methodology which should accompany any demonstration. Actually it is hoped that the Research Utilization Specialist will serve as a link between the rehabilitation research program and the delivery of rehabilitation services. As such a link and catalyst, the RUS hopefully will bring about changes in both the character of services delivered and the nature of the research pursued (Bourgue, 1969). It is further hoped, in line with Leonard and Skipper's implications for the practitioner-researcher, the RUS should also help the field counselor see himself as a source of program innovation.

The RUS in his linking and catalytic roles should help in foreshadowing social policy for the 70's through States' awareness of the need for technology transfer to help in the answer to problems of social welfare. Social change through legislative action on a national basis provides justification for practice-oriented research both to the professional graduate school and to the academic campus research culture.

As Alfred North Whitehead has noted:

"The tragedy of the world is that those who are imaginative have but slight experience, and those who are experienced have feeble imaginations. Fools act on imagination without knowledge; pedants act on knowledge without imagination. The task of a university is to weld together imagination and experience" (Whitehead, 1929: 138).

Learning Engineers

Mackie and Christensen were concerned with an effort to enable the Navy to gain more practical applications from the research it sponsors. The study describes the processes involved in translating the results of laboratory research in psychology into forms that would be meaningful and useful in operational settings. Interestingly enough, the authors found that learning theory has been particularly barren of useful predictions about human learning behavior in the operational environment. Apparently the reason lies in the fact that theory development is undertaken in laboratory experiments with tasks bearing no known relationship to "real-life" learning requirements (Mackie and Christensen: 5).

These authors support the current Field Testing Laboratory approach mentioned earlier in this chapter, which aims to transform existing service agencies into sites for technology transfer. "There should be more emphasis on how to cast operational problems in a form that can be investigated by research rather than on how to relate theoretically inspired research to operational problems" (Mackie and Christensen: 7).

Instead of the title, "practitioner-researcher," Mackie and Christensen feel that "there will be an increasing need for a corps of professionals who may be described as 'learning engineers' " (Mackie and Christensen: 10). They add that this new breed should be trained as "constructive critics of learning research, and as experts in the learning processes." Somehow there is always the pious note included which seems to expect the formation of a new profession or a profession to be related to the world of research.

The remaining description of the "learning engineers" includes specialized knowledge of the subject matter and operational tasks in the field where application is to be attempted. The required training in research will be as a generalist rather than as a specialist.

The authors hope that this new breed will avoid the trap of research specialization but at the same time inculcate specialization in the field of application. They conclude that the only way that is effective currently is for the researcher to be involved in an ongoing program or perhaps something like a field testing laboratory. Thus we come full circle to the "no man's land between laboratory and classroom" as Leonard and Skipper describe it. Mackie and Christensen see the need for an operational setting which they call a "training environment," but deplore the small number of psychologists who might be willing to operate in a practical or functional setting wherein to conduct their research. This concern is not held in the field of rehabilitation where the demand for service is so overwhelming that the research demonstration is the order of the day, and theoretical conceptualization lags far behind empirically based programs throughout the country.

Research Briefs and Research Trends

Translation of findings to practical application "is almost nonexistent" according to Mackie and Christensen. One of the recommendations on the Task Force on Research Utilization was to publish concise digests for the practitioner. The first "Research Brief" was issued on August 15, 1967. The major focus is on usability, with significant findings of the studies made available for innovation by the practitioner. The Research Brief consists of one page printed on both sides, highlighting new results that can be absorbed into ongoing techniques of the practitioner. The one sheet Brief attempts to bring research into effective focus by presenting results which have definite implications for use by practitioners. They are designed to be read quickly, easily digested, and readily kept for continuing use. The Briefs are issued every two weeks and are intended to be stimulating as well as useful. Each project must upon completion not only submit a Final Report but also a Research Brief and an accompanying abstract of the project.

The "Research Trends" series will begin in the Fall of 1969, reporting developing or emerging patterns of both theory and practice from several ongoing projects dealing with similar problems. Several "Trends" are underway dealing with problems of biomechanics in the field of prosthetics and orthotics, blindness, and correctional rehabilitation. In addition, "Trends" will deal with the following concepts which have undergirded the rehabilitation process for the severely disabled as he enters the community as a first class citizen after years of treatment, restriction, and institutionalization:

1. The Individualization Concept within a Relationship Setting.
2. The Socialization Concept within a Work Setting.
3. The Ambulation Concept within a Multi-Service Setting.
4. The Family Integration Concept within a Secure Income Setting.
5. The Vocational, Social, and Psychological Concept within a Therapeutically Realistic Setting.
6. The Training and Placement Concept within a Regular Job Setting.
7. The Follow-Up Concept within a Housing and Community Setting.

These concepts have been obtained from the outcomes of research and demonstration projects over the past fifteen years within the framework of vocational rehabilitation.

Research Utilization Progress

In December of 1966, future plans for research utilization were listed at a meeting in Florida (Joint Liaison Committee). At this date, it might be well to review those items to see what has been accomplished.

1. *Research Utilization Task Force*
   The Task Force Final Report was submitted in January 1968 to Miss Mary E. Switzer, Administrator, Social and Rehabilitation Service, and at her request its recommendations are now in the process of implementation.

2. *Research Utilization Unit*
   This Unit is now a Branch, one of four within the Division of Research and Demonstration Grants in the Social and Rehabilitation Service of the Department of Health, Education, and Welfare. Its staff is developing plans and materials for an eventual Data Retrieval and Information Center in the field of rehabilitation and social welfare.

3. *Summaries and Outlines Abolished*
   Not only were outlines preceding the final report abolished, but Summaries of Final Reports were also abolished. In their place, a Research Brief is requested with every final report; in addition, an abstract of every final report is also requested.

4. *Research and/or Technical Briefs*
   The Research Briefs have now been occurring for two years. Distribution of each is over 25,000, with reprintings in various other publications from time to time. Instead of Technical Briefs, "Research Trends" have been substituted, and the first publication of one of them will be in the Fall of 1969.

5. *Revised Final Report Guidelines*
   The revisions of the Final Report Guidelines have been accomplished. The last version includes a request for a Research Brief and an abstract of the Final Report.

6. *Highlights of Research Findings*
   On the inside front cover of every Final Report, highlights are clearly listed, making immediately visible the outcomes of the project.

7. *Project Research Conferences*
   A number of conferences have been conducted during the final year of the project, bringing together projects of a similar nature, and also sharing some of the implications with practitioners.

8. *Data Bank and Retrieval System*
A contract to obtain the abstracts of 1300 Final Reports is underway. Subsequent steps in the preparation of an automated data processing system have been outlined for implementation.

9. *Distribution of Currently Approved Projects*
Projects just approved are listed with States and Regions within the Department of Health, Education, and Welfare complex of agencies. There is a far closer relationship between the projects within social welfare areas and rehabilitation areas since the Office of Research, Demonstrations and Training has been established.

10. *State of the Art Monographs*
The Regional Rehabilitation Research Institutes have published as their first monograph in the series of their core research, the state of the art in relevant research. The newly created Regional Research Institutes on Social Welfare are planning to publish a first monograph in the same fashion.

11. *Special Projects on Research Utilization*
The Research Utilization Branch has formed a Research Utilization Advisory Council which reviews projects relevant to dissemination, innovation, and utilization of research outcomes. There are several projects now underway concerned with such topics as the utilization of documentary films accomplished with rehabilitation support, and the innovation of research outcomes within State Divisions of Vocational Rehabilitation. Field Testing Laboratories have been started concerned with utilization of innovative techniques.

12. *Mobile Rehabilitation Research Utilization Units*
While there have been no specific projects of this nature, perhaps the closest demonstrations would be those underwriting the role of the Research Utilization Specialist. In many ways, he is a human mobile rehabilitation research utilization unit!

13. *Dissemination and Utilization Aspects of Research Projects*
A display presentation has been worked out for research utilization purposes. It can be transported to conferences or conventions. Project Directors are urged to present findings at various State, Regional, or National Conferences if results can be shared.

14. *Information Bulletins*
The initial applications as well as the Final Reports both request approaches which the project director has in mind for the utilization of his findings. Information Bulletins were decided not to be requested; instead, Research Briefs were initiated.

Summary

Integrating theory and practice for innovation and utilization purposes is a major goal of any research and demonstration program, especially one with the essential task of social change for members of disabled and disadvantaged groups in inner cities. The very purpose of the Social and Rehabilitation Service has been to coordinate those agencies involved in services to people. Despite problems and difficulties a good start has been made. What is now necessary is to coordinate these various services on the State level, where the "SRS" concept as yet does not truly exist. Combined services to people to minimize individual problems and promote human growth is the goal inherent in agency and Departmental priorities within the Department of Health, Education, and Welfare.

One necessary ingredient, which we can all agree should be included, is the optimal input of technology transfer so that innovations utilizing what is significantly better than current practice can improve our future effort. That future should allow the integration of theory and practice through a Research Utilization Specialist (Research-Practitioner) so that social policies can benefit all sections of the population.

Notes to the Chapter

1. Personal Communication from Dr. Richard O'Toole, January 14, 1969.
2. In the Leonard and Skipper Paper, pp. 269–291.

References

Bourque, Ellsworth J.
    1969   "The research-practice gap in vocational rehabilitation what's being done about it?" Paper presented at American Personnel and Guidance convention. Las Vegas (March 31).
Joint Liaison Committee of Council State Administrators of Vocational Rehabilitation and the Rehabilitation Counselor Educators
    1966   *Communication, Dissemination and Utilization of Rehabilitation Research Information.* Conference Report (December).
Cooper, CoCilia, and Archambault (eds.)
    1968   *Proceedings: Communication, Dissemination, and Utilization of Research Information in Rehabilitation Counseling.* Department of Guidance and Psychological Services. Springfield College. Springfield, Massachusetts.
Duff, Raymond S., and August B. Hollingshead
    1968   *Sickness and Society.* Harper and Row.

GOLDIN, GEORGE, KENNETH MARGOLIN, and BERNARD STATSKY
1969   *The Utilization of Rehabilitation Research.* Monograph No. 6. New England Rehabilitation Research Institute. Northeastern University (February).

HOOKER, SUSAN, PATRICIA RILEY, and NINA MASAR
1968   "Introducing RUS — a link between research and service." *Rehabilitation Record* (November–December).

LEWIN, KURT
1952   "Group decisions and social change." In Guy E. Swanson *et al.* (eds.), *Readings in Social Psychology.* New York: Henry Holt and Company.

LIPPITT, RONALD, *et al.*
1958   *The Dynamics of Planned Change.* New York: Harcourt, Brace and Company, Inc.

MACKIE, ROBERT, and PAUL R. CHRISTENSEN
undated "Translation and application of psychological research." *Technical Report* 716–1. Human Factors Research, Inc., Santa Barbara Research Park. Goleta, California.

PINES, MAYA
1969   "Why some 3-years-olds get A's — and some get C's." *New York Times Magazine* 12: (July 6).

REGIONAL REHABILITATION RESEARCH INSTITUTE
1968   *Research and Demonstration Projects. A Bibliography* — 1968. Gainesville, Florida: University of Florida.

SUSSMAN, MARVIN G. (ed.)
1965   *Sociology and Rehabilitation.* Washington, D.C. American Sociological Association.

TITMUSS, RICHARD M.
1968   *Commitment to Welfare.* London: George Allen and Unwin.

WHITEHEAD, A. N.
1929   *Aims of Education.* London: Benn.

CHAPTER FIFTEEN

Another View on Integrating
Theory and Practice

A. D. Puth

Leonard and Skipper have suggested that theory and practice can and should be further integrated through the use of special schools and personnel having special functions related thereto. This may well be the best of all solutions, but I am not quite sure for whom. It seems to me that their notion of a "buffer zone" does not really integrate theory and practice, but rather "links" them, particularly in light of the many dichotomies that their paper suggests exist on either side and the ongoing "wars" between these interests. The solution which Leonard and Skipper suggest is based on the politics of the organization of the different social, behavioral and physical sciences and on its value to sociology and the other sciences. Sociology, for example, will benefit more than rehabilitation and the other helping professions.

In his daily work the practitioner deals with the problems of the total person and the total system which influences change. The researcher's perspective and his methodology do not deal with the complexity of total man, his background and environment. To attack problems that are relevant to practice we must develop new methods and theories which integrate different perspectives.

The Underlying Difficulties in Integrating Theory and Practice

It is my view that there can not and must not be any conflict between scientific theory and professional practice, if theory is designed to guide us to increased levels of predictability and if practice is directed toward the achievement of specific measurable goals in the most efficient way possible. I hold that good (super-saturated-with-predictability) theory is the very essence of applicability and the quintessence of operationality or functionality. If conflicts exist between the two (theory and practice), I believe they come to pass for the following specific reasons (alone, or in combination):

A. The theory is wrong from conception;
B. The theory is incomplete;
C. The theory has been incorrectly applied;
D. The theory has been inappropriately applied;
E. The factors or objectives sought for or to be achieved have not been (or as yet can not be) quantified (measured) and, therefore, cannot be related to the theory in question.

In my mind, I believe I see very clearly many of the breakdowns in A, B, C, D, and E as listed above that create the seeming disharmony and disunity between potential, good (usable), scientific rehabilitation theory and related professional rehabilitation practice. Steady now! I did not say I saw crystal-clear answers, but that I saw many of the breakdowns, i.e., the problems. These problems are many and complex and so fixed in tradition (including scientific tradition) that they are not only difficult to solve or resolve but also difficult to even identify and accept (or even consider) as problems!

In the page limitation imposed on me (for your protection) I am going to pick *just one* of these problems, address myself to it, and propose some *possible* answers. More important, I will try to imply or show the complexity of the consequences of new and different answers which we must be willing to deal with if we are truly to unite theory and practice in fundamental ways that transcend "politically" bridging answers between institutions, parts of institutions, professions, and humans with problem-creating needs. Such "political" answers, it seems to me, tend to reject the problem as not our own and project it into other people and institutions.

In dealing with problems of theory among all concerned with rehabilitation, I can accept the answers "I'll try" or "I haven't yet tried." I will not accept the answer that "I won't try." Such an answer, it seems to me, represents the height of irresponsibility and pure arrogance on the part of either the "creators" of knowledge or the "utilizers" of it. (If both groups are not equally interested and concerned, we simply do not have a shared reality and can never meet on the common ground of what we call disabled people.)

More importantly, I believe all professional practice is based on theory. All that is at question is the source of the theory and the degree and nature of its testing. The lines between assumption, hypothesis, theory, and law are exceedingly fine — almost undetectable, since the amount and quality of supportive evidence for each is not fixed. To me, all people are theorists. All that is at question is whether they are knowing or unknowing theorists, authoritarian or democratic theorists, open or covert theorists, and the unique universe of circumstances to which each believes his own theory apply. After all, theory is, at best, a function of one's self-defined reality, and in the absence of more predictable theory, there is no other recourse or referrant but self and its reality. The intensely practice-oriented person who denigrates or belittles theory or theorists is simply evidencing fright at having his own theories held up to the scrutiny of others, i.e., his own reality held up for public comparison with the reality of others. This is the same fright of the "pure" theorist as he faces the expanded protocol data of the many practitioners. Each lives in fear of the other, and cannot admit it to anyone, least of all himself. If dialogue on theory did not demand so much exposure of self, I do not believe we would be so testy and defensive about it. In the final analysis, debate on theory is a confrontation of different self-realities. I will have more to say about this later.

The Power and Politics of Knowledge

We have failed to realize that knowledge, particularly scientific knowledge, is laden with power and has been and continues to be politically organized and that depending on our training we are each enmeshed in a part of that politics. When man first gained the insight (knowledge) that a stick of wood and a wheel and axle gave him added power, he began to organize, codify, and "husband" that knowledge. When later other men gathered other knowledge about fire, brass, the heavens, etc., they, too, organized, codified, and "husbanded" that knowledge. Then, as now, they used this knowledge to control or manipulate their environments, producing products and circumstances with which they bartered depending on their needs. In the intervening years, knowledge has exploded and has been organized on a variety of bases and for a variety of reasons . . . none the least of which is accident, further discovery, and a desire for exclusivity with regard to its use or application. Some of the early and rigid arbiters of the organization (division) of that knowledge have given way, and others, using different organizational patterns, have taken their places. Matter, as a referrant base, has also influenced the patterns of organization. An elementary beginning of the horizontal "merger" of knowledge has taken place, resulting in many new disciplines. While somewhat over-generalized, these disciplines have emerged for largely utilitarian reasons. One of the most interesting recent horizontal "mergers" has been the aero-space technology.

Much though we would like to deny it, adherence to any one of the above organizations of knowledge gives us a bartering power — a survival mechanism (very much like the Gypsy secrets for cleaning and repairing copper pots and pans). The politics of our well-being and survival are hopelessly enmeshed with our choice of vocation and represent one of our strongest survival mechanisms. We tend to approach, see, cope with, and respond to our reality with and through our chosen knowledge system, and to the degree possible, we position ourselves accordingly.

These self-aggrandizing, myopic, political overtones applied to knowledge systems tend to inhibit us from entering into other areas or systems (other people's knowledge-politics) for fear they will transgress into ours. Academic, professional, and vocational exclusivity is rationalized in every conceivable way and on all levels.

What the knowledge makers, organizers, and users have all too often failed to realize is that *knowledge is already organized* in the sense that knowledge is largely a symbolic replication or construct of the way a given organism *is* organized or the way the universe *is* organized in relationship to that organism. The politics of a given knowledge-organism is almost hopelessly infected with its own well-being. This is equally true of the theoretician and the practitioner. Only the self referrants are different (Theoreticians really are human!).

The larger politics of all human nature have not as yet prevailed. The horizontal integration of knowledge is not simply beyond the well-being of the "system-bound" theorist. New, larger, more comprehensive theory, which can reconcile and integrate, must, to a certain extent, await man's ability to forge a larger and much more complex self-survival weapon or mechanism. He is as yet uncomfortable with these larger tools, which, among other things, require larger self-mastery and larger responsibility.

The Practitioner's View

In the field the practitioner deals with the problems of the total person, his background, and his environment. He must work within a system of helping services and must understand the total array of forces, including his own interaction with the client, which affect the process of change.

Therefore, most of what is researched seems trite compared to the array of problems which the practitioner encounters on a day-to-day basis. It does not deal with the complexity of the total man, his background and environment. Over concerned with complexity, researchers just seem to be digging little holes. They do not research basic human problems. Instead they study only small bits of behavior, and in so doing they miss the total aspects of life — so necessary in order to build viable, workable theories to guide practice.

Behind a methodology there is a particular concept of man. Often methodologies so divide man that they lose the total picture. In addition, their research for the most part is static, not focused on change. Thus, research does not seem to be related to the goals of rehabilitation.

What I am really asking is for researchers to get involved in the total problems of men. While researchers have methodological sophistication, they seem to lack human value in their work. The goals of helping men must be given more consideration. From the appearance of their work, researchers don't seem to care if research is going to help or hinder man. Sociology and the other social and behavioral sciences must be relevant. A viable social science can live in the street as well as in the ivory tower.

I have the view that theory and practice are made up of the same "stuff" — knowledge. I hold that the process of the distillation or crystallization of knowledge into patterns which enables us to possess an increased capacity for predictability cannot, so to speak, be farmed out or assigned politically in an authoritarian manner to a select few. To do this would be living life through surrogates. Further, specialization, under circumstances, may be an escape which may lessen our capacity to deal with the problems which confront us.

We must also develop methodologies which are capable of dealing with the complexities which the practitioner faces. We must develop means to measure the objectives sought in practice.

We need integrationists who can bridge the gaps in the political divisions of the sciences and between science and practice. To accomplish this we must overcome the tendency to view problems only from our limited perspectives.

Two prevailing, yet poorly understood, practices and concepts in science seem to stand in our way: A. the current use (or misuse) of probability theory, and B. (and far more fundamental) the basic reasoning (or symbolic logic) process in "science" as it attempts to deal with the *man-created* issue of the conceptual continuum of identicalness — similarity — differences. Both of these concepts and related practices represent profound epistemological problems and resulting complexities in the areas of mensuration and taxonomy. We are unable to treat these two problems fairly, short of several chapters and the inappropriate skewing of the general content of this book itself.

Suffice it to say, however, that there is a growing number of people who call themselves scientists who are disenchanted with the current referents for scientific truth and who are beginning to hold that the ultimate referent for space, matter, motion, and time — may well be life itself. This is a little hard for the "atomist" to swallow, and it always will be, until such time as he realizes that all notions of *disorder* are dependent derivatives of a yet larger concept of *order*. And pray tell, is there a referent for *order* beyond life itself? I, for one, doubt it. Yet the referent *life* is a difficult one to comprehend as it demands that we eventually get beyond self to the larger concept of *all*, via the complex multi-systems route of sustained yield.